The reviews are in on "Total Control: The Michael Nesmith Story."

Television chronicles #12: A masterful job of weaving together her source material, much of which comes from interviews conducted by various Monkee scholars.

J. Amazon.com Rating=10: Total Control: The Michael Nesmith Story is the finest entertainment bio I have read in some time. Ms. Massingill in doing her homework has brought an understanding to a very complicated man, performer, producer, director, writer and entrepreneur. This is recommendable to anyone curious about the Monkees, Mr. Nesmith even the 60's music and television scene in general or the beginning of video music as we know it today, but especially any and all Monkee fans who have been extremely critical of Mr. Nesmith in most recent past. "To Read About The Man Is To Understand The Man."

P.A.: Just (received) my copy of "Total Control-The Mike Nesmith Story" by Randi Massingill and it is a fine, well thought out piece with a few typos in it. It will make you realize just how much a genius Mike is, although you'll cringe at the legal BS the man has gone through and is continuing to go through. A wonderful book!!!

P.P.: I agree! I read that whole thing right when I got it (which took up most of day). It's a wonderful little thing for people like me who obsess, er... admire Nez greatly. :-)

V.B.: From an unhappy childhood, to the incredible, yet damaging fame The Monkees brought him; to his pioneering of MTV and his creative solo career, to his other career as an executive movie producer, to his troubled personal life - it's all here. For those who like steamy, bloodletting biographies, this book will be a let down, but for those looking for an insight into a very private person this work is a revelation.

C.H.: I got my copy last week - Thanks so much Randi. I'm only up to page 100, but I think it's great. It's cool to read peoples quotes from who were actually there. It's got great photos and is very professional. Those of you who were undecided on buying it, you really should!

R.W.: I'm reading Randi's book on Nez - I recommend it to everyone on this list.

B.B.: I've just finished reading the book. It was great reading. Being a Monkee fan for the past 30 years, it gave me a lot of information that I didn't know. I really enjoyed reading it.

A.R. Amazon.com: Fabulous book! Anyone who hates this book is a starry eyed fan who can't see that Nesmith is human. God bless authors like Massingill who put up with this nonsense and write the truth.

V.L.: I received Total Control at around 11:00 a.m. yesterday. I began reading it right away and finished the main text at around 7:00 last night. I even took it to the bank and grocery shopping! What a powerful book about an interesting man. Congrats!

Copyright

Total Control: The Monkees Michael Nesmith Story

MICHAEL NESMITH

By Randi L. Massingill

Table of Contents

INTRODUCTION 7

TOTAL CONTROL 10

FIRST NATIONAL RAG 12

LIFE, THE UNSUSPECTING CAPTIVE 14

THE KIND OF GIRL I COULD LOVE 20

CRUISIN' THROUGH THE JUNGLES OF L.A. 25

A JOURNEY WITH MICHAEL BLESSING 30

HOLLYWOOD 36

HORSERACE 47

I'LL REMEMBER YOU 75

RUNNING FROM THE GRAND ENNUI 76

LADY OF THE VALLEY 87

WRITING WRONGS 89

THE UPSIDE OF GOOD-BYE 93

SUNNY GIRLFRIEND 95

"IT LOOKS LIKE WE'VE MADE IT ONCE AGAIN" 97

KEYS TO THE CAR 103

WHAT AM I DOING HANGIN' 'ROUND 106

HERE I AM 113

HEAR ME CALLING 120

ONLY BOUND 123

TWO DIFFERENT ROADS 124

I WON'T BE THE SAME WITHOUT HER 127

DIFFERENT DRUM 129

NEVER TELL A WOMAN YES...132

I'M HEARING THE LIGHT FROM THE WINDOW....................................134

I AM NOT THAT...138

MORE THAN WE IMAGINE 139

ROLL WITH THE FLOW 142

LIVING INSIDE OF A LITTLE GLASS ROOM 147

THIS ALL HAPPENED ONCE BEFORE 154

WAKING MYSTERY 158

THANX FOR THE RIDE 164

RAINMAKER..166

NEVERMIND THE FURTHERMORE, THE PLEA IS SELF DEFENSE 168

YOU JUST MAY BE THE ONE..173

RELEASE...176

LAUGH KILLS LONESOME 180

LISTEN TO THE BAND...189

ZILCH..194

I NEED HELP, I'M FALLING AGAIN...197

DANCE AND HAVE A GOOD TIME 199

I FALL TO PIECES...202

HEY, HEY, HE'S A MONKEE...209

HILLS OF TIME: 2005 UPDATE...215

APPENDIX 1: 2005 MONKEES UPDATE..229

APPENDIX 2: MICHAEL COMMENTS ON 9/11 234

APPENDIX 3: THE PRISON STORY..235

APPENDIX 4: MICHAEL NESMITH AS MUSICIAN 238

APPENDIX 5: MICHAEL NESMITH AS MUSIC PRODUCER 255

APPENDIX 6: MICHAEL NESMITH AS SONGWRITER 256

APPENDIX 7: MICHAEL NESMITH AS LIVE PERFORMER 259

APPENDIX 8: WICHITA TRAIN WHISTLE PERFORMERS 262

APPENDIX 9: MICHAEL NESMITH AS RECORD PUBLISHER 263

APPENDIX 10: MICHAEL NESMITH AS VIDEO PUBLISHER 264

APPENDIX 11: MICHAEL NESMITH AS VIDEO PERFORMER 274

APPENDIX 12: MICHAEL NESMITH AS FILM MAKER/PERFORMER 276

APPENDIX 13: MICHAEL NESMITH AS TELEVISION ACTOR 279

APPENDIX 14: BIBLIOGRAPHY 288

Introduction

Seven years have passed since the first version of this book was released. When the book was originally released, The Monkees (including Michael) were about to tour and all was well. I very much wanted to have a happy ending even though I had my suspicions that things would not be happy for long. I don't regret my decision to end on a positive note, as there was hope. It was only in 1997 after Michael's departure from the group did the dirty laundry really fly in the press.

On the Internet, I read several theories about my book and several "facts" relating to Michael's involvement with Total Control, with the majority being completely incorrect. For the record, I am not a former employee, family member, girlfriend, etc. The fact is that I had written Michael on January 8, 1996 regarding the book and wishing his cooperation. I had also asked about the whereabouts of John London as I felt he would an extremely important interview for the book. Michael replied the very next day stating that he was "very distracted with business affairs. If you can wait for some time I can be of more help to you." He also said that, "you are starting this a bit early in my life. I am embarking on some new projects which will seriously alter the landscape of my life, i.e. Neftoon. Neftoon will be published by a regular publishing house. I am through with self distribution. In addition to LSHONZ I am setting up other works just as broad in scope and impact. Any thing you write now will be almost instantly old and behind the time, wasting your good efforts." As for John London, Michael said that, "I have no idea where John is...but he may not be useful once you have digested all of the works and know what to write, so tracking him down might be costly and inefficient in the last analysis."

I waited a full year for Michael's promised help as I did research and collected photos. I did locate John London, who was living in Texas under his actual name of John Kuehne. I called him and we spoke about how he couldn't talk to me regarding Michael, even though they had parted ways at least ten years earlier due to a bad investment which lost a few million dollars of Michaels in a land deal. He said that he had home movies, photos, unreleased music dating back to Michael's pre-Monkee days but he would only share them if I could patch things up between he and Michael. I contacted Michael and made the request that he contact Kuehne. I never heard back from Michael but I heard from Kuehne a few months later stating that he never heard from Michael. Kuehne would pass away a few years later.

Other un-named people had scheduled to loan me photographs and give interviews, but out of the blue they would all cancel out and claim that they had never spoken to me despite my being at their residences and selecting the photos to use. Michael's two ex-wives were located but both would not speak about Michael. Even though Michael no longer is active in these people's lives, his power & influence lingers in the air. I waited one full year and e-mailed Michael, he was not returning my e-mails anymore. His involvement in the project was over and I was on my own.

Since the first edition I have added some new photos, switched out old photos and added an update on what Michael has done since the first version of Total Control.

It is easy to understand why Michael is wary of the press as he is consistently asked about The Monkees and little else. This television phenomenon, which was on the air for only two years and producing eight albums, has continued to dominate most or all of the rest of Michael's life. His work since that time is significant and certainly worthy of appreciation, if not fame, so that is the focus of this book.

I've had to depend on the kindness of brave strangers for help researching the life and career of Michael Nesmith. These people have become trusted friends and I thank them dearly for their help. These people include: Joanne Caravello, who provided me with so many wonderful print articles from the seventies as well as radio interviews from around the globe. Henry Diltz, Michael's official photographer, whose great photos were at my disposal and quite a few appear in this book. Pat Smith, who opened the way for me to obtain access to the Diltz Archives. George Gimarc, a disc jockey, author and record collector/dealer extraordinaire, who discovered the first ever Michael Nesmith single on the Highness label. Maggie McManus, editor of Monkee Business Fanzine, who provided me with recent articles about Nesmith, as well as giving me support when I really needed it. Maggie also became a proofreader of this book and corrected a few errors that popped up along the way. Chris Mezzolesta, who loaned me many issues of Monkee Business Fanzine from the early 1980's. Gary Strobl, who once worked on a book about the Monkees and shared his 200+ interviews with me. Carolyn Thomas, who provided me with invaluable information about Michael's mother, as well as being a big supporter of this project. For my friends and family, I give my heartfelt thanks for putting up with my Nesmith ramblings as well as not hearing from me for weeks at a time.

My thanks go to Brad Waddell. He was there for me whenever I got frustrated and kept me from quitting the project. Actually he kept me from throwing my computer off the balcony. I am eternally grateful for

8

his love and support.

Total Control

Total Control
By Michael Nesmith

I want total control of the airports
Total control of the sea
Total control of the freeways
Total control of police

I want total control of the subway
Total control of my life
Total control of all variables
Total control of your wife

Total control
Total control
Total control of machines
Total control
Total control
I'm sure that's what happiness means

So I know that I'll need lots of money
To get where I'm trying to be
I've read all about it in magazines
I've heard all about it on the radio
I've seen all about it on TV shows
I've got to grab all the gusto
And I know that means total control

So I want total control of the oceans
Total control of the moon
And total control of the children
Total control of my room
I want total control of emotions
And total control of the wind
Total control of beginnings
Total control of the end

Total control
Total control

Total control of machines
Total control
Total control
I'm sure that's what happiness means

So I want total control of emotions
And total control of the wind
And total control of beginnings
Total control of the end
Yes I want total control of beginnings
Total control of the end
Of the end
The end
Of the end
The end

First National Rag

Ask people who know Michael Nesmith to give their opinion of him and you will probably get a different answer every time.

Dean Jeffries recalled Michael as, "A rotten person. He was a very bad person. That's my personal opinion of him. . . because I had run with him quite a bit. He was just nasty with people. I thought he was a prima donna but he had no reason to be that way. Mike Nesmith was just up and down. One minute he was pleasant to be around and then you would leave him, and two hours later, you'd come back and he'd be a rotten son-of-a-bitch to be around. He did that way with me a couple of times because he used to hang around all the time at my auto shop. He did it a few times with me and that was enough."[1]

Bill Chadwick said, "He saw it (The Monkees) as an opportunity, as a stepping stone. He took every advantage he could. Mike was a very intelligent guy. He was a real good businessman and a real talented person. He was going to make the best of it no matter what the situation was. *The Monkees* was a vehicle."

Lester Sill said, "I hold Mike responsible for breaking The Monkees up. That was his intention and I tell him this when I see him. We don't see each other that often, but when he came up here to buy some of his songs back, which I refused to sell him, I told him that I thought he played the part of a cold-hearted Rasputin that did not consider Davy, Peter or Micky. I feel he was the catalyst in helping to destroy the group because he felt that the other boys were inadequate."[2]

Micky Dolenz observed, "He was always kind of the loner out there. He always had some problems with The Monkees."

David Pearl said, "Mike has always been outspoken and more often than not, Mike has pretty much been right."

David Jones said, "Mike could be quite tall when he wanted to be. Not to mention rude, arrogant, belligerent and aggressive, and that was on a good day."[3]

Shorty Rogers said of Michael, "He's a very groovy person, a great guy. He's one of the good guys. In my case, Michael couldn't have been nicer to me."

Steve Blauner recalled, "Mike was interested in music. Not a very nice person, but he was interested in music."

---

[1] Gary Strobl's interview with Dean Jeffries 10-18-84.
[2] Gary Strobl's interview with Lester Sill 12-6-84.
[3] David Jones- They Made a Monkee Out of Me.

Marilyn Schlossberg said, "Michael was half and half. When he was good he was very good. When he was bad he was a horror."[4]

Ward Sylvester said, "Michael always had an approach avoidance attitude toward the group. He resented it succeeding and he resented it failing. The Monkees didn't present Michael the way Michael wanted to present Michael."[5]

To understand why everyone would have such a different opinion of Michael, we need to go to the start of it all.

Photo by Henry Diltz

---

[4] Gary Strobl's interview with Marilyn Schlossberg 1-19-86.
[5] Gary Strobl's interview with Ward Sylvester 3-30-84.

Life, The Unsuspecting Captive

Michael's mother Bette Claire McMurray Nesmith Graham.
Photo from The RLM Archives.

Bette Claire McMurray was born on March 23, 1924 to Jesse Thomas McMurray and Christine DuVal McMurray. Jesse was in the wholesale auto business while Christine had her own knitting shop, along with her own local radio program where she would sing. Entrepreneurship was common in the family, as Bette's great-great grandfather, John Darby, was a co-founder of Wesleyan College in Macon, Georgia, one of the first women's colleges in the country.

Growing up in Houston Texas, Bette was known around town for her independence as well as her rebelliousness. Bette was also known to be a real wild woman. She enjoyed drinking and staying out on the town all night with various men, until a brush with uremic poisoning nearly claimed her life. A relative, who happened to be a Christian Science practitioner, stopped by the McMurrays' house to pray for Bette's health, and Bette quickly recuperated. Bette, who had been a Baptist, immediately quit her wild and wicked ways and became a devoted follower of Christian Science.[6]

Mary Baker Eddy founded the Christian Science religion in 1878. Her teachings were written in the best-selling book *Science and Health with Key to the Scriptures*. The goal of the religion is to bring the unreal material body into a condition of perfect harmony with our spiritual condition. Being made in the Divine likeness, we are geared for spiritual perfection.

It is stated in the religion that right prayerful thinking and a dutiful attentiveness to Eddy's commentaries on the Scriptures may overcome the disharmony of sin, sickness and

---

[6] Michael Nesmith- The Long Sandy Hair of Neftoon Zamora.

death. Instead of medicines and drugs, spiritual truth must be affirmed, error denied, and the distinction made between absolute being and the frail mortal life. Devout Christian Scientists do not celebrate birthdays, as they are taught not to record age.

After dropping out of Alamo Heights High School in San Antonio, Bette got a job at a law firm in a typing pool, even though she didn't know how to type. The law firm liked her so much they sent her to secretarial school. In the evenings after work, Bette earned her high school diploma.

After a brief courtship, Bette married Warren Nesmith on March 4, 1942. Since World War II had erupted, Warren left for Hawaii to fight after only two months of marriage. Unfortunately, there is a history of millions of hasty marriages before men went off to war, and when returning home the marriages would rarely last. Warren was still stationed in Hawaii when he received word that Bette had given birth to a son named Robert Michael Nesmith in Houston, Texas. The child was named Robert after Warren's father, but Bette preferred to call the child by his middle name, Michael.

Warren came back home after the war, but the couple found themselves incompatible and Bette divorced Warren in 1946. Warren deserted his family, leaving Bette and the child to suffer in poverty. This was definitely the beginning of hard times for Bette and Michael. It didn't help that Bette had been rebellious at one time, and everyone could easily have blamed her for her own problems. Regardless of her situation, Bette, confident with the religious beliefs that she was teaching Michael, was determined to build a life for her and Michael, and decided they needed a change of location.

Michael and his mother in Dallas, Circa late 1940s. Photo from The RLM Archives.

15

In the early 1950's, Jesse McMurray died and left his daughter Bette some land in Dallas. Moving to Dallas with Michael and her

mother Christine and sister Yvonne, Bette discovered the land was in a poor section of town where only the 'colored people' lived. Michael remembered in an interview, "There was all this pressure from the white folk for us to move out of the area...but we didn't want to budge. It was our home and we've always felt

that home is wherever you feel you ought to be.

"So because of the strange zoning regulations back home I went to this all colored high school. We didn't care because we didn't see anything wrong and anyway it was our home."

For years stories have been told of an incident where Michael seriously injured one of his hands. The main story told was that a firecracker had gone off in Michael's hand when he was young. Michael now discounts this by stating that what really happened was that he and some neighborhood kids were smashing rocks with a sledgehammer. Michael was holding one of the rocks and the sledgehammer came down

on his hand breaking the bones. Due to Bette's Christian Science beliefs, no doctor was summoned and the bones were not set in the hand. Because of the accident, Michael is unable to make a fist with his right hand, and he lost the use of the third finger on the same hand.

Michael attended Thomas Jefferson High School in Dallas where he was not exactly a model student. He made it clear that he did not like being

there, so it was not a huge loss to most of the staff when Michael quit school during his senior year. It was almost like Michael was begging to get expelled anyway, as he would just get up out of his seat and walk out of the classroom. No one knew what was going on in his head. The only

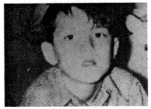

class in school that he ever talked about years later was the choir class, where he sang first tenor. The teacher, Annalee Hufaker, recalled Michael in an interview, "Mike got along very well with his peers. He kept them entertained for which they loved him. If he had a vice, it was his bid

for attention. He was never boisterous or loud, but could cause others to be so with his witty quips and antics, which were done so subtly. Many a time in getting him to stop this I would remind him to quit 'acting the monkey.'

16

"He was an actor. He showed a definite talent in this field and especially from a comedy standpoint. Each year the choir did a Broadway musical. Mike's junior year we did 'Oklahoma' and he was cast as Andrew Carnes, the father of Ado Annie. At each rehearsal he would give a new interpretation to the part especially when he came to his line, 'Nevermind the furthermore, the plea is self defense.' This naturally 'broke up' the rest of the class. On the night of the actual performance, he did a superb, authentic interpretation of the part. His senior year he was in 'The King and I.'"

Michael in his junior year of high school, circa 1959. Photo from The RLM archives.

On rare occasions Michael has talked about his years in Texas.

"I had a wretched childhood," He said. "We were dirt poor, just miserable. I hated school and I hated it at home. There wasn't any real difference, you went from one to the other and they nagged you both places. You couldn't have any fun at school, they were always teaching you the wrong things, just a lot of useless information. They never taught you how to get along in the world.

"I grew up in Texas where Hank Williams was coming out of the radio and Bobby Bland was coming out of the bars. I took in both with about equal enthusiasm. I remember I had to tell my mother that Bo Diddley was a Harvard graduate so she'd let me play his records at home."

"I remember having a list of 13 girls who might just conceivably go to the school dance with me. One time I'd rung up 12 of them and they all said they didn't want to go. Not to the dance that is, they just didn't want to go with me. Anyway I got to the 13th girl and rang her and I said, 'I suppose you wouldn't like to go to the

The house Michael grew up in when he lived in Dallas in the late 50s. Photo by Randi L. Massingill.

dance with me?' And she said, 'I'd love to go to the dance with you, Mike.' I'll never forget her name, it was Carol. I was dumb struck, I just didn't know what to say. Finally I just blurted out 'That's great, gee, I wish I had asked you first.'"

17

While Michael either suffered through school or insulted girls, Bette was working as an executive secretary for the chairman at the Texas Bank & Trust. Bette was a great secretary except for the problem of the brand new electric typewriters that had replaced her manual typewriters. Making one mistake after another, Bette kept erasing the mistake but would make the error worse as it would then smudge. Working on a freelance art project for the bank, Bette realized that when painters make mistakes in their painting they just paint over it. Bette then realized that perhaps one could paint over a typing mistake?

Bette Nesmith becomes the hero of secretaries everywhere by inventing Liquid Paper correction fluid. Photo from The RLM Archives.

At first using a small bottle filled with white paint and a brush, Bette, trying to improve on her idea, then went to Michael's chemistry teacher for help in developing a formula for tempera paint. She then learned how to grind and mix paint from a worker at a nearby paint manufacturing company. Using the product in the office got the attention of her fellow secretaries and they requested bottles. Bette then got the idea that maybe others would want her product.

Obtaining a patent, Bette set up her kitchen as a factory and started production of her product called 'Liquid Paper,' with Michael and his friends helping stir the paint and fill the bottles. Bette wrote the electric typewriter manufacturer IBM about marketing her product. IBM turned it down asking Bette to improve on the product and to contact them again in a couple of years.

She never did write them back as she took to marketing the product herself, calling her company The Mistake Out Company. Taking a small ad in the October 1958 issue of *The Office* magazine, Bette received over 500 orders from ecstatic clumsy secretaries from all over the country.

Staying up all night working on her product made Bette unable to concentrate on her secretarial day job. That problem was quickly solved when she accidentally signed her name as well as the Mistake Out Company name on the bottom of a letter to IBM for her boss. It infuriated him so much that he fired her immediately. Worried about her future as well as providing for Michael, Bette just placed her faith in God and pushed herself harder to make 'Liquid Paper' a success.

In 1962, Bette met and married Robert Graham, a frozen food salesman. This union did not please Michael, who in retaliation ran away to California, taking the family car with him. Michael went to Los Angeles where he made a little money doing odd jobs before returning home to Dallas to face a very upset mother and stepfather.

When Michael came back home, Bette had him enlist in the Air Force in hopes of him learning some discipline. Sent to Sheppards Air Force Base in Wichita Falls, Texas, Michael did not learn much discipline. The entire time at Sheppards was a miserable experience, as Michael was very much a rebel, but he would be able to get a weekend pass now and then.

On one of these weekends, Michael went to Oklahoma to a club where he saw Hoyt Axton perform with his guitar. Michael felt that he wanted to play the guitar, but, with his stubbornness, Michael would teach himself and not use any instructors. Shortly after Michael's return from Oklahoma, he managed to tip over a general's airplane while he was cleaning it. It was then decided that the Air Force was better off without Michael Nesmith and Michael Nesmith was better off without the Air Force.

Michael in High School program for "Oklahoma." Photo from The RLM Archives.

Discharged from the Air Force, Michael headed back to Dallas where he earned his GED. Then he moved to San Antonio, where he lived with his uncle Chick Adair and his wife and attended San Antonio College. Uncle Chick would later be a developer of the Seneca Estates in the Leon Valley suburb of San Antonio. Located between *Cammie Way* and *Trone Trail*, he placed *Mike Nesmith Street*.

The Kind Of Girl I Could Love

Phyllis Ann Barbour was 16 when she went to join her family in San Antonio where her father, an army officer, was stationed. Right after the start of her second semester at San Antonio College, she saw a sign up on campus saying "Folk Songs by Michael Nesmith in the Auditorium." He had been playing the guitar for only three-and-a-half weeks and had written several songs, all with two chords.

Phyllis then went to her friends in the Student Union Building and asked them, "Who is this upstart?" but none of her friends had ever

heard of him. Phyllis didn't catch his performance, but a few weeks later as she walked into the Student Union Building between classes, David Price, a friend of hers, was sitting with (as she described) "a scrawny, funny looking guy with a Brillo pad mop of black hair."

David said, "Phyllis, this is Michael Nesmith. Michael, Phyllis."

Turning to Phyllis, Michael said, "Nine is brown."

One of Michael's earliest promotional photos circa 1963-1964. Photo from The RLM Archives.

Phyllis replied, "Three is red."

From that moment a friendship was born and by the beginning of their second year of college, Michael and Phyllis were a couple.[7]

Bruce Barbour, Phyllis' brother said "I liked Mike, from the time he started dating my big sis. Gosh! I guess I was maybe 14 or something. He had a Triumph Bonneville motorcycle, which to this day, is one of the fastest bikes. He said, 'Do you want to go for a ride, kid?' I

---

[7] Gary Strobl's interview with Phyllis Nesmith 2-13-85.

said 'You bet.' He said 'You better hold on.' 'Naw, I'm fine.' And he blasted off.

"He was my hero for years and years. We were on Fort Sam Houston in a big old house because my dad was a staff officer. Mike would show up and he was. . . whatever car he was driving that year. . . but it was always hot. It was always neat. He was just really laid back. Real quiet."

While both were attending San Antonio College, Michael and Phyllis would go to the house of a blind History professor in order to read aloud to him. They were there for dinner one night and it happened to be the night of the first Beatles' performance on *The Ed Sullivan Show*. Standing in front of the TV as they watched the Beatles, both Michael and Phyllis began jumping up and down and started screaming, which hopefully did not frighten the blind professor too much.[8]

Phyllis finished her second year while Michael left long before the second year was over. He just didn't care about school or his studies as all he wanted to do now was pursue a singing career. He also wanted to marry Phyllis, and they were engaged in the early spring of 1964. One night when Michael went to pick up Phyllis for a date, he was greeted by Phyllis' father who asked, "How do you intend to support my little girl, Mike?"

"Well, I think I'll go to Hollywood and become a star," answered Michael.

As Bruce remembered, "Well, being a musician in San Antonio, Texas, that was probably the wrong thing to say to my dad. Well, I thought my dad was going to take his head off. I thought 'Oh God!!! Don't say that.'"

Trying to be a star would be no easy task, as David Price recalled, "I really don't know how he ever got to San Antonio, but I was involved with a group of people there. This is around '62-'63. We

Michael and John Kuehne in San Antonio after they won the San Antonio College talent show circa 1963-1964. Photo from The RLM Archives.

were the folk crowd and considered ourselves to be fairly esoteric folkie types. Mike just sort of showed up. I don't where he came from. He came from outer space maybe.

---

[8] Gary Strobl's interview with Phyllis Nesmith 2-13-85.

"He started playing around town with his friend John Kuehne. Mike and I got to know each other back then, but there was a lot of animosity between the pure folkies and Mike as he was very commercial. He wore the striped shirt and the clean-pressed wheat jeans and tennis shoes with no smudges on them. And he forced poor John Kuehne to do the same but if you knew John, he is a wonderful guy, but one of the great slobs of the world. Mike always had his act together. All of us were fairly derivative but then when you're that young, everyone's terrific. His stuff was sort of the Kingston Trio-ish.

"Anyway, Nesmith had this thing where he played guitar and sang these tunes and John played upright bass. We all thought he was a tad crass and commercial. Of course, he was making money and we weren't.

"So, he started booking himself and a revue that he built out of a number of us into grocery store openings and stuff like that, and we usually called ourselves 'The Mike Nesmith All-Stars.' I did a couple of the shows. There were some others who did more of them with him.

"One person of great note at this time who was part of this revue was Phyllis Barbour. She was singing with a guy named Mark Wheatley. He played guitar and she sang. She had this beautiful pure voice. I guess the comparison at the time was sort of a Joan Baez type. That was the act and Mark was this very interesting guy and very nervous guitar player.

"So, that's where we met. I'm told by both Mike and Phyllis that I introduced them but I couldn't come up with a story on that if I had to. We used to hang out at the Student Union at San Antonio Junior College. There was about 10-15-20 people in this basic group of people and back then we were fairly off-the-wall, we were not hippies at that point even though a lot of us became hippies later. We were sort of the artistic crowd.

"And somewhere along the line there eating french-fries between classes, I'm told I said, 'Mike, this is Phyllis. Phyllis, this is Mike.' I can't really think of a specific moment that I met either one of them. I know I knew Phyllis before Mike, but any rate, Mike always fascinated me and he still does to this day. He and I are kind of different types. I do know that Mike stood out in the crowd in those days.

"There was a great deal of animosity directed toward him and I think a lot of it was, in retrospect, was that he had it together and we didn't. We were pretending to be something and he was actually going for it. He eventually left San Antonio in an old MG Sprite that was a little teeny car. Bug-eye Sprites they were called. The car was as long as this coffee table.

22

"He and John Kuehne packed up all of their belongings and John's big old bass and a little U-Haul that was tacked on to this dumb little car and drove to L.A. to make their fortune. When he did that we all said 'Well, hasta lumbago to that.'

"I think somewhere in there prior to his leaving for L.A., he went as a solo act and played around Cape Cod one summer for a few months. Just before he left for L.A., he came back to San Antonio and I remember he had either a Yale or Harvard sweatshirt and was feeling a lot more confident because he had obviously done well. If you know Mike, he would always do well.

"I think that was the point where he probably came back after that and worked a little bit more around town with all of us Bozos and he said, 'Hey, these guys (chuckling) are clowns. I'm out of here.'"

Record labels in San Antonio at the time were a dime a dozen, and Michael took advantage of it by recording his very first single on the Highness label, featuring the songs; *Wanderin'* and *Well, Well. Wanderin'* featured Michael alone on guitar with a very simple arrangement of a song about wanderin' down the highway, and *Well, Well* was strictly a filler piece with a simple chant of "well, well" throughout.

Michael also wrote a song called *Go Somewhere and Cry* that was recorded by Denny Ezba and the

Michael auditioning for WFAA-TV. Photo from the George Gimarc collection.

Goldens which featured Michael whistling in the background.

Michael also recorded several songs with Michael Martin Murphy and John Kuehne under the name of the Trinity River Boys for Phil Spector's Prospector label. The Nesmith compositions included on the album are *East O' Texas, Dawn Broke Clear in the Morning, How Can You Kiss Me?, The Black and Blues,* and *All The King's Horses.* The record had a limited pressing and is difficult to locate.

After his recordings went absolutely nowhere, Michael needed to earn some money, so he went to Dallas and worked briefly for his mom Bette. Bette was still working on her Liquid Paper product, and she had moved the company out of her kitchen and into its own building in a desolate part of Dallas. Bette also hired her first full time employee, Judy Canup, who became the office manager as well as the official feeder for Bette's dog Buttercup.

Michael returned to San Antonio in June of '64 where he and Phyllis were married on June 27, 1964. As a wedding present for the

Phyllis and Michael on their wedding day. June 27, 1964 photo from The RLM Archives.

couple, Bette gave them a brand new MG 1100, but, in an absurd move, all she did was make the down payment for him.[9]

So, there they were, a newlywed couple with no visible means of income and strapped with three years of new car payments.

---

[9] Gary Strobl's interview with Keith Allison 9-89.

Cruisin' Through The Jungles of L.A.

Four days after the wedding, Michael and Phyllis headed out to Los Angeles. Accompanying them was his friend John Kuehne and John's stand-up bass guitar. John and Michael rode in the front with the pregnant Phyllis riding in the back, sharing the back seat with John's bass. They were going to Los Angeles with a few sheets and towels, and close to $400 in cash, but no job, no contacts, and most importantly, no place to live.

They didn't know anybody out there except for John's friend, Keith Allison. When they got into town, they stayed one night with Allison in his apartment, and the next day went to North Hollywood. They were told that the rents were cheaper there, so they went out and found an apartment at the corner of Lankershim and Cahuenga that cost $105 bucks a month. The apartment was furnished with, as Phyllis described it, "hideous" orange Naugahyde furniture. They had no TV, no radio, no nothing.

Every morning was the same as Michael and John would get up and Phyllis would starch and iron their identical outfits. The standard was that if you played together as a folk group, you wore the same thing, the same color baby blue chino pants and the same color striped, button-down shirt.

Wearing their matching starched shirts, Michael would take his guitar, Kuehne would take his bass, and together they would walk up and down Sunset Boulevard. They would walk into publishing places and agents' offices and ask if they could play their tunes. They had been there about a week-and-a-half and were down to $3.65 and hadn't

Michael & John Kuehne as a folk duo, 1964. Photo from The RLM Archives.

eaten for nearly two days when they walked into Frankie Laine's office on Sunset. There they spoke with Jackie Sherman, who would hang around at agents' offices trying to find talent to represent. She was, coincidentally, the daughter of their landlord. She listened to them

25

perform, and Laine happened to be in the back. She called him out and had him listen to them play. It was decided then that he would record one of Michael's songs called *Pretty Little Princess*, a slow folk number featuring a rapid fire auctioneer type lyric delivery. Laine took $50 out of his pocket and handed it to a very happy Michael, who immediately took Phyllis and John to the grocery store to buy food.[10]

Throughout the years Michael's story has changed about his contact with Laine. In an interview in the late 70's, Michael stated, "We were discovered playing in a club by Frankie Laine's girlfriend, who really liked the way we sounded. She recommended us to Frankie, who was starting his own label at the time called Omnibus."[11]

If Michael was worried about providing for his wife and his future offspring he didn't ever let it show as Phyllis explained, "It was 1964 and I was a little wifey. It must have been so scary for him. He accepted that responsibility of providing for us and he had an enormous drive and an enormous sense of destiny, of direction. I think it would have been much easier on him to not have had a wife and to not have been expecting a child. Maybe when you're trying to shoot for the moon, it helps to have one person in all the world who adores you without reservation, who says, 'You hung the moon. You can do it. I believe in you.' Maybe it helps."

Jackie Sherman saw great promise in the team of Michael and John, and she became their manager with their first gig being a tour of high school assemblies in the most ironic of places, Texas. Michael and John proceeded to trek back to Texas in a white Chevy station wagon with their instruments. They also took a map of Texas with a million little towns that they would have to find so that they would be able to perform two assemblies per day. They would play one in the morning, and then drive to a whole different city by the afternoon for the second.

Meanwhile Phyllis stayed in the apartment for a month by herself. When Michael's mother and her husband came out to California to visit and found Phyllis pregnant and living alone, they took her back with them to Texas. Phyllis spent that time from September to the beginning of January going back and forth between her parents, who still lived in San Antonio, and Michael's folks who lived in Dallas. Every couple of weeks, Michael would be close enough to San Antonio or Dallas that they could be together. The tour finished right before Christmas and Michael joined the family in Dallas. Then, at the beginning of January, the newlyweds packed up, and went back to

---

[10] Jason Humphrey's interview with Frankie Laine
[11] Blitz, September/October, 1978.

California where they rented another apartment at the same complex they had lived at before.

At 6:30 a.m. on January 31, 1965, Christian DuVal Nesmith entered the world. Not much is known about Christian's birth except that it was at the Griffith Park Maternity Home where a Christian Science Practitioner looked over the proceedings. Michael had been taught the ways of the Christian Science religion by his mother and would teach them to Phyllis, who, in turn, would pass them to her children.

Michael's association with Sherman began to unravel. There was a feeling that while they were on the tour she had cheated them out of some of the money they had earned. She would tell them, "You know, you can only keep this much for expenses. Send it all back here, I'll keep it. I'll hold it for you and we'll settle up at the end." When Michael and John returned, there was nothing left over at the end. Michael then disassociated himself from Sherman and went on his own again.[12]

It has been reported in many articles and printed in many books that Michael at this point was a session musician for Stax/Volt Records. This information is inaccurate and Michael has called the story 'hogwash.' This bit of misinformation originated in an interview with Tony Everett in the early Seventies for *Phonograph Record* magazine.

Another bit of misinformation is the appearance of a certain "Tony" on the Nesmith single on the Edan label featuring the songs *Just a Little Love* and *Curson Terrace*. Although the A side was credited just to Michael, the B-side *Curson Terrace* was credited to "Mike and Tony". When asked whom Tony was Michael answered, "I'd like to know that one myself! I have no idea who Tony is. I never played with anyone named Tony. I was amazed when I found out that this single had been released. It most definitely is me on there, but I have no idea who is behind the release of it."

Bill Chadwick, a musician and songwriter around Los Angeles, had been working for Randy Sparks, a promoter in the Los Angeles area, and Bill was putting together a group for him called The Survivors. One night in 1965, Randy was out of town so he asked Chadwick to go to the Troubadour "Hoot" amateur night for him. Bill was instructed to scout it out and see if there was anybody new in town that he thought was interesting. Michael was performing there and made an immediate impression on the songwriter. Chadwick suggested that Michael contact the Sparks' organization. Willing to follow up on a possible job opportunity, Mike went down and was hired on the spot, as the staff liked him immediately.

---

[12] Gary Strobl's interview with Phyllis Nesmith 2-13-85.

Randy Sparks held a songwriters' workshop each day for three

The Survivors from left to right: Del Ramos, Bill Chadwick, Niles Brown, Carol Strong, Michael, Owen Castleman and John Kuehne. 1965 photo from The RLM Archives.

or four hours. Other members of the workshop were Michael Murphey and Owen Castleman from The Survivors, and John Denver. Mike and Bill got to be pretty good friends right off, and, since Mike was sitting in on the workshops each day, during free time he and Bill would get together and write songs which they performed at night. Soon, on their own, they started going into the Troubadour on Monday nights where they would perform with John Kuehne on bass.

It was around July when Michael started with The Survivors. With a weekly salary, Michael, Phyllis, John and baby Christian moved to an old Spanish duplex in the Hollywood Hills, right behind the Hollywood Bowl. It had a little yard and they added a dog to the family. One night, the couple along with Kuehne sat in the front yard and listened to the Beatles concert that was going on at the Hollywood Bowl. Unfortunately, The Survivors didn't survive, as member Del Ramos remembered the fire at Ledbetters, "We had just finished doing three concerts that night and the crowd had been out of the building for at least five minutes, and somebody must have left a cigarette burning in the trash can, and the place went up in like seven minutes. I watched it burn. I couldn't believe it. I was just across the street sitting in my car with some girl and this building burns down."

Nobody was hurt in the fire, but almost everyone's musical instruments were in the building and they were destroyed including Michael's guitar. The Survivors went their separate ways. After the fire,

28

Michael, who quickly replaced his guitar, John Kuehne and Bill Chadwick started performing at the Troubadour Club every Monday night.

A Journey With Michael Blessing

Bob Krasnow was searching the clubs to find a singer to record a Tom Paxton song called *The Willing Conscript*. Deciding that Michael had the sound he was looking for, Krasnow became his manager and also had him signed to the Colpix label for two singles. Krasnow had a problem with the name Nesmith. "You gotta have a different name because Nesmith stinks," he said.

Going to the phone book, and finding nothing in the A section that pleased him, Michael replied, "Well, how does Blessing sound?"

"Not much better but I will go with that."

Barry Friedman, a former record distributor, worked for Randy Sparks as a publicity man. He was a Hollywood hotshot who would run around town and get things done such as getting concert tickets and getting jobs for people. One day Barry read an ad that appeared in the entertainment newspaper *Variety* that said, "Madness, Auditions, Folk & Roll Musicians Singers for acting roles in a new TV series, Running parts for 4 insane boys, age 17-21 Want spirited Ben Frank's-types. Have courage to work, Must come down for interview. Call: HO 6-5188." Barry recommended that the guys go down there and try their luck.

Bill Chadwick remembered, "He had been sending us out on a lot of stuff like that. We said, 'Oh, yeah. OK, another one of these.' We went to the interviews in an old Colpix Records office on 1347 N. Cahuenga Boulevard above an electronics supply store."

Another version of the audition story comes from Doug Weston, who owned the Troubadour club. Weston stated years later that Screen Gems came by the Troubadour to see Michael as well as asking Weston about any possible people for their TV series. Weston said that he recommended Michael as well as Peter Tork, a folk musician from Greenwich Village.

The producers of the show, Bob Rafelson and Bert Schneider had an idea for a TV show with a brand new style. The idea was a comedy with the main characters being young men in a rock and roll band. The idea had been used in the movies very successfully with The Beatles in *A Hard Days Night* back in 1964. The movie was a major hit and the reasoning in show business is that if you see something successful then you copy it and milk as much money as you can with the idea.

The producers didn't want to use any established bands or any professional actors. They wanted men who were interesting, exciting

30

young personalities with a natural sense of humor. They also wanted each guy to have a look that would set the young girls' hearts a flutter. Among the men auditioning were Stephen Stills, John Denver, Paul Williams, Tim Rooney (son of Mickey Rooney), Micky Dolenz, John Kuehne, Bill Chadwick and Michael, who at the audition wore his green wool hat that he used to keep his long hair out of his eyes while riding his motorcycle.

Throughout the years it was rumored that Charles Manson auditioned for the show, but this is not true as Manson was in prison at the time of the auditions and was too old to qualify. Manson would be very famous a few years later, but unfortunately it would be for the Tate/LaBianca murders.

There were hundreds of auditions that consisted of Rafelson and Schneider quizzing, heckling and in some cases, angering the applicants just to see what they would do. During the audition, they stressed that they wanted the four men who would be chosen to have some musical experience, ad-lib and most importantly, be original.

The auditions filtered out the weak from the strong, and before long the search had been narrowed down to eight men. One of the eight was Nesmith, who was mostly interested in writing songs for the TV show. The producers then filmed screen tests of Michael and the other seven finalists that included; Peter Tork, Nyles Brown, Micky Dolenz, Bill Chadwick, and David Jones, who was already under contract to Screen Gems and was already chosen to be in the group.

Then Rafelson and Schneider used an audience research division of Screen Gems called Audience Studies Inc. to test and rate each finalist. When they were finished, the decision was made that the four insane boys would be Mike Nesmith, Micky Dolenz, Peter Tork and David Jones.

British born David Jones had been a child actor in England appearing on the soap opera *Coronation Street*. His big chance at stardom came in 1964 as he performed on Broadway in *Oliver* playing the Artful Dodger. He was nominated for a Tony Award for Best Supporting Actor, but lost to David Burns who was appearing in *How to Succeed in Business Without Really Trying*.

After *Oliver*, David appeared in *Pickwick* where he was spotted by Screen Gems executives, who saw a gold mine of talent and charm in the British teenager. Determined to find a showcase for David, Screen Gems signed him to a seven-year contract.

David was proposed for a television series where he would play twin cousins, but the show was given to Patty Duke instead. David recorded an album for Columbia's Colpix record label that did not sell that well but earned him a small fan following as well as mentions in the fan magazines. Guest starring on *Ben Casey* and *The Farmer's Daughter* was the training ground for his future work, and he was a true professional in posing for publicity photos as well as recording and filming.

Micky Dolenz had been a child actor for Screen Gems, playing the title role in the NBC show *Circus Boy* back in the fifties. His first name was really George, but he was billed as Mickey Braddock so as not to confuse television audiences, as his father George Dolenz had his own television show, *The Count of Monte Cristo.*

After *Circus Boy*, Micky guest starred on *Peyton Place, Mr. Novak* and an episode of *Playhouse 90* entitled *The Velvet Alley.* Micky would be no

problem for the producers, as he was a professional actor who was accustomed to waiting between filming scenes and he was willing to take orders from directors. He knew that this was just another role for him.

Peter Tork was an accomplished musician who could play nine musical instruments. He was a folk musician from Greenwich Village working as a dishwasher, who chanced upon the audition by word of his friend Stephen Stills. Stills had been turned down by the producers because of his thinning hair and his crooked teeth. Peter was not an actor, but he was a quick study with nice hair and good teeth. He was very glad to be working and would hardly be any trouble for the producers.

Then there was Michael, who was not an actor, but a high strung perfectionist musician who did not want to be told what to do, and did not want to sit in a make up chair for long periods of time. This one would be a problem for the producers.

Now that the actors for the band had been picked, the producers had to find a name for them. They tossed around names like The Creeps, The Parrots, The Inevitables and The Turtles before settling on the name The Monkees. The misspelling of the band's name was the trend at the time, and Screen Gems found themselves unable to copyright the word "monkeys." After the name was picked, Screen Gems set a budget of $200,000 for the pilot episode. The amount was unusually high considering there was not even a written outline for the show yet.

Bob Krasnow managed to get Colpix records interested in Michael, and they agreed to release two singles. The first single to be recorded was *The Willing Conscript*, but the name of it would be changed to *The New Recruit*. The song, Michael's first released song with a full band, was a war protest number given a satirical twist, with the new recruit in the Army stating his eagerness to learn his new job because he had never killed anyone before.

Shorty Rogers, recalling the first meeting with Michael said, "Bob Krasnow called me on the phone. Lester Sill told him to call me. Bob had discovered a new young singer that they were going to record on the Colpix label. The singer's name was Michael Blessing. We had a date set and I lived in Van Nuys. We were just going to do two sides, and, as the arranger, I needed to get with the singer and set what keys we're going to do it in.

"I talked to Michael on the phone and he said, 'I'll come Monday.' I said, 'Great. Monday's fine. Here's my address.' Monday came and he called me and he said, 'I can't get out there.' Something like, 'I'm busy.' I said, 'Fine. Come tomorrow.' Well, this went on each day and it was finally Thursday or Friday. . . the whole week went by and finally he came out with Bob Krasnow. He got out there and he later kind of leaked the information to me that he wanted to come over in the week, but he said that he was living in his car and that they had no gas! It took till Thursday for him to get a ride out to the house.

"So, we got in there and we working on the key and he had his guitar. . . he was playing some beautiful things. I made a little tape of Michael performing the song it so I'd be prepared to write it into sheet music. In the middle of it, the phone rang and it was a phone call to Michael. He spoke on the phone in front of me and he just got very

elated. He hung up the phone and said, 'I just got the news. I'm going to be with The Monkees.' I was there and I witnessed it.

"We did the recording session the following week. . . a Buffy Saint-Marie tune called *Until It's Time For You To Go* along with *What Seems To Be The Trouble, Officer?* He did a wonderful job. I really knew this was a special guy."

To promote *Until It's Time For You To Go*, Michael appeared on the local Los Angeles program, *The Lloyd Thaxton Show*. Wearing a denim jacket and blue jeans, looking forlorn, like he had lost his last friend, Michael sat on a stool and lip-synched the song. After the song, Thaxton, who appeared to be a carbon copy of Ed Sullivan in his mannerisms, interviewed Michael. Unfortunately, the single sank without a trace until it was re-recorded and became a hit for Elvis Presley as well as Buffy Saint-Marie.

Reflecting on his early recordings, Michael said, "The early material is more about producers trying to catch a hit, rather than the message or artistry of a singer or a song, and that's why it's so poor and why it makes me cringe a little. Baby pictures, but in some weird make-up."

In November of 1965 the pilot film for The Monkees was filmed in five days. The show was a wacky comedy about four unemployed musicians who lived together in a California beach house filled with wacky props. They spent their time trying to get gigs and find fame. The songs included in the show would alternately feature film of the band playing and "romps" showing the boys running around and causing wholesome mischief.

The guys were told to go home and wait for news that the show had been sold. It was around that time that the guys began to hang out together and really get to know each other. Peter came to live at Mike and Phyllis' Hollywood Hills home, and Micky was there all the time, even though he didn't live there. In March The Nesmiths and all of their houseguests moved to a house on Sunset Plaza Drive, where Davy lived with them, along with Phyllis' brother Bruce, and David Price.

On Thanksgiving Day in 1965, Bill Chadwick's mom Iris made a great big Thanksgiving dinner for all of Bill's musician friends, who were all made to feel like part of the Chadwick family. She had a big oak dining table where all of the guests, including Michael, Owen Castleman, Mike Murphey and John Denver would sit around talking about what was going to happen with their future.

Denver suddenly said, "I'm going to make it."

Mike said, "You're not going to make it any faster than I am. I'm going to make it bigger than you are."[13]

---

[13] Gary Strobl's interview with Bill Chadwick 9-25-87.

Hollywood

In January of 1966 the news was that NBC had picked up the Monkees for their fall season. The studio contracted the four actors for $400 a week. Michael was still under contract to manager Bob Krasnow who sold the contract to Screen Gems and got quite a bit of money for it.

Marilyn Schlossberg was hired as a production assistant for The Monkees and recalled her first day on the job, "I was wearing a chain belt that day. Michael, for some reason, was standing behind me in the office and suddenly, I found that he had chained me to the file cabinet. That was my introduction to the boys."[14]

To turn the boys into comedic geniuses, actor Jim Frawley, who would also direct some episodes of The Monkees TV show, gave the guys classes on improvisation. At first the boys didn't know what to do, and they appeared awkward until Frawley started giving them instructions.

Typical instructions were having Michael talk the way a teapot would, or having Micky imitate a gangster. It was exercises like these that helped the guys loosen up and become more comedic. They would

---

[14] Gary Strobl's interview with Marilyn Schlossberg 1-19-86

also sit and watch countless hours of Three Stooges and Laurel and Hardy movies. The producers were very happy with the way the boys were coming along in the humor department, but they needed a unique visual impact.

Gene Ashman was given the task of coming up with costumes for The Monkees to wear on their TV show. Ashman recalled the design of The Monkees famous eight button shirts, "It was through the influence of Mike Nesmith. . . we were talking about something that was interesting. . . something that would be a move away from what was then considered the Mods. We came up with the idea of doing like a John Wayne shirt. . . so, in a way, Mike Nesmith had quite a bit to with its conception. I took it and then made it practical.

"I took a contemporary shirt and I added a plastron front which made it into a Western shirt and made the cuffs wider giving us that ambiance . . . feeling of being a Western shirt and then added eight buttons. Actually, Mike Nesmith and I came up with it. We were talking about a look and I just happened to mention using a plastron shirt. He said 'Hey, that would be terrific.' So, we made one up real quick. . . about 10 minutes. He put it on and he loved it. And by him liking it, the other kids liked it."

In addition to the shirts, Michael would continue to wear his green wool hat. The producers liked the hat so much that they even had his character's name as "Wool Hat" for a time, but as Bob Rafelson recalled, "By using their own names on the show, there was some identification. We had a fight with Mike Nesmith because we called him 'Wool Hat' on the show and he said 'I will not be called 'Wool Hat.' Mike was pretty rebellious when it came to the whole image thing. I would say that Mike was the most independent. He enjoyed the success of it, but he took his measure of it very seriously and said 'I'd rather do it my way and have less.' I doubt if anybody thought that they would have less."

Photo by Gene Trindl

The early episodes shaped the boys' personalities. David, the tambourine and maracas player, would be the dreamy Monkee with the stars in his eyes, falling in love at a drop of the hat. Micky, the drummer, was the wacky Monkee who couldn't stay still or stay serious. Peter, the bass player, was the dumb Monkee who would always manage to get the guys in trouble somehow. Michael, the lead guitarist, was the smart Monkee with a quick wit and appeared to be the leader of the group even though no leader was officially named.

To show his loyalty, Michael got his friends various jobs with the show. Bill Chadwick would sing background vocals on some of The Monkees' songs, while David Price and John Kuehne became stand-ins for David and himself respectively. John Kuehne joined the Screen Extras Guild and changed his name to John London when he discovered that there was already a John Kuehne in the guild.

Michael thought that at least The Monkees could be a real band, but Screen Gems had the boys busy filming episodes, posing for publicity photos and giving interviews for the press. There were not enough hours in the day to rehearse as well as record music on a regular basis. But despite this, according the Michael, the first song recorded by the Monkees was his own composition, "The Girl I Knew Somewhere". Still, after hearing a few recordings, Bert and Bob said that they liked the music enough, but they knew there was not enough time to mold the guys into a flawless band. They felt that the boys shouldn't be bothered by the music portion, but their decision upset Michael since he was a singer/songwriter and musician.

They brought in several music producers such as Mickey Most, Snuff Garrett and Leon Russell, but they all left intimidated by Michael, who even called some of their work "garbage" to their face. Gerry Goffin and Carole King flew in from New York to try their production skills. After a fiery confrontation with Nesmith in the studio, King burst into tears and flew back home that same day.

38

In desperation Bert and Bob called on Don Kirshner to be the music supervisor. He was the president of the Columbia Pictures/Screen Gems music division, where he was the music supervisor of such shows as *Bewitched, I Dream of Jeannie* and *The Farmer's Daughter*. He was also in charge of a successful publishing company, and Kirshner had his own stable of songwriters that punched a timeclock in an office, wrote songs all day, and then went home at five o'clock. These people included Neil Diamond, Goffin and King, Carol Bayer Sager and Neil Sedaka. The first act of business for Kirshner, known in the industry as "The Man With The Golden Ear", was to find a producer for The Monkees. As time went on, Michael would make an effort to try and chop off the golden ear.

Songwriting team and singers Tommy Boyce and Bobby Hart were working for Screen Gems at the time. They thought that they would get the job of being The Monkees' producers, if they could just show Kirshner what they could do. They assembled tapes that they had made of The Monkees performing and played them for Kirshner. Kirshner was impressed enough to go ahead and hire the team to be The Monkees producers. With that accomplished, Boyce and Hart set out to listen to each Monkee and figure out what they could do with their voice.

They found Micky's voice the easiest voice to work with, while Michael was trying to pass himself off as a country singer. Davy had a voice pleasant enough for ballads but not much else, and with Peter, well, they never figured out what to do with his voice.

Boyce and Hart went to the recording studio with Davy and Micky, and they recorded song after song for the television show. The producers' job was to assemble a band for the recording sessions, and Boyce and Hart used the finest musicians in the Los Angeles area. It was a common practice by major record companies and singing talent at the time, but one that would come back to haunt the guys later.

Even though Michael may have made her burst into tears, Carole King came back to L.A. and the two collaborated on a song called *Sweet Young Thing*. Michael told an interviewer about his experience, "Carole came out here after she broke up with Gerry Goffin and we had dinner together. She said 'Do you think we could write together, think we could be a writing team?' I said, 'Boy, you can't imagine how much I wish we could.' We sat down and wrote the song together. Gerry and Carole and I wrote four or five things together. Some of the stuff is still stuck in New York. They came out and stayed at my house. I loved her, always have loved her, but I just hate her records. God! I just can't stand her records! But I told her when we talked about getting together, you see I connected with her on a personal level, I just loved her, but I just couldn't connect with her on a musical level."[15]

Michael's passion about the honesty of his music had caused friction with the producers as Wayne Erwin, a singer who had worked with Boyce and Hart recalled, "The Monkees had done not only the pilot but they had about another four or five shows in the can. So it was really going full force. I heard through Boyce and Hart that they were having hassles with Nesmith because he was very independent. He was always very by himself and righteously so. . . the guy's talented cat and didn't just want to be a little puppet guy down there. Some of the other guys were a little more willing to just be a puppet and to go along with the moves just to have a show. But, he was a little more headstrong than that.

"So he's giving them trouble and always bitching about this and demanding that. . . and this is before the show was on the air. One night after a session up at RCA, Boyce and Hart

---

[15] Interview with Michael Nesmith from Zig Zag #39, 1973.

come over and say, 'Hey! Wayne, come out with us tonight to dinner. Don Kirshner's going to take us to dinner.' I said, 'Oh great, man. Let's go.' So, me and Boyce and Hart and Kirshner went to a restaurant in Hollywood. I thought, 'Well, gee, this is nice asking me along with the bigwigs on this. How cool.'

"So, we're sitting there having dinner and Kirshner says, 'Wayne, we've been having these problems with Nesmith and we're thinking about bumping him off the show. If we do, we're thinking about having you replace him. Would you be interested in that?' I said, 'Yeah, I'd be interested in that. Absolutely.' So, I sit around for a couple of weeks still doing the sessions and just wondering if Nesmith was still fucking up. . . enough to get bounced off that show and hoping he was. I was wondering if there's any way I could help it along. . . instigate some shit."[16] Nothing happened. Michael was never dropped from the show, but that didn't mean he had stopped bitching.

As a way to make Michael happy, he was allowed to play guitar on his songs and produce his own compositions. As Bill Chadwick

recalled, "My feeling was that Mike wanted to make sure that he didn't get buried in somebody else's sound. He wasn't trying to take the group in any particular direction. He was just trying to be sure that he wasn't dragged into some direction that was totally foreign to him. He wanted to express himself, and he was led to believe that he was going to have an opportunity to do that. Once Mike set his mind to do something, he was a pretty hard guy to dissuade from doing what he wanted to do. He was a man with a goal. He knew how to achieve that goal."

With the musical success of TV related theme songs such as *Rawhide*, *Bonanza*, and *Dobie Gillis* and the performances of Ricky Nelson on *The Adventures of Ozzie And Harriet*, among several others, the producers thought that they might sell a few copies of an album of

---

[16] Gary Strobl's interview with Wayne Erwin 2-13-86.

Monkees songs. Kirshner, however, believed that with a great promotional push, there could be a great business with Monkee albums. The money for the promotion would come from Screen Gems, and by building up the music, it would promote the TV show and vice versa. In preparation for The Monkees project, the Colpix label was shut down and a new label was started called Colgems, named after the partnership between Columbia and Screen Gems, with a major distribution deal with RCA Records, and with The Monkees being the first act signed on the label.

The Monkees music promotion plan was going smoothly, but the Screen Gems TV promotion strategy hit a snag when they made a disastrous mistake of having The Monkees appear at Chasens restaurant for the annual meeting of the NBC affiliates during the presentation of the new fall season. Not allowed to perform music, the boys were told to "be funny" which turned into an unrehearsed session of childish pranks and goofing off which involved Micky switching the power off inside Chasens and the boys stopping traffic by playing a game of volleyball in the middle of Beverly Boulevard using the NBC symbol, a stuffed peacock, as the volleyball. And this was before they were on stage.

Finally the world's oldest teenager introduced them, host of the *American Bandstand* TV show Dick Clark. The boys resorted to lame comedy bits such as Micky pretending to shave with a microphone and Davy imitating a duck. All of the humor wore thin with the affiliates who did not find these long haired kids amusing at all, and the end result was that at least five major markets turned down The Monkees TV show. The lack of affiliates would affect The Monkees in the future when it came to the national weekly ratings.

With a budget of $100,000, Kirshners's great Monkee campaign began. "Monkeemen" visited thousands of disc jockeys around the country, showering them with preview records and bumper stickers announcing "Monkee Business is Big Business" and "The Monkees Are The Greatest." Carole Shelyne and Shelley Farrell were picked to be the "Monkee Maids." Their job was to travel around the country and be interviewed on radio and television about The Monkees and their upcoming television series since The Monkees were too busy to promote themselves. Ads started appearing in magazines everywhere to call attention to both the records as well as the TV show. Screen Gems and Colgems were hoping The Monkees would be as big as Beatlemania had been. The joining of the music business and the television business had never been done before, and it was showing promise of huge profits for all involved.

Ed Justin was in charge of the merchandising for the show, and his job was to make every imaginable related product available for sale.

42

He had the teen magazine editors under contract to pay a fee for Monkee photos, which was unheard of at the time. Not even Colonel Tom Parker had been able to do that with Elvis back in the Fifties.

If any of the magazine editors made a fuss, they were threatened with being forbidden to have any coverage on The Monkees, or even worse, not being allowed on the set of the show for exclusive interviews. They reluctantly put up with the hassles of Screen Gems because they knew that the teenage girls would like The Monkees. They knew that the guys were very cute, especially Davy, who was British and had a "groovy" British accent. Thanks to the Beatles, this became a very big asset for the show.

The other guys had teen idol potential as well, except for Mike who was the odd man out since he was married. Being a married teen idol was not good for business, but then it didn't hurt Beatle John

Phyllis and Michael posing for Henry Diltz circa 1967-1968.

Lennon's standing with the fans. They just simply hated Cynthia Lennon with a passion since she stood in the way of their having a chance with Lennon. It was wondered how Michael would handle the issue of his marriage with the fans. Phyllis' brother, Bruce Barbour, remembered, "For a long while, Mike didn't want anyone to know that he was married. He usually felt that young kids would not identify with it. It was much more desirable to have a young eligible guy to worship than to have the teen magazines saying, 'No, this guy is married, and he's out of reach.' I never wanted to play upon that relationship. But, I also wanted to stand by my sister."[17]

Pretty soon the teen magazines had ads for everything from Monkees sweatshirts to Monkees pillowcases. There were hundreds of items with The Monkees on them, and they were all approved by Screen Gems to make certain that there were no shoddy items with the boys' faces on them. Mike's wool hat was even mass marketed in several different colors (including fluorescent pink) with tiny Monkees logos sewed on them.

---

[17] Gary Strobl's interview with Bruce Barbour 6-24-86.

There was also Chuck Laufer over at *Tiger Beat* Magazine, who had signed a contract with the option of having an all Monkees magazine, which would pay Screen Gems even more if this show succeeded. There were also exclusive Monkee photos that Laufer would pay a fee on. According to a memo to a business executive from Ed Justin, Laufer was a first rate client and should be given the fullest cooperation possible. It's unknown how much Laufer paid Screen Gems, but it must have been a good amount, as he would have a contract with them to handle David Cassidy a few years later.

JC Penney, a popular mass market clothing store, got on the bandwagon by creating a line of Monkee wear. There were sections in both the men's wear and the women's departments, each being called The Monkees Pad. Photos were taken of The Monkees wearing the line of Monkee clothes, and plans were made to include these photos on a future album cover. It was estimated at the time that the clothing line would gross at least $20 million. Of the millions of dollars that could potentially be made off of The Monkees merchandising, the actors had nothing in their contracts regarding royalties from their likeness.

In exchange for promotion, Pontiac donated a car to create the Monkeemobile, a souped-up fire engine red Pontiac GTO, modified by Dean Jeffries especially for the show. Pontiac got even more promotion out of The Monkees deal by loaning each of The Monkees a Pontiac GTO convertible for a year. Michael managed to get into trouble in his new car as he was caught speeding one evening. The cop discovered that the white GTO was not registered in Michael's name. It took a quick call to Pontiac to keep Michael out of jail.[18]

On August 16, Colgems released a single of *Last Train to Clarksville*, a song that would be featured on The Monkees debut album as well as on an upcoming episode. Before the show was even on the air, the single was on the *Billboard* magazine record charts.

On September 1, The Monkees were sent out on a ten day promotional tour visiting major cities around the country. Thousands of teenagers were given tickets to these events through the local radio stations, and they responded enthusiastically to The Monkees who appeared on stage clowning around and playing music. Barbara Hamaker, who worked at KHJ during the last date on the promo tour remembered, "I worked at KHJ, which was *the* station in L.A. in 1965-66. Their big thing at the time was to promote listenership by huge promotion giveaways of tickets, they would create an event. I think Bert and Bob approached KHJ. They wanted to promote *Last Train To Clarksville*. So, Don Berrigan, who was the promotion guy/publicity guy at KHJ, devised a promotion in which we rented a train from Union Station down in L.A. and we created a fictitious Clarksville. We used some podunk town called Del Mar, California, that was on the beach,

---

[18] *Car Review* magazine December 1986.

between Los Angeles and San Diego. It had a little old-fashioned train station and we put a big Clarksville sign over the station and we gave away tickets on the air. The tenth caller would get two free tickets to the 'Last Train To Clarksville.' To this day, I don't know how we did it. I was the one who had to type up all the releases and all of the stuff that was involved in getting kids onto the train. It seems to me that there were hundreds, it was like 400. They flew the four Monkees in by helicopter to Clarksville, they had a bandstand all set up. It was on the beach as I recall. So, all the kids got off the train, The Monkees did a couple of songs, the kids got back on the train, and we came back to L.A."

Horserace

Finally after all of the chaos, *The Monkees* TV show debuted. It won second place for its time slot losing first place to ABC's *Iron Horse*, a western show about a gambler who wins a partially completed railroad, which was also produced by Screen Gems. The Monkees unexpectedly beat out the hit series *Gilligan's Island*. The series, about seven people who were stranded on an island after a storm interrupted their three hour tour, was a huge hit for CBS and had been moved opposite *The Monkees* specifically to deflate some of the younger audience. In the national ratings the show reached number 70. It would never get into the top 20 due to the number of NBC affiliates who refused to pick up the show. It was the boys' long hair, as well as the disastrous Chasens incident, that kept them from getting into the top ten.

The first episode that aired, *Royal Flush* featured the boys saving Princess Bettina from her evil uncle, the Archduke Otto, who plans to kill her so he can be the ruler of Harmonica. The episode showed the viewers something that had never been attempted before on

TV. Entire songs from the first Monkees album were joined with "romps," which were injected into the storyline with quick cuts.

One other unique thing about the show's concept was the fact that there were four long-haired teenage boys living alone with no authority figure. This had never been attempted before, since long hair on boys was usually synonymous with drug usage, but The Monkees were four teenage boys who just wanted to be happy and find regular work somewhere so they could pay the rent on time, even though they had the coolest car on TV.

Each Monkee had his own dressing room to go to after filming a scene. Each room had a distinct personality. Micky's room had a shag carpet that covered the walls as well as the floor that was covered with dozens of paisley pillows. Peter's room was filled with musical instruments and sheet music and assorted musical knickknacks. Davy's room was the ultimate star trip, the mirror was surrounded by light bulbs and telegrams, letters and photos lined the walls. Michael's dressing room was the strangest of them all, as Micky recalled, "I still can't figure out where he was coming from. He had real hi-tech psychedelia. Mike, who was down home country-western, and yet, he had the walls solid aluminum foil. He'd taken Reynolds Wrap and just papered all the walls around with that. And then he put in colored light bulbs and Christmas lights. And he had one whole wall that was safety pins. And he'd stuck safety pins. . . prelude to punk, all through the wall. There were these flashing lights, you'd walk in and 'Oh God!' Really psychedelic."

The Monkees cast and crew group photo. Photo from the Charlene Nowak collection.

There was also a converted meat locker that the guys could go into when needing to relax. Each Monkee had his own corner where he could do any illicit thing he wanted to and nobody at Screen Gems cared. Each Monkee was also assigned a colored light bulb and, when his bulb would light up in the locker, it would indicate that he was needed for filming.

The Monkees' self-titled debut album was released on October 10. The cover featured the soon to be teen idols flashing their pearly whites, except for Michael, who was verbally counting the seconds. He had told the photographer that he was only allowing him five minutes to take the cover photo and that was it. When the five minutes were up, Michael stormed away.

The songs on the album were catchy tunes spotlighting the guys' different musical styles. Micky was the wild one in the group, starting off with The Monkees' theme. This song originally was to feature the other Monkees singing as well, but that particular recording session ended when the boys got into a wrestling match.

Micky dominated the album with *Saturday's Child, Tomorrow's Gonna Be Another Day, Take a Giant Step, Last Train to Clarksville, Let's Dance On,* and *(Theme From) The Monkees.* Davy would get the girls to swoon by singing the romantic ballads *I Wanna Be Free, I'll Be True To You;* his tracks also included the bouncy *This Just Doesn't Seem To Be My Day.*

At the end of the record was a novelty cut that showcased the boys' humor on the TV show called *Gonna Buy Me A Dog.* The song featured Micky and Davy joking while trying to record a Boyce and Hart composition. Michael was allowed to contribute two of his own compositions to the album, *Papa Gene's Blues* (originally titled *Happiness* and *Brand X*) as well as the collaboration with Goffin and King, *Sweet Young Thing.*

The song *Papa Gene's Blues* included Michael verbally hinting at the fact that a non-Monkee is playing on the track by saying, "Pick it, Luther." The 'Luther' was a reference to Luther Perkins, and Johnny Cash used the line in one of his songs. The line was barely heard on the original release, but is easily heard on The Monkees re-mixed CD box set *Listen to the Band* from 1991.

Photo by Henry Diltz

The song was also an example of Michael's somewhat annoying habit of choosing song titles that are rarely, if ever, related to the song, and are often never mentioned in the song itself, perhaps his

49

own attempt to thwart the commercial nature of the music business. It had also caused a problem for the record manufacturer, as they didn't know how the "Gene" should be spelled. In a state of confusion, the manufacturer started printing the first covers with the title *Papa Jean's Blues* until it was decided that it had been right all along and it was corrected.

The teenagers and pre-teens of America liked what they saw in The Monkees. The guys were becoming the biggest thing in the music and television world. The stores were reporting that their Monkees merchandise was flying out of the stores, and they just couldn't get enough to meet the demand. Most of the major magazines of the time period such as *Newsweek, Time* and the *Saturday Evening Post* did articles on the new phenomenon.

As if it couldn't get any more hectic, Screen Gems decided that they could make more money by having the guys go on tour as a real performing band during their winter and summer hiatus. The idea of the guys touring was to promote record  sales, which were skyrocketing. The problem in all of this was that the guys had never played music together, except for a brief time in-between the filming of scenes for the pilot. Screen Gems now expected them to perform live, so on top of filming the episodes during the day and recording the vocals for the songs at night, they had to also rehearse for live performances to be played without the benefit of backup musicians.

The popularity of The Monkees did not go unnoticed in Hollywood. Gene Roddenberry thought that a cute Davy Jones type character would boost the sagging ratings of his series *Star Trek*. Walter Koenig was hired as the Russian "Ensign Chekov" for the second season, and a new teen idol was born.

Michael didn't think that he was much of an actor, but he showed a genuine innocence as well as a sharp wit in the episodes. One of the numerous Monkee directors, Bruce Kessler recalls an episode he directed, "One of the early episodes in the season was called *I've Got A Little Song Here*. It was about Mike Nesmith being taken advantage of. .

. thinking somebody was going to publish his song or put his song in a movie. I knew immediately, when I read the script, it was going to be a terrific show. Treva Silverman wrote a great script for it. When the show got started, Mike's wife came to me and asked me to please try to encourage him. This was the first episode that really focused on him. He was terrific."

One of the Monkee Maids, Carole Shelyne was on the set of the early Monkees episodes and recalled one moment with Michael, "I saw Mike do a dramatic scene one time in which he was talking to Davy's grandfather who was supposed to be trying to take Davy away. He was so great that I walked over to him and said, 'You know, you really have the makings of a great actor!' He turned to me and smiled and gave me a hug. That was all he said about it, but you could tell just how important that was to him."

Another moment Carole describes just how entertaining Michael could be to the crew and not realize it, "We were on the set one day, and Mike wasn't involved in any of the shots they were setting up. This particular set used a backdrop, which was a picture of the ocean, which is supposed to be behind the house in which they live.

"I guess Mike just got bored, and since they were shooting on the other part of the set at that time, he walked over to this backdrop and he started talking to the backdrop! He started talking to the water and to the boats, in relation to himself and to The Monkees, and how silly the whole thing was that grown boys 'our age getting in front of a camera and playacting is ridiculous!' He even started composing a song about the whole thing!

"Pretty soon, one by one, everyone stopped what they were doing and just sort of filed over him to watch. And he was completely oblivious to all of them! He was carrying on a genuine conversation with a backdrop!

"After a while, just about everybody had stopped what they were doing to watch, and they were all sort of holding their laughter in. You know, standing there behind him and watching this whole thing, but with their hands over their mouths!

51

"Finally, when Mike was finished with his conversation, he just picked up and walked off! He was completely unaware that we were watching! That conversation at that time was very important to him."

The show was becoming very popular and it began to affect the way Michael lived his life. As Phyllis recalls, "I do remember that right after the show went on the air there was a wonderful modern art exhibition at the Museum of Modern Art, Academy Museum. We went into the museum we started to walk around. We were looking at the pictures and, all of a sudden, I'm looking at Michael and Michael is looking at everyone looking at him and then people stopped doing what they were there to do. They began to talk and you could feel the hum and you could feel the tension and people just began to converge, 'It's him! It's him!' It panicked him. It freaked him out. 'Let's get out of here.' Instead of being able to say, 'Oh, that's great! You've seen the show. How are you? Thank you very much. But look at this. This is great stuff, too. Let's all look at this. Of course, I'll sign the autograph.' I think that infringed upon his privacy really. . . [sighing] he just wasn't prepared for it. Of course, we couldn't go out anymore as private persons. We couldn't go out to a movie, to a museum. We couldn't really just go out and bop around a shopping center. We continued to shop at the Food Cart

market in North Hollywood. We'd make a run once every three weeks or a month and stock up massively on food. It was a quiet little place so that we wouldn't be recognized."

As Michael said about his newfound celebrity status, "Well, it was interesting. Certainly full of a lot of adventures and excitement. But it's nothing that I think I'd like to repeat. It got old pretty fast because fame is time consuming, and I just wasn't able to do the things that I wanted to do.

"I couldn't go to the national drag racing finals; I couldn't go to Los Angeles' Museum of Contemporary Art. They had an exhibition at the Chicago museum one time where they had a 1938 Dodge covered with purple flocking. In the mid-'60s that whole Pop Art movement began to develop and had gotten very interesting by the late '60s. Of course, it was during those years that The Monkees were white hot.

"They had assembled all of the Rosenquists and the Rauschenbergs and the Oldenburgs and Warhol. There were all of these

52

great Pop artists at a Chicago exhibition in 1968. You can see that, to me, it was an important experience. I couldn't go, because of the furor it would cause. I tried to go, but I couldn't stand in one spot.

"So I just got very testy and pushy and called up the museum and said, 'How can we do this?' And they closed the museum so I could go to that exhibition. I thought, 'Boy, this is idiotic.'"

Spencer Davis recalled one of the perks of Michael's celebrity, "We (Spencer and his then wife Pauline) called Mike when we got into town. And Mike said, 'Let's go down to Disneyland.' I had never been to Disneyland. So, off we went down to Disneyland. We get to the gates and I'm with Mike Nesmith and the guy at the entrance said, 'You can't come in. Your hair's too long.' So, Mike went over to a phone and called Walt Disney's brother Roy Disney. After that we got in with no problem."

In-between everything, the boys were still recording music. OK, the boys were still recording their voices to the music. Nesmith was now very much the hothead every time he entered the recording studio. One of the songs they were working on at the time was written by Neil Diamond. Although Diamond had no major complaints about The Monkees recording his songs, he had different plans for this song. Kirshner who liked Diamond's hit *Cherry Cherry* managed to persuade him with the reality of making a lot of money in royalties.

Each of The Monkees listened to Diamond's version of the song as a reference, so they could get the feel of how the song should go. Everyone said that they liked the song except for Michael, who declared that the song would not be a hit. He stated that he was a songwriter and a producer and that he knew it was not a hit and that it was never going to be a hit.

As a joke, Jeff Barry, the producer of the song, suggested adding strings to it, but to his surprise Michael liked the idea, taking the idea seriously. When everybody started laughing, Michael realized that everyone was laughing at him, and that infuriated him. Phyllis was there visiting and witnessed the incident. Michael threw such a tantrum over the joke; Barry kicked him out of the studio for the rest of the day.[19]

Shortly after the recording, the version of *I'm A Believer* sung by Micky was released. As a single, the song had over one million copies ordered before it was even released. The song spent seven weeks at the number 1 spot on the Billboard charts. The song also went on to be one of the biggest songs of 1967 and the biggest Monkee hit ever.

On the set of the TV show, Michael was deadly serious most of the time while the others would goof off. Jackie Cooper, former president of Screen Gems told the story, "He had a baby already, and a prop man went to lift up his guitar and he didn't like the way the prop man set it back down again. This was a story that came back to me while they were still on location. There was quite some altercation between the property master and Mike. Mike started  screaming about how his baby went without milk so he could have that guitar so he could get out and make a living with it. . . it ought to be paid respect. . . not that it was possible. All the property man might have done was to set it down just a little bit too harshly."[20]

Talking to reporters was not one of Michael's favorite things to do. He didn't like their stupid questions and was known to storm off

---

[19] Gary Strobl's interview with Jeff Barry 5-13-86.
[20] Gary Strobl's interview with Jackie Cooper 11-25-85.

during an interview more than once. Hollywood columnist Marilyn Beck recalled the first time she was given access to The Monkees for an interview and she came back with less than desirable results. The boys generally goofed off and wouldn't answer any of her questions. Instead the boys decided to tell off-color jokes such as Michael's joke, "Did you hear about the guy who thought syphilis was fine cause it came from abroad?"[21] It was enough to make any Screen Gems executive cringe. When asking for an interview for an upcoming issue of *Tiger Beat*, Ann Moses recalled Michael saying, "I will give you an interview if I can fuck you."[22] Not certain that he was joking, Ann didn't even try to get an interview from Michael for that issue.

In realizing that their performing Monkees were still in need of musical training for the upcoming live performances, Bert and Bob had them practice constantly. The guys would have to be dead solid perfect in performing all of the songs that they appeared to have already recorded for the album that was number one on the charts.

It was decided that The Monkees would have their concert debut in Hawaii December 3 at Honolulu's International Center Arena performing at a teen beauty pageant. The site of the appearance was so far away from the States on purpose, because if The Monkees bombed, who would know about it? The concert turned out to be a smash, although the audience could not hear anything but the screaming of the fans.

The performing Monkees embarked on their first tour produced by Dick Clark Productions. During the tour rumors started flying from jealous peers that The Monkees were not really playing musical instruments during their concerts, but a real band behind the curtain was. Michael would deny the rumors during an interview segment at the end of a Monkees episode, but he would not be silent for long on the subject.

The Monkees wound up getting into trouble out on the road, whether it was their fault or not. Disc jockey Robert W. Morgan went on the road with The Monkees for a couple of dates and colorfully described

Photo by Henry Diltz

---

[21] Marilyn Beck- Marilyn Beck's Hollywood.
[22] Gary Strobl's interview with Ann Moses 6-25-95.

55

one incident,   "For whatever reason, we left the hotel. It was midday. I think they'd been through sound checks and everything. . . maybe not. I go out and all of sudden there's girls scattered around the hotel. They're chasing us. It was funny at first. Then, literally, you're running for your life. This was a lot of girls. . . 50 or 100. . . and they were crazed and they were going to rip our clothes off. We'd all been through this for two days. We're running and outdistancing these fucking girls. They're starting to come from different directions now. They're just hanging around downtown. . . around the hotel. Nesmith said, 'Here. In here. Quick. Over here!', hollering. We jumped into this fucking Cleveland police car. Peter Tork was there and Nesmith and, I think, Davy Jones. There were four us because they thought I was one of The Monkees. They jump in this police car. These two redneck Cleveland cops. All of a sudden, the squad car now is surrounded by girls. They're rocking it. These cops don't what is going on. They have no idea. They don't know Monkees from zilch. All the cops know is these hippies the girls are chasing. We're scared to death, man. Michael's trying to explain we're The Monkees. These cops said, 'Yeah, right. You're the fucking monkeys and I'm a fucking giraffe and we're going to the fucking station.' We go down to the station. We would have to get ahold of Steve Blauner to explain to these people who we were. That we weren't some kind of drug-crazed hippies that were causing a riot. They were going to arrest us.

"While we're in the police station, I'm standing at the typical desk in this police station. They're ready to book them. Somebody's on the phone to get ahold of Blauner to come down and explain who they are. Michael's standing and nudging me. He says (whispering), 'Stand in front of me. Stand over here.' What he's trying to do, as I later figure out, is that he's trying to get me to stand between him and the cops because he and one of the other Monkees were walking over to the wastebasket to drop a handful of joints. That was next. Right? 'Let's search these fuckers.' Then it would be all over for their careers. . . literally. The Monkees, at that time, getting busted for marijuana, would have been history. The show would have never aired again. It would have truly been canceled and they would have been in the slammer.

"I can still remember them walking over to the waste basket there and this empty waste basket going, 'Thump. Thump.' A metallic thud as these joints hit the bottom of the waste basket. I'm thinking, 'Fuck, man. How are we ever going to get out of here?' I wasn't as scared because I didn't have any dope. . . by that time it was in the waste basket. Having a joint was heavy-duty bust. I'm thinking at the time, 'These stupid fuckers. If you're in a hotel room, fine. But Jesus Christ. . .' We literally jumped into a squad car to save our ass. It was like frying pan to the fire. . . because these heavy, thick set, redneck type prototypical cops that don't know the fucking Monkees. If they had known who they were, it probably would have been worse. Blauner came down and straightened it all out. By that time, some of the women around the police department. . . the employees. . . slowly it unfolded

these were indeed celebrities in there and there was a little different attitude. But, at first, explaining in this car to these cops with girls chasing and rocking the car. . . that 'Yes, we are indeed big deal, fucking rock stars and we are here to perform in your fair city. We need your protection.' They didn't want to hear any of it."[23]

While on tour in January, The Monkees were in a record shop looking around when, to their surprise and horror, they discovered a new record by The Monkees! The album, *More of The Monkees* was released without their knowledge and was filled with songs they had recorded for the TV show.

---

[23] Gary Strobl's interview with Robert W. Morgan 3-7-88.

More of The Monkees is in all regards a record directed at a teeny bopper audience, and not for someone who wanted to be taken seriously as a musician. The songs for the album were picked by Kirshner to make the girls swoon while they read the latest issues of *16* and *Tiger Beat Magazine*.

She and *Sometime in the Morning* were Micky's moments to shine, whereas Davy got the girls all screaming at their stereos in ecstasy with *Hold On Girl, When Love Comes Knocking (At Your Door), Look Out (Here Comes Tomorrow)*, and the nauseating narrative *The Day We Fall in Love*. Michael was able to get two songs on the album *The Kind of Girl I Could Love* and *Mary, Mary*, featuring Micky on vocals and session musician Glen Campbell playing lead guitar.

Peter was finally given a track on a Monkees record, and it was a novelty song called *Your Auntie Grizelda*, which was featured in a couple of episodes. The bouncy dance tunes on the album were *Laugh, (I'm Not Your) Steppin' Stone*, and the big hit single *I'm A Believer*. *More of The Monkees* was exactly what the pre-teen girls of America wanted at the peak of Monkeemania and became the best selling Monkee record ever, despite Michael calling it "the worst album in the history of the world." Some of the hatred probably came from the fact that the cover features The Monkees wearing selections from the dreadfully ugly JC Penney Monkees clothing line. They hated wearing the clothes, and they were posed in a way that was reminiscent of the Beatles *Rubber Soul* album cover. The liner notes on the back of the album were written by Kirshner, profusely thanking all of the songwriters and producers for their great work, and mentioning The Monkees as an afterthought.

Michael started getting more vocal to the outside world on his unhappiness in camp Monkee. He didn't want to take the credit for someone else's work, and he wanted The Monkees to become a real band, but nobody wanted to rock the boat, as the records were selling just fine. He did not trust Kirshner, and he couldn't get his way unless he raised his voice. It got to the point where Michael would typically be in a different studio across town from the other guys with his own musicians recording his own songs.

As he said at the time, "I produce my own stuff. I mean, I won't let anyone touch my music. I won't let it go to the hands of those stupid muckrakers." Everyone was asking Michael that if he were so unhappy, then why would he accept their songwriter royalty checks? He never really gave an answer to that.

Displeased that things were not going to change with The Monkees' music unless drastic measures were taken, Michael finally reached the boiling point late in January of 1967 with the event that changed The Monkees forever. The Monkees met at Don Kirshner's private bungalow at the Beverly Hills Hotel for a ceremony in which they would be given gold records as well as million dollar royalty checks. The Monkees, along with Kirshner, posed for the photographers present.

When everyone from the press left, Kirshner presented The Monkees with acetates of four new songs from which one would be chosen as the next Monkees single. The only thing that would be needed from the boys would be their voices. Michael, unable to contain himself, burst out that he was sick of having his name on work that other people had done and that he wouldn't have anymore to do with it.

Herb Moelis, a Screen Gems executive, insisted that Kirshner had the right to pick out what songs he considered to be the hits of the bunch. Michael then replied that The Monkees were so popular they could record *Happy Birthday* with a beat and it would sell a million copies, and that if something didn't change he would quit. Moelis then made the mistake of telling Michael that he had better read his contract. With that Michael exploded in anger and WHAM! He put his fist right through the wall of the bungalow. In the midst of the dust and the shock of it all, Michael turned to Moelis and said, "That could have been your face, motherfucker." With that point made to his satisfaction, Michael left in a huff. Quickly Kirshner ran out after him and sheepishly gave him his gold record.

The man with the golden ear proved that he still had the touch, for one of the acetates Kirshner tried to present was of a song called *Sugar Sugar*. The song was later recorded by a Kirshner creation that could not talk back or put a fist through a wall; the animated cartoon characters from *The Archies*, a Saturday morning cartoon show based on the popular comic book series.

The next day Michael met with Schneider, who, although he was not present, had been inundated with different stories of the fist through the wall incident. Michael said that he was sorry about it, but he felt that he just couldn't go on being so deceptive with the recording. He had expected to be fired and he had thought of moving to Mexico or Tahiti, being completely broke and letting everyone sue him while he ate coconuts for the rest of his life. Schneider consoled Michael, siding with him when faced with losing a Monkee or Don Kirshner.

Michael, still mad as hell over the musical direction and assured of a job by Schneider, made a play for control by making waves through the press. He called all the magazines in town and announced that he would be holding a press conference. Only *Time* and *Look* showed up, but it was enough press to get the message out. He announced to the reporters, "We're being passed off as something we aren't. We all play instruments but we haven't on any of our records. Furthermore, our company doesn't want us to and won't let us."

Warren Nesmith with his son Michael.

The press took off on the story and immediately Screen Gems held an emergency meeting to determine how to handle the onslaught of negative publicity created by Michael's statement. The newspapers all were proclaiming The Monkees to be a disgrace to music, but of course The Monkees were a TV show and not a real band anyway.

Michael would give several comparisons through the years such as, "I don't mean to burst your bubble, but Marcus Welby is not a doctor and Starsky and Hutch are not cops and Mary Tyler Moore is really not a single woman having her own career and Laverne and Shirley don't really work at the brewery. Tom Selleck is not really a detective. He's an actor. When you go to a motion picture, we so seldom fail to realize that Henry Fonda and Katharine Hepburn were not really married. They really didn't go to a summer resort where they encountered their children. E.T. is really a three million dollar puppet."

Michael, John Kuehne & Micky recording the Headquarters album.

Michael believed that he could gain total control of a major recording organization by gaining the public's sympathy for their powerlessness as they were being manipulated by Screen Gems. He was, however, woefully mistaken, as this act of rebellion destroyed his and the other Monkees chances of having a solo career, as well as destroying their credibility. While the studio was debating the issue, Michael went out to find a producer that he could control, believing that the powers that be would never let him have full production responsibilities.

Chip Douglas was playing bass with the Turtles at the Whisky-A-Go-Go one night when Michael walked up to Chip and said, "Do you remember me?" Chip had seen him once before at the Troubadour when Michael was playing he club with Bill Chadwick. He had mentioned at that time that he was getting involved in a new television series. Michael was also a fan of another group Chip was in called the Modern Folk Quartet. Suddenly this guy he hardly knew was asking him, "How would you like to be our record producer?"

Chip, in disbelief, said, "I don't even know how to do that. What do you mean? Produce records?"

"Don't worry about it, I'll teach you everything that you need to know. You'll be making six figures in six months, I guarantee it."

"This must be a joke. Do you really mean this?"

"Yes, yes, I do."[24]

With an offer that he couldn't refuse, Chip immediately quit his $125 a week job with the Turtles and became the producer for the most popular band in the music business. It could be assumed that since Michael was Chip's teacher, Michael now had a puppet of his own and could give orders through Chip. Not all of The Monkees were happy with Michael's choice of producer as Peter explains, "I would have chosen Stephen Stills. I had considered him and I then asked him, and he said, 'Yeah, I'd love to do it,' and then, before I got to say that, Mike said, 'Oh, I got Chip.' Because I was not in those days capable of any kind of self-assertion, I was capable of bitterly complaining, but in terms of rational assertiveness, I had no notion of what that was all about. So, when somebody else said, 'Well this guy would. . .' I went (slowly) 'Okaaaay.'"

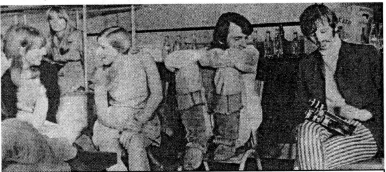

Cynthia Lennon, Phyllis, Michael and Ringo Starr in London 1967. Photo from The RLM Archives.

The first song produced by Douglas was a re-recording of *The Girl I Knew Somewhere*. When handed over to Colgems to be released as the next Monkee single, Kirshner refused to even listen to it. The musical director had already determined that the next single would be one featuring his favorite Monkee Davy, the one Monkee who never complained.

Schneider disagreed with Kirshner, but it obviously did no good. Kirshner went on without approval and had the single pressed. The song was *She Hangs Out* with the flip side being the Neil Diamond penned *A Little Bit Me, A Little Bit You*. It was hastily withdrawn,

---

[24] Gary Strobl's interview with Chip Douglas 11-24-84.

although some copies were released in Canada, and it angered Screen Gems enough that they fired Kirshner. He then responded by filing a $35 million breach of contract lawsuit against Columbia and Screen Gems.

Kirshner settled out of court for the biggest settlement in the history of Columbia Pictures, an amount that he is not allowed to say to this day, although Phyllis Nesmith had heard that the settlement was $12 million. Schneider then proceeded to make the next single *A Little Bit Me, A Little Bit You* with the B side being Nesmith's *The Girl I Knew Somewhere.*

As Davy recalled about losing Kirshner, "Colgems didn't really want to get rid of Kirshner, but they did want to have more input into the music. It wasn't all or nothing, but they didn't realize that. We could have done it a lot better without going to the wall. Mike Nesmith had a plan. He was heir to a multi-million dollar fortune, he knew that was there, so he could make as much trouble as he wanted to. But he was the one, in the end, who was bad-mouthing The Monkees and he always thought that we weren't as qualified as we actually were. I don't know how qualified we were supposed to be. Mike Nesmith knew about three chords before The Monkees first started. He was a great musician. Fabulous songwriter. But he wasn't a studio musician."[25]

It is true that Michael might have had some backup money in case he was fired or he quit The Monkees. His mother's Mistake Out Company had earned one million dollars the previous year and was expected to double that in one to two years.

As Steve Blauner recalled, "Mike and Donnie were working together, but I guess Donnie had always intended to do whatever he wanted to do, which made it even worse as he was leading Nesmith on. And, eventually, that would be the cause of the break-up of the group. Because, when he didn't really work with Mike, it created this insanity in Mike, who single-handedly destroyed the group."[26]

The four Monkees were finally given some time off in early February for a vacation, and Michael did not waste any time getting out of town to spend some major money. Stopping off in New York, he and Phyllis stayed at the ritzy Plaza Hotel in New York, and Phyllis ran off to shop at Saks 5th Avenue.

The Nesmiths next stop in England turned into a promotional trip, as the record company wouldn't have missed a chance to interview him and to promote sales of The Monkees records and the television show that had just debuted in England. It turned out that regardless of

---

[25] Gary Strobl's interview with David Jones 10-9-87.
[26] Gary Strobl's interview with Steve Blauner 1-21-86.

the Beatle roots, The Monkees were just as big in England as they were in the USA. The press in the UK also repeated the statements that Michael had made regarding The Monkees not playing their own instruments, but the fans didn't care.

When they arrived in England, Michael and Phyllis wound up at the Grosvenor House in London. Some RCA representatives came over the first morning after they arrived and planned the itinerary, which would include an appearance on the popular music show *Top Of The Pops*. Later on that day, Michael sent a telegram to the leader of the most popular band in music, John Lennon. According to David Price, the telegram read, "John, we would be pleased to have you and Cynthia over for dinner, God is love, Mike." Later that evening, Michael and Phyllis went to the "Bag O' Nails" nightclub and ran into Lennon. John apologized for not answering the telegram, but to make up for it, he invited Michael and Phyllis to attend an upcoming Beatles recording

Ringo Starr, George Harrison, John Lennon, Donovan, Michael and Phyllis.

session, and invited the couple to spend their remaining days in England at The Lennons' home. Michael and Phyllis were delighted. John sent his Rolls Royce to pick them up. The car, which was customized with a bar and a TV, took the couple to Weybridge where John and Cynthia had their home.

During their visit, Michael and Phyllis went with John to a London disco called Sybil's that was in a dark basement with loud music. Phyllis remembered being crowded into a booth sitting next to

Paul McCartney. She said, "The Beatles were all there. Paul, George, John and Ringo. I guess it must have been their hangout." At one point in the evening John Lennon leaned over to Michael and was heard to say, "You know, there used to be only four of us to know what it feels like to be in this position in the world, and now there are eight of us."

Reminiscing about that evening, Phyllis remembered, "There was a place that the Beatles could still go without being mobbed. I don't know whether they owned part of it or whether it was a private club or what it was. It might have been a membership club at that point. I have one absolutely crystal clear vision and that is of walking out of the club up the steps and, as you came to the top of the steps, in front of you was a street corner and there was a street lamp and there was the proverbial pea soup fog shrouding the light and giving it a really mystical glow. George and John and Paul were dancing with hands clasped around the street light singing, 'Hari Krishna, Hari Krishna, Krishna, Krishna, Hari, Hari.' They had just gone through their Eastern religion thing. They had just begun to get in touch with that. They were dancing around singing this chant in the moonlight in the fog. In the street light. Well, I'll just never forget that. It's like a still photograph in my mind with sound. Not like an action thing at all. It's fixed in time."

The next night on February 10, the Nesmiths attended a Beatles recording session of a song called *A Day In The Life*, which was to be included on the *Sgt. Pepper's Lonely Hearts Club Band* album. Also attending the session were Marianne Faithful and Mick Jagger. When Michael noticed Jagger, he asked Phyllis, "Doesn't he have charisma? Look at him. Don't you think he's sexy?" To which Phyllis responded, "Ehh. No, he's kind of little. Big lips. Looking a little scroungy. Who cares. So, so."[27] At the end of the session, the artists who attended, including Michael, were asked to record "hmmmm" for the end of the track. Unfortunately, the "hmmmm" was not used.

---

[27] Gary Strobl's interview with Phyllis Nesmith 2-13-85.

Reminiscing about dinner with the Lennons, Phyllis said, "I remember a Sunday dinner that John and Cynthia fixed for us. I remember how she did the potatoes. I still do my roast potatoes that way. These potatoes were unbelievable! You cook the potatoes in their jackets. Boil them. When the skins start to pop a little bit, take 'em out and take the skin off of them and cut them into pieces and position them on a rack underneath where the roast is. And cook them the rest of the way at the same high heat that the roast is cooking at. The juices and the grease from the meat that's spattering around coats the potatoes and then they get a crust on the outside of them and they're soft inside and crusty on the outside."

Not all of the time in the kitchen was golden as mentioned in Cynthia Lennon's book *A Twist of Lennon*, as she talks about Phyllis, "A short stay by Mike Nesmith of the Monkeys (sic), with his wife, was fascinating. Until it came to breakfast and she hovered over me while I was cooking, inferring all the time that I wasn't doing it right. 'Mike doesn't like it like that. I always cook it for Mike this way.' How I kept my cool I'll never know."

When Michael and his fellow Monkees came back from vacation they didn't know that Kirshner had been fired. Michael was sitting in his car waiting for Phyllis and her brother Bruce while they shopped for groceries. As Michael recalled in an interview, "I turned on the radio and the guy said, 'That was one side of the brand new Monkees single, I'll be back to play the other side.' So I told Phyllis to hurry and get back to the car to witness a moment in history. I said to her, 'If this ain't my song,
I'm out of a job. I'm gonna be out on the streets looking for work.' So we twiddled our thumbs until the opening chords came on, and I realized it was my song. It felt like such a tremendous victory after all that fighting."

The Monkees were so popular in the fan mail department that there was a team of girls hired to answer all the fan mail. Their main duty was to send out postcards inviting the fans to join The Monkees fan club. For $1.50, a Monkee fan would receive an orange folder with the Monkee logo. Inside the folder was a welcome letter from the president Lynn Martin, a membership card, a button with the Monkees logo on it, a pen with the same Monkees logo, a biography of each Monkee, a photo of each Monkee, a group shot of The Monkees, a photo with several different shots of The Monkees, and a book cover with, you guessed it, The Monkees photo on it.

One of the main girls in charge of the fan mail was Charlene Nowak who recalls an encounter she had with Michael, "It was around Valentine's Day. . . February '67. I had been given two all-day suckers in the shape of a heart. They were the clear red candy that you could look through. I put one in my desk drawer. I decided I was going to go on the set and visit and I was going to take one of my lollipops down there to lick on it and chew on it.

"I had just barely nibbled the rim of the lollipop off and I walked across the stage, minding my own business. Mike came off the set and he was heading towards the dressing rooms. He came off the set past me and the next thing I knew my lollipop was gone. He just ripped it right out of my hand and went around the corner to run into his dressing room. But he was still within arms' reach. I reached up and I grabbed that green wool hat right off his head. I figured, 'Hey, you got my lollipop. I got your hat. I want my lollipop back. I'll give you back the hat.' He threatened to break my lollipop. I threatened to shred his hat, which I couldn't do because we're talking the original green wool hat here.

"We're standing there looking at each other. He's going, 'If you don't give me back my hat, this lollipop is history.' I went, 'If you don't give me my lollipop back, this hat is history' knowing damn well it wasn't. We had this little Mexican stand-off for a few minutes. He raised the sucker above his head. He made a gesture like he was going to throw it to the floor. I went, 'Alright. Alright.' I reluctantly turned over the hat and he gave me back my sucker.

"Well, me and my big mouth. I had to ask him 'Would you really have thrown this lollipop on the floor if I hadn't given you back your hat?' He said, 'Yep.' I couldn't leave well enough alone and this time I told him, 'Well, I think it would have been okay because I have another one just like it up in my desk drawer in the office.' Next thing I knew the lollipop was back in his hand and then all over the floor. Bits and pieces of lollipop just went scattering all over the floor.

"I'm standing there looking at all these little chips of red candy with a stick with a little corner of my lollipop still stuck to it. He turned around and gave me a big smile and walked into dressing room and shut the door. I'm standing there among all this candy. I wasn't mad because this was totally unlike Mike. I had never seen Mike do anything like this. He was always so. . . the leader. Always real quiet. Always really together. And here's my lollipop all over the floor."[28]

The biggest night of 1967 in the music industry was on March 2, when the Grammy awards were presented. The Monkees were nominated for two awards for *Last Train To Clarksville*, including Best Contemporary (R&R) Group Performance, Vocal or Instrumental and Best Contemporary (R&R) Recording. The Monkees would walk away empty handed, losing both awards to the Mamas & The Papas and the New Vaudeville Band respectively.

Peter, Davy, Chip Douglas, Micky and Michael in the recording sessions for Headquarters. Photo from The RLM Archives.

As soon as Michael could, he got his fellow Monkees into the studio along with producer Chip Douglas to work on their third album, and he was determined that this be a real Monkees album, entirely recorded by the four band members. With their newfound control, *Headquarters* was recorded in six weeks and cost $25,000. *Headquarters* sold 2 1/2 million copies, half the sales of its predecessor, but the guys were proud that they had finally become a real live band. The album was number one on the charts for three weeks until The

---

[28] Gary Strobl's interview with Charlene Nowak 4-16-88.

Beatles *Sgt. Pepper* album was released, and the two stayed together in those first two positions for several months.

Headquarters was an uneven but enjoyable mixture of The Monkees tastes in music, and it was unable to generate even one single release. Michael's voice lacked the styling of Micky's, as everything he sang sounded country, as evident on *You Told Me* as well as *You Just May Be the One*. Strangely enough, there is only one track written by Peter, which Michael named *For Pete's Sake*, that ultimately became the closing theme for The Monkees television series second season.

The recording engineer Hank Cicalo recalled the making of a Monkee song on *Headquarters*, "I was getting a lot of pressure from Lester Sill. We were in Studio C at RCA for almost six weeks. We couldn't see out the glass of the control booth anymore because everybody came in with tempera paints. It started with Micky drawing and Davy was very artistic doing flowers. . . so, this watercolor appeared that covered the whole glass and we couldn't see. There was no more contact out. I kept saying 'Leave a little hole so we can see what's going on.' When you do a date, the eye contact is important to be able see players. I kept telling the guys 'There's no more time. We don't have any time. There's no time. No time.' Because they were saying 'We'll get another song.' 'You don't have time to go home and write a song. We got to finish.' And all the RCA execs coming out from New York. . . Joe Diemperi. . . all these people were coming to hear the album. . . and this was something that wasn't planned. Again, like they were pressured into that 'We got to be finished by a certain date.' Well, the day came and went. Next week. Okay, next week. They were struggling plus Screen Gems was giving them all the songs. We had enough material for two albums but it was the thing that they wanted to pick the songs they did. . . to get down to the point where they were really not happy with some of the tunes that they'd already done. And I kept screaming 'No time, no time, no time.' And that went on for two days. I was really starting to get frustrated and I'm starting to scream at guys. And they knew when I started screaming, something's wrong. Because I started losing my patience.

"Michael said 'Give us a couple minutes. . .' And they went in the studio and they were gone for an hour or so. Peter had taken off. Micky was around and Davy was around. They started working on lyrics and Chip went out and worked on it. . . and out of that came the song *No Time*. They came in and they were doing vocals and I leaned over and I gave them a couple of lines for the song. I had the title. I never thought anything of it. When the song was done and everything was over with. . .we did it. The next morning we mixed it. It sounded great. Lester came over. . . Lester, I think out of pure relief of having the album done, he said 'It's terrific! Let's take it!' Michael, Micky, Davy and Peter and Lester came in and they said 'Hank, thanks a lot. That's your song.' I said 'What?' Michael said 'That's your song.' He said 'For all the time over the last year and a half, you've really been great for us

Michael, Bert Schneider, Bob Rafelson, David, Micky, Anissa Jones and Jimmy Durante backstage at the Emmy Awards telecast, 1967.

and you've stuck it all out and all the craziness and we wanted to give you something. Here's a song.' Well, you know what a song was on that album. You know what it meant financially? Now I have a house in Woodland Hills that I purchased for 50 grand at that time and it's now worth $250,000-$300,000. And I owe that to them and I owe that to Michael for doing that. That was one of the nicest things that anybody ever did for me. It was just their way of saying thank you."[29]

One of the other songs on the album was *Shades of Gray* in which Michael wrote the cello and horn parts. Not being able to read or write music, Michael would sing the parts to Peter, who would write them down and then give them to the musicians who would perform it. As Peter noted, "What we didn't realize at the *Headquarters* period was that Mike was the timekeeper. If Micky on drums had followed Mike, we would have had splendid time because Mike was very correct. . . rigidly correct. . . and he despised the fact that I couldn't hit pitches as well as he could. He gave me all kinds of shit for that. Micky's time is

---

[29] Gary Strobl's interview with Hank Cicalo 3-15-85.

70

only so-so. . . it's not bad but it's not like Mike who has excellent time."[30]

When the boys noticed that Michael was getting royalty checks bigger than theirs because of his added songwriters' royalty, they began to write songs. The songs were hardly hit material, but with their new musical control they were good enough to get on The Monkees albums.

Michael was also branching out with other artists. When The Butterfield Blues Band recorded a version of Michael's song *Mary, Mary*, fans of the blues band wrote to the record company Elektra to complain, 'That sellout jerk Mike Nesmith is taking credit for writing the song *Mary, Mary*.' The fans got letters back from the president of Elektra, Jack Holzman, stating that, indeed, Michael Nesmith did write the song. Michael was very slowly gaining some respect for his

Peter, Michael, and Tommy Smothers at the Emmy Awards telecast, 1967.

songwriting abilities, but he was still considered by most to be a no-talent Monkee, largely because of his own bad publicity.

Having some trouble with his throat around this time, Michael had his tonsils removed on May 23, at Cedars of Lebanon. After the operation he immediately checked himself out of the hospital due to his Christian Science beliefs. It was reported that after the operation, a nurse took off with the removed tonsils. It is probably the one souvenir

---

[30] Gary Strobl's interview with Peter Tork 1-14-87.

71

item that rabid Monkee fans are not that anxious to get their hands on. Michael's surgery caused him to miss a concert gig in San Jose, and it was canceled. Davy remarked to an interviewer that Michael's voice changed permanently after the operation.

It was Emmy Awards time in Hollywood and *The Dick Van Dyke show* had ended its long run on television, along with a four-year streak as Best Comedy Show. All of the other comedy shows of the era were relieved at the loss of the *Dick Van Dyke Show,* as they figured they would finally have a shot at the award. No such luck, *The Monkees* in their very first season beat out *Bewitched, The Andy Griffith Show, Hogan's Heroes* and *Get Smart* for the award. The same Emmy Awards found James Frawley winning the award for Outstanding Directorial Achievement in Comedy for the Monkee episode *Royal Flush.* Hollywood was shocked that these brash young newcomers had beaten the top rated sitcoms, but, if the music industry shunned these new hit makers, at least the TV industry appreciated their talent and success.

June also had The Monkees recording the tracks for their fourth album. This time the boys did not enjoy the recording sessions very much as it became a tedious exercise between shootings. As Peter recalled, "Davy had come to me and said 'Listen, it's all right for you guys. . . it takes you 50 takes to get your parts right. I'm playing the goddamn tambourine. I got my part right first take. I'm breaking my hands waiting for you guys to get the part right. . . so I'm not going to do this anymore, if you don't mind.'" Also, the boys had such eclectic tastes in music that they were having more and more arguments in the studio. There was little Chip could do to control them, as their egos were inflating to astronomical sizes.

One day in the studio Mike said to Peter, "You know, you're not singing flat anymore."

Peter, all excited, said, "Thank you, Michael."

"You're singing sharp now."[31]

Another problem that plagued the recording sessions was the fact that Chip was unhappy with the echo in the RCA studio they were using. Using the men's room at RCA, Michael recorded the vocals for *The Door Into Summer* and *Don't Call On Me.* The album was recorded in nine days but as Michael said, "How creative can you be in that amount of time?"

The Monkees also toured the UK in the spring to very receptive audiences, but the effects of stardom were beginning to take their toll on the guys. Michael complained that due to the screaming of the fans, some of his hearing was gone, twelve percent in one ear and eight

---

[31] Gary Strobl's interview with Chip Douglas 11-24-87.

percent in the other ear and he now had to start wearing ear plugs. After an afternoon show at the Empire Pool at Wembly, Michael and Peter collapsed backstage. They were revived by oxygen and both said that the incident was caused by the heat. They held a second concert that night without any incidents. Michael and Peter were also suffering from fatigue and strain. The other Monkees, Micky and Davy, were not faring much better as Micky was suffering a bad cold and Davy was just plain grumpy.

Evidence of Mike's self-deprecating wit was definitely apparent in London as Micky, Peter, and Davy were standing on the balcony above their screaming fans. When asked by Davy if he would want to join them on the balcony, Michael replied, "Naw, I'm saving myself for them at the concert, anyway it's so embarrassing when I go out onto the balcony and no one screams."

Michael did not get along with the English press, and he was sullen at The Monkees press conference in which he would get questions such as "Why are you so rude?" The answer Michael gave was all his own, "Perhaps it's because I have set high standards for myself, and I tend to react to anyone who falls short of my ideals." After that remark all of the questions were then directed to Davy who always tried to be gracious to the press. Michael remarked that he had suffered more abuse

Photo by Henry Diltz

from the English press than anyone else. The incident at the press conference did little to improve his already shaky relations with reporters. One British reporter who did like Michael proposed a "Society for the Prevention of Cruelty to Mike Nesmith."

Michael was able to cheer himself up over his problems with the British press by taking some of his friends over to a car dealership called Radfords to see his latest vehicle acquisition, a customized Morris Mini with aircraft seats, stereo tape deck, perspex tinted windows and illuminated 'No Smoking' sign. Costing about nine thousand dollars US, it was one of the most expensive Minis ever built, since the basic Minis were at least three thousand. A few days later, he took a reporter from *Flip* magazine for a drive to test it out. While driving, Michael remarked, "This goes like a scalded cat. Holymotheragod was that 7000 revs? I drive like a little old lady." After the test drive, Michael needed a drink at a local pub to get prepared for the drive back.

I'll Remember You

Michael had first heard about Jimi Hendrix through John Lennon when Lennon played a tape of Hendrix performing *Hey Joe*. By sheer coincidence, Micky had also seen Jimi performing, while he and Peter attended the "Monterey Pop Festival", and was amazed by his guitar playing. Michael and Micky got Hendrix signed on to go on the

Jimi Hendrix and Peter on tour in 1967. Photo from The RLM Archives.

next Monkee tour, much to the hesitation of tour producer Dick Clark. At the beginning of each concert, Michael would often sneak to the front in the midst of all the screaming fans and watch Hendrix perform. In an interview, Michael said, "I listened all the way through *Purple Haze*, and at the end, I broke into this shrieking, yelling, cheers of applause. I was the only one out of 10,000 people shrieking and yelling, and I suddenly realized that I was calling attention to myself, which was dangerous to some degree."

The Monkees audiences' reaction to Hendrix was one of shock, and the young fans didn't know what to make of this black person on stage who would set his shrieking guitar on fire and sing songs such as *Foxy Lady*. Parents didn't like Hendrix, as he was loud and blatantly sexual in his singing as well as his guitar playing. Hendrix didn't care much for performing on The Monkees tour, as he was sick of having to compete with screaming fans yelling for The Monkees. Finally at Forest Hill in New York, Hendrix tired of it all, threw his guitar, flipped off the audience, and yelled "Fuck you!" He then proceeded to walk off the stage and off The Monkees tour. Witnessing the incident, Michael turned to Micky and said, "Good for him."

Running From The Grand Ennui

Always the loner as well as the standoffish Monkee, Michael would take his six-passenger Lear jet and fly separately from the rest of the guys during the tours. As Steve Blauner explained about Michael traveling separately, "Mike comes to me and says that he can't deal with these people anymore, the rest of The Monkees. He couldn't stand it, he was going home, he wasn't going to play the tour. They couldn't do that many personal appearances 'cause of the show. We'd go out on some weekends, play two dates. And even though they were young and they could stay in that gear, this was the big tour for the summer. [30 cities in 40 days] And I knew all the tickets had been sold out, what am I going to do? But, I got up and I said 'Fine. Do what you have to do.' And I got to the door, I turned around and I said 'It's too bad. It's too bad you're gonna make Donnie Kirshner right.' And shut the door and went to my room. His wife was on the phone calling the airport. Nice lady. I always liked Phyllis, she was nice. That saved the tour. That line, that I threw out of left field. . . 'cause I got to the room, the phone was ringing. [imitating Michael with an attempted Texas drawl] 'Well, okay. I'll go on the tour but I'm gonna take my own plane. I won't fly with 'em.' 'Well, fine. I don't care what you're gonna do. You're gonna pay for it.' So he did. He flew separately, I think, the whole tour. He rented a jet. The Kirshner line worked magic."[32]

As Rick Klein remembered, "I heard a story from the pilot that Michael and Ward Sylvester got drunk on the way back from a concert and Mike had the pilot do a loop! Mike was always removed from the other three."

Drug usage in the rock groups during the sixties was common, and The Monkees were no exception. Dom Demieri from the Sundowners, one of the numerous opening acts for The Monkees, recalled, "There was acid. I don't know about Mike. He used to just talk a lot. I think he was taking No-Doze or something. Every time he'd sit down, man, he was like talking to everybody. . . there'd be like ten people around and he'd be like coming up with all this philosophy things and talking a mile a minute. And here is Mike saying in his Texas drawl, 'I assume that maybe if that wagon didn't have the right wheel on it. . .' He was like going on and on. He cracked me up. I said 'What's he

---

[32] Gary Strobl's interview with Steve Blauner 1-21-86.

talking about?' It was funny though, because I was listening to him. It sounded interesting. And he was going on and on. . ."[33]

Rick Klein remembered Michael's drug usage, "Mike's got a great sense of humor. Mike never did drugs. Mike was into Ritalin, an anti-depressant. It was mood elevator they gave to schizophrenics and manic depressives. In those days, it was a bitch to get. Obviously, you got it from a doctor, and now it's next to damn near impossible unless you're committed. I don't think he abused them. I think he used them to get himself up. He gave me a couple of them on occasion and they would like power your head out. We went to Nashville and he and I started smoking dope. He might have done it before, recreational joint smoking. We were in my room, we had rooms adjoining in this hotel, we smoked a joint and we got real goofy and we were laughing. And he got up and went to his room to go to bed, and as soon as he closed his door I forgot to ask him something. I went over to the door and I heard this woman's voice, 'Who is it?' It was totally odd, off-the-wall shit but real quick wit. It took me about 30 seconds to figure out where the hell I was after that."[34]

Michael listening to music on his state of the art sound system, 1968. Photo by Henry Diltz

---

[33] Gary Strobl's interview with Dom Demieri 5-93.
[34] Gary Strobl's interview with Rick Klein 10-89.

Publicist Don Berrigan accompanied the guys on tour and recalled an incident, "I'm going down the hall and I'm hearing something going on in Michael's room. So I went in there and Michael had all these reporters in there. He was telling them, 'Naw. We can't play our own music, instruments, or sing anything. It's all tape recorders backstage.' Which was the rumor, but he was aiding and abetting this rumor because he was bored. So then I had to take all these reporters backstage during the concert and show them that there were no tape recorders. This rumor was coming out in the press, and so I was supposed to keep the boys away from the press. Nesmith had all the press in his room. So I was on the cross again. Michael wasn't doing this against me, but he just wanted to have some fun."[35]

Michael lounging in his stereo chair, 1968. Photo by Henry Diltz.

On July 30, after a concert in Chicago, Michael flew home to Los Angeles for Phyllis' birthday. He spent the night and went back on the tour the next day. It was this sort of extravagance with money that was alarming everyone. As The Monkees' fame grew to gigantic proportions, so did Michael's bank account. Michael was the first Monkee to live lavishly with at least seven cars, countless motorcycles and a boat designed by Dean Jeffries named Carnation. A photographer who was on the set regularly, Allen Daviau, recalled, "I remember him having sort of an attitude about the money from The Monkees. That he

---

[35] Gary Strobl's interview with Don Berrigan 3-2-92.

was spending it and not worrying about it because he said in a Texas drawl, 'This is dirty money.'"

When asked seriously about his financial status, Michael said, "Now my bank manager says hello to me. Fine. But really, money is unimportant. I know what I'm worth and I like to buy things that I know are good value. Like I still go to the Army and Navy store and buy surplus clothes. Jeans are $3.98 a pair. Clothes don't mean anything to me, they're just something to cover my nakedness. So when I'm in London you don't see me rushing out around Carnaby Street, stocking up. I've got my clothes and I can remember only too well what it was like when the soles of my shoes fell off and there was no money in the house to go out and buy myself some new ones. Food and shelter. That's what's been most important to my mother and to me. Okay, so now my 'shelter' costs me $150,000. But that's all it is is shelter. If I eat two pounds of steak instead of a can of beans, all it is is 'food.'"

To contradict himself, Michael also told a reporter once, "When The Monkees are all over, I guess I'll just sit down with my scrapbooks and cry all the way to the bank."

As publicist Don Berrigan, who left L.A. radio station KHJ to work for Screen Gems, was visiting Michael at his house he recalled, "Mike called me over, 'Come here. I want to show you something.' He took me into the garage and here were all these tools, man. He had bought four grand worth of car tools. I said, 'That's great, Mike.' I thought, 'Man, why is he buying $4,000 worth of tools?'" Phyllis said,

"There was so much material abundance in those days. There was more money practically than you knew how to spend. You had to invent things to buy. It had nothing to do with need. Every need had long ago been met and almost every whim satisfied and you had to come up with new whims."

As Bruce Barbour remembered, "He called my mom and dad. He had been kind of a smart-ass when he said, 'I'm going to go to Hollywood and become a star.' And they went, 'Uh-huh. Right.' Almost eight or nine months after the show had started, he called my dad and said, 'What's your favorite kind of car?' My dad had no idea what he was talking about. He said, 'I'm partial to Fords.' He bought him the top-of-the-line Ford LTD, with everything you can hang onto the damn thing, and had John Kuehne drive it back for him. Until John dropped it off at their door at about 11 at night and woke them up, they had no idea it was coming. He was just that kind of guy."

Jim Edmonson the special events coordinator for Continental Security Guards, a security company that contracted 100 security guards and four personal bodyguards for The Monkees 1967 tour remembered, "Mike liked to be flamboyant. We went to a little restaurant in Dallas. They were open all night. He ordered a hamburger but the guy didn't have any mayonnaise. Mike told this black kid that I would give him $50 to get a jar of mayonnaise. I said, 'Don't be ridiculous.' To me, that was ludicrous. To Mike, it was nothing. I finally talked Mike out of it. I said, 'Eat it with ketchup. Eat it with anything. Don't be that foolish with your money.'

"One night I went to dinner with Mike, his brother-in-law Bruce, and someone else. We went down the beach where there's a Diamond Jim's, a luau type Hawaiian place. We walked in and it really had to be kind of funny looking because Mike is dressed to go to the concert, here I am in black sharkskin suit with a crew cut while Mike had fairly long hair and Bruce and the other guy with real long hair. We're walking in for dinner. They set the menus down and Mike said, 'I don't want any menus. I want the Chefs' special.' We proceeded to have about a 12-course dinner that was incredible. They had two waiters on us at all times as well as the maitre'd. They treated us like royalty. At the end of it, Mike wrote down $200.00 dollars for the gratuity. These little Oriental guys were falling all over themselves. Mike wanted $50 for each one of the waiters. $50 for the maitre'd and $50 for the cook. They thought that was the greatest thing that ever happened. . . at least to a working stiff. For Mike, it was peanuts. He liked to be flamboyant like that."

Rick Klein remembers, "Mike used to throw parties and we would rate them on a scale of 1 to 10. And Mike was always more concerned about how I rated one of his parties than how it actually came off. If he had a party for six people, he would have valet parking, a maid and a butler all dressed up, and a full bar, just as a goof to see if he got a 10 from me."

The Monkees tour also was not without its share of thrills, as Jim Edmondson recalled, "Well, this one particular night on the way to Des Moines, we had gotten into an electrical storm. They were having such a good time throwing pillows and drinking. I was up in the cockpit and the pilot says, 'you better tell them to sit down. We've got some rough weather coming up.' So I got on the intercom and I said, 'the pilot has informed me we've some got rough weather. You better take your seats and buckle up.' Here comes a pillow at me. They wouldn't listen to me. I said to the pilot, 'they're not listening. I don't know what the hell is going to happen.' He says, 'I'll get them in their seats.' He takes the gears and we dropped about 500 feet and came back. After the pilot did that, everybody went, 'Oh, shit!' They all jumped in their seats and buckled up.

"Then, we hit the electrical storm. The plane was getting tossed around. I went back to my seat and I'm sitting across from Mike who was just white as a T-shirt, I mean he is scared. Lightning would hit and it would look like daylight outside. The plane is just getting tossed around like fish. I've always been a fatalist thinking, '. . . it's my time, it's my time. There's nothing I can do about it. Let it happen if it's going to happen.' Mike's sitting there. . . he's trying to talk and he's trying to be funny but he's scared shitless. He is scared to death. He said, 'All my life. . . my mother's a wealthy woman and she's never really helped me out a lot. I've struggled. Now, I'm a millionaire. I'm going to die tonight.' That kind of cracked me up. It took the edge off of my fear."[36] Needless to say, Michael did not die that night and the plane did arrive safely in Des Moines where The Monkees performed.

Other thrills came courtesy of the fans, who would show their undying love to The Monkees by throwing items onto the stage. Peter got hit in the face with a banana in San Francisco, while Michael got hit by a can of hair spray at one concert. The can hit right above his right eye and required stitches, but it is not known if Michael actually went to get the stitches.

Avoiding flying objects on stage as well as not being able to hear the music he was playing on stage due to the fans screaming left Michael frustrated that he couldn't prove to the public that he was talented. He said in an interview, "There was a feeling of consistently being on the brink. Of what I don't know. It's that strange anticipatory feeling you go through before you get laid, before you have a great meal, before you get into a fight. It's an incredible anticipatory feeling that continues, but it's never satisfied. The concerts were not orgasmic for me."

While checking into a hotel in Dallas before a concert, the guys had to fight through the usual onslaught of fans at the door. When the band got inside the hotel, a Texas state trooper called over to them.

---

[36] Gary Strobl's interview with Jim Edmondson 7-2-87.

The trooper said, "Come here, boy. Let me see a little ID. Look at what we got here, Lester. Come here. Look it there. There's a live one. What makes you so special?"

Michael said, "Oh, nothing really. We're just different from you in the fact that we have more money, more prestige and get nicer women."

After saying that, Michael walked on much to the delight of the guys with him.

At one of the final concerts on the tour, Michael threw his wool hat into the crowd and a very happy fan grabbed it. He wasn't rid of the hat yet, since Screen Gems had stacks of wool hats for him to wear.

Henry Diltz was a member of the Modern Folk Quartet, which also included The Monkees producer, Chip Douglas. He was also a photographer who took photos of rock musicians. Henry got a job with *Tiger Beat* going down to The Monkees set at Screen Gems and taking photos. The guys warmed to Henry immediately since he was young and not pushy as the other photographers were. Henry became the official Monkees photographer supplying thousands of shots of the guys for all the teen magazines.

The Monkees second season of episodes began. Screen Gems, in a gesture of great generosity, raised the boys' salaries from $450 a week to $750 a week. The boys now sported longer

Photo by Henry Diltz.

hair and hipper clothes. The wool hat was now a rare sight as Michael was tired of wearing a piece of clothing that he was so identified with and that had been commercialized.

The boys were also becoming more vocal. They complained to anyone that would listen that the scripts they were being given were rejects from the first season. When they threatened not to do a third season, the scripts got better. Always the complainer, Michael was quoted as saying, 'We don't learn scripts...hell, we don't even read them.' The boys even developed attitudes with the crew as publicist Don Berrigan recalled, "It became the kind of the job that's the worst kind of a job, having responsibility for the boys, without having any authority over them. So, I would come down with a directive from Bert and I would tell Nesmith to do this. He'd say, 'Screw you.' And then, I'd tell Davy and he'd say, 'Fuck you.' And then, I'd have to go back and tell Bert that they wouldn't do it."

Rebelling against Screen Gems at times, Michael would not show up for the filming of certain episodes during the second season. In the first episode without Michael, *99 Pound Weakling*, there are several times where the other Monkees would face the camera and say, "I wish Mike were here." The second episode sans Michael, *Card Carrying Red Shoes* would only feature Michael at the end during a performance clip of *She Hangs Out*. Another episode, *Monkees Watch Their Feet*, would feature Michael only at the beginning as he introduced Pat Paulsen. Rebelliousness was not the only reason Michael would be absent from episodes, as Henry Diltz explains about the filming of the episode

Hitting the High Seas, "Mike got seasick right away on the boat they were filming on. He was feeling bad, and they said 'Well, you better go lie down, Mike.' He actually started feeling squeamish and they had a little boat come along and take him off. I have a picture of Monkee director Jon Andersen holding on to both boats while Mike steps in."

Sneaking onto the set day after day for months was a young student filmmaker named Steven Spielberg. Finally he was asked if he would

Photo by Henry Diltz.

like to direct an episode and he quickly said that he would want to. Unfortunately, The Monkees had director approval and they refused to have someone new direct them. Years later Spielberg, now a successful film director, would ask Michael why he was refused to direct them. Michael told him that he would have agreed, but the others were

83

swaying him to say no.[37] It is hard to imagine Michael being swayed by someone and them changing his mind.

On his thoughts as an actor Michael said in the Seventies, "I don't consider myself an actor, never have been comfortable in playing a role. I was never involved enough in the television series to know what was going on. As far as writing music, it wasn't really stimulating. I exercised more self-discipline and control just to stay out there and do the job to which I was contracted. It's like I got drafted. I'd just gotten out of the Air Force, the most horrible experience of my life, and I thought 'Boy, I'll never sign a contract like that again!' Ended up signing one. Except the punishments were much more severe, I think I would rather have spent time in the brig. They have clauses in there to keep you out of work the rest of your life. You simply can't work. You can't work for anybody."

Michael may have insisted he was not an actor, but he was given moments in episodes that proved that he had promise. One episode, *The Devil and Peter Tork*, featured Monte Landis as the Devil who gives Peter the ability to play a harp in exchange for his soul. The plot was certainly not typical of situation comedies. In the episode it is even joked that the boys can't even say the word "hell" on television, which of course is bleeped out. In the climax of the episode Landis goes to collect the soul and Michael challenges him in court. As Landis recalls about the filming, "Jim Frawley did the directing. But, in the court scenes, Bob Rafelson was there. When we were doing the court sequence, Bob Rafelson directed Mike in that. In fact, before every take that Mike did, he took Mike aside and they worked on it until they got it right. They really put a lot of work into that. He psyched Mike up for

Photo by Henry Diltz

every take of that show. Bob would come on the set and he'd coach Mike to do it a certain way. He took Mike under his wing. Bob Rafelson had a

---

[37] Gary Strobl's interview with Dave Evans 6-23-87.

84

very big thing for him and he was very impressed with Mike as well as being very attached to him. He wanted to create some special kind of moment. Mike became Bob's child. Mike was his creation. I got no direction at all."

Also in the second season The Monkees began bringing guests onto the show. Nesmith's guest was Frank Zappa, who appeared on the show dressed as Michael, complete with a green wool hat, while Michael impersonated Zappa with wild hair and a fake nose that kept falling off.

Zappa (*as Nesmith*): C'mon I'm one of those unpopular musicians. Teach me.

Nesmith (*as Zappa*): No, you've got it the other way around. You're a popular musician. I'm dirty, gross and ugly.

Zappa then proceeded to destroy a car while Michael conducted

Photo by Henry Diltz

the destruction as if it was a symphony. Michael was trying to show the rock community that he was not just a kiddie show guy, and that he really wanted to have some credibility no matter what the cost.

For one of the episodes, The Monkees traveled to Paris and basically romped around the entire episode. Bill Chadwick recalled the trip and the trouble only The Monkees could get into, "We were driving along in a bus doing a whole bunch of stuff for two or three days. While we are doing this, Mike is phonetically trying to teach this French girl how to say, 'I don't understand you,' in English. But he was teaching her with a Texas accent. (speaking with a Southern drawl) 'Ah doan

85

unnerstaynd yew.' This is the only English she could speak. So we get these mini-cars and we go out and we make a traffic jam. These Parisian officers are flipping out because it's right dead in the middle of the rush hour. So they're taking their hats and throwing them down, and you can see it in the episode, but it's not acting. They're serious. They're really pissed off. And here's this officer going up to the girl and he's shaking his finger at her and she's sitting with Mike in the mini-car and she's saying in her best Texas drawl, 'Ah doan unnerstaynd yew.' You can't tell in the film, but the guy's going 'What?' It was just crazy. We had eight or ten mini-cars all just clogging things up and creating this planned confusion. Then, we found out that night that it was practically an international incident because it caused such a traffic foul-up that it delayed some presidential speech for three hours because the president couldn't get to where he was speaking. While we were in Paris we stayed at the Hotel George V, a dynamite hotel. The hotel told us that Mike's suite was the one that Hitler stayed in during the occupation of Paris. He made it his field headquarters. It was a beautiful suite. It looked like something out of a 1940s movie."

Lady Of The Valley

While Michael and the other Monkees were being featured in the teen magazines, Phyllis Nesmith also became somewhat of a teen idol. Teen magazines would have pin ups of her as well as articles on her marriage to Michael and the raising of their child. *Tiger Beat* even featured Phyllis in a fashion layout that was photographed by Henry Diltz. As Phyllis said, "I remember a quote from Michael when the proofs from this session of Henry's came back. He said, 'I never realized you were so beautiful until I saw these pictures.' I thought, 'Well, thanks, I guess.' That part was fun because I wasn't

Photo by Henry Diltz

personally on display. I didn't save any of them. I felt very, very much a watcher in all this. They said, 'We need some pictures of you.' I said, 'Okay. Good. I'll play dress up.' It was fun. I still think it's fun to look and say, 'Look how pretty someone made me look. Look what an experienced photographer can do.'"

One issue of *Tiger Beat* even listed all of Phyllis' vital statistics and when asked what her professional ambition was, she replied that she wanted to be a country and western vocalist. This did not occur as she had to cater to Michael's needs. Her hobby was listed as "the care and feeding of temperamental musicians."

Michael's plans for his son Christian were also fodder for the teenage magazines. Michael revealed one of his ahead-of-his-time ideas in an interview in 1967, "My son is two years old and next year I'll put him in boarding school if I can find the right one. I'm very much interested in the Montessori method, where the child is taught in a way entirely different from the American system. Actually I would like to set up my own preparatory school sometime and put my ideas about

87

education into effect. I think the entire public education system is terrible."

The Monkees' fourth album, *Pisces, Aquarius, Capricorn and Jones LTD*, was released during the Fall of 1967. It was a flawless record, blending Michael's country taste to Davy singing his usual schmaltzy songs about love. Peter provided the novelty cut *Peter Percival Patterson's Pet Pig Porky,* which was then followed by the anti-suburbia rocker *Pleasant Valley Sunday* with lead vocals from

Phyllis and Christian Nesmith. Photo by Henry Diltz.

both Micky and Michael. As Peter explains, "I always thought, and I believe I was vindicated in this, that the ideal lead vocal was Micky and Mike double tracked. Micky was just a little too faint and Mike was just a little too stern and you put those two vocals together to the point where they're balanced so you can't tell who is exactly singing and you really will get each one bringing the other one there. And on *Pleasant Valley Sunday* you hear that. You hear that lead vocal combination. I think you hear Mike sounding strong and Micky sounding young and naive. There's a naiveté to Micky's voice that's very appealing in many ways. An easiness, that's not the right word, but it's a quality that Micky had that Mike lacked. And that sternness and rigidity. I mean Michael's pitch was (sternly in a growling voice), 'It's fuckin' right, motherfucker!' (laughing), kind of an attitude, and that drew Micky into better pitch and that kind of combination and I think it worked. I think you hear it on *Pleasant Valley Sunday*."[38]

The album barely sold a million records, but it showed that The Monkees could still record on their own and be successful without being in the shadow of Kirshner, or so they thought.

It was also revealed that The Monkees had sold more records in 1967 than the Beatles and the Rolling Stones combined. Although true, this is not exactly a fair comparison, since The Monkees had released three albums as compared to the Beatles and the Stones releasing one album each.

---

[38] Gary Strobl's interview with Peter Tork 1-14-87.

Writing Wrongs

Frustrated with being unable to showcase his own talents, Michael now began to develop and finance his own projects, leaning towards being an entrepreneur of the entertainment business, with little interest in whether the project would succeed financially.

He told a reporter that he had written a couple of books but he was going to have them published under a pseudonym so he would not have to hear the comparisons between himself and John Lennon, who had also written a few books. One of the books was a long poem of about 300 words in which a little boy falls into a camera and sees that everything is reversed. Michael also stated that he didn't want to cash in on the Mike Nesmith of The Monkees name. Of it Michael said, "If my work has any value it should stand up under any name." These books were never published.

Upset that Screen Gems could profit from everything he did, Michael turned to the one thing they couldn't profit from: producing albums for another record company. According to Monkees recording engineer Hank Cicalo, "Michael had this idea. It came out of nowhere. We had talked about it a couple of times and he kept telling me about he always wanted to do this big orchestra thing with tunes that he had written. He wanted to do it with a big orchestra and the best players he could find. Some of the ideas were pretty bizarre. It started off with trying to get 150 guys in the Grand Canyon and can you mike it? There were some really absurd trips going down. He wanted that big sound. He wanted it to sound spacious and big and gigantic. And he wanted it to sound like a wall. I listen to the album now and there are things about it that I don't like because of the fact that it sounds so open. But, that was part of the sound that Mike wanted. He wanted it real open, overhead microphones, and wanted it splashing."

On November 18, Michael assembled at least 50 of the finest LA musicians he could find and had them record an instrumental album of his own tunes. Michael had it planned that when the project was finished, he would then present the completed recording to several record companies with hopes of one distributing the album. Originally called World War Three, and then titled The Pacific Ocean, the project ended up being called The Wichita Train Whistle. The album *The Wichita Train Whistle Sings* cost at least $60,000 to produce, which came out of Michael's own pocket. In addition, he had the session food catered from the ritzy restaurant Chasens, reportedly because he needed the tax write off. Hank Cicalo remembers about the recording session,

"Michael was at times musically not able to express certain things and Shorty Rogers, the music arranger of the project, had the ability and the patience to work with something as momentous as that. . . and when you change a couple of bars. . . you're changing a couple of bars for 50 guys. Shorty always was able to go right through that and say, 'Sure, Michael. I'll do. . . wait a minute. Give me a couple of minutes.' I'd be in the booth with Michael and Michael said, 'Jesus. How is he doing that?' I said, 'Carefully.' We were able to do it.

Michael with Hank Cicalo during the Wichita Train Whistle recording sessions. November 1967 photo from The RLM Archives.

"Michael was, of course, being the perfectionist. . . at times. . . I'll never forget that with Manny Klein. . . that one the piccolo trumpet. . . and Michael kept wanting to change it. There was something that bothered him with the take. In those days, we didn't do much editing and putting a piece together. Although we did it, Michael said, 'I want to hear the whole thing.' And Shorty kept coming in, being a trumpet player, they're seeing Manny Klein. . . what's going on with Manny? So, Shorty said, 'This is really trouble.' After it was all over, Manny Klein. . . he's playing piccolo trumpet and he's bleeding. . . he was blowing up there in the stratosphere and he's blood all over his lips and everything. Michael saw that, and he felt so bad because he didn't realize that was happening to him playing the piccolo trumpet and playing up that high. . . and that ending went on forever. He went nuts and he said, 'What can

I do for you?' Manny Klein said, 'I'd sure like a bottle of vodka.' He sent somebody out and got him a bottle of vodka. And then Manny spent the rest of the afternoon blitzed."

Ever the consummate party giver, Michael previewed the *Wichita* album for all of his friends as well as for members of the press at his lavish Bel Air home. At the party, Michael told a few reporters that this album was made to prove to himself and to everyone else that 'he was not just a member of a no-talent, manufactured group.' After managing to put down his Monkee cohorts, Michael succeeded in

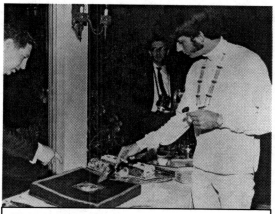

startling some of the young girls who were guests by telling them that if they were already drinking, that they would end up being middle aged alcoholic housewives. Leave it to Michael to liven up a party.

Michael then signed a contract with Dot Records to handle

Michael at the Wichita Party

the album, and it is not known if Dot actually heard the record before they agreed to distribute it. He did, however, warn them that it would not sell in the same quantity of copies as a Monkees record, but it is doubtful Dot believed him. With the cover's dark lettering and lack of photographs, it bombed on the record shelves and peaked at #160 on the charts before falling into oblivion. The magazine *High Fidelity* called *Wichita*, "One of the all-time clumsiest attempts at combining the big band brass with rock and roll rhythms."

Michael avoided responsibility for its commercial failure, instead blaming it on managerial problems at Dot. He stated that it wasn't promoted right and that it wasn't distributed right and also that no one would buy a record associated with a Monkee. Years later Michael would say that hearing one of the '*Wichita*' songs performed by a college band in the Rose Bowl Parade in the early '90s was one of the highlights of hearing his own music played back to him.

Michael also signed an agreement with Dot to produce 12 demos of prospective artists for the label. The project was called The Pacific Ocean, and had Michael producing records for a group called

The Corvettes as well as for his friend Bill Chadwick. A couple of singles of each artist were pressed, but they did not make it past the promotional stage. Any other work that Michael may have produced remains unreleased.

The Upside of Good-bye

On November 22, the 'no-talent manufactured' Monkees filmed the last episode of the second season. They were not eager to be renewed for a third season. The guys were tired of the teenage love, spies and vampire stories, and wanted to change the format of the show from a sitcom to an hour long show with a changing theme each week, varying from western sagas to science fiction stories. They even intended to do some filming around the world on their concert tours.

The problem with this was that NBC was not interested in the idea of a revamped Monkees show. They were very happy with the ratings, not to mention the money they were making with advertising, and they didn't feel the need to change anything. The Monkees could not reach a compromise with NBC, so *The Monkees* television show was canceled. The announcement was made publicly in February, and the fans responded with a letter writing campaign that was the largest in history, even surpassing the infamous *Star Trek* letter writing campaign that same year.

There was an agreement with NBC for The Monkees to make three variety specials for the next TV season. It was a decision that at least Micky regretted a couple of years later, when in an interview he sighed and said, "Maybe we should have done a third season." It was too late. Monkeemania was on the downhill slide, and, with the TV show off the air, it would prove impossible to revive.

But Michael Nesmith was busy putting his Monkee earnings to good use, as Jim Edmundson remembered, "Michael told me he had done a Twelve Days of Christmas thing for Phyllis. The first day he bought her a ring. The next a fur. The next day something else, building up to a big home that they bought." The house, originally owned by Doris Day, sat high on top of a hill in Beverly Hills and cost Michael $200,000. Then he proceeded to spend an additional $50,000 in remodeling the house that he named "Arnold."

The house had a 60-foot indoor/outdoor swimming pool, as well as four fireplaces. There was an indoor barbecue pit, and Michael had a little electric train set up to run along the edge of the bar. Michael said in some interviews that the doors in the house were voice controlled to open when one said the word "love."

The Mistake Out Company officially changed its name to the Liquid Paper Corporation in 1968. Bette was named chairman of the board, while her husband Robert Graham was named president. The company was now advertising on television during *The Tonight Show* and *The Huntley-Brinkley News Report,* as well as in the magazines *Fortune* and *Glamour.* The advertising worked and the company reaped the rewards by making millions with their Liquid Paper product.

On February 4, 1968, Phyllis gave birth to Jonathan Darby Nesmith. All the teen magazines were waiting for the new arrival, and they wasted no time trying to out-scoop each other. *Tiger Beat* was the winner as they printed a photo of Jonathan still in the hospital. All *Flip* magazine could do at the last minute was give the time of birth in the corner of the table of contents.

Keith Allison recalls trying to visit the new baby, "I hated going up there. He used to have this German Shepherd named Fraak. It was the most terrifying thing you've ever seen. Oh my God, man! One day. . . I had a motorcycle back then. Sonny Bono had one, too. So, Sonny would call me up and say, 'Bring Judy over and we'll go riding bikes.' We got to their place. Judy says, 'You got to see this house that Michael Nesmith just redid.' She told them about what was going on and Cher says, 'I want to see it.' So, she called Phyllis. . . said, 'We're coming up.' Chastity must have been an infant at the time. They went up to the house. Christian, I guess, was a toddler and then there was Jonathan. They had two kids. When you got to the gate, you had to yell in or buzz in saying, 'Is Fraak out?' because he would, 'Hooh. Hooh. Hooh. Hooh.' And when he started doing that, you better just freeze. Because he wasn't attack-trained. He was killer-trained in Germany. It's against the law to have those dogs in this country. He would build up, 'Hooh. Hooh! Hooh! Hooh! Hooh! Hooh!' As the pitch went, man, you better freeze and not move a muscle. You stand there and wait. Cher and Judy went up there and that dog is like this the whole time. He doesn't take his eyes off of her. . . staring at Cher and then he'd stare at the babies. Staring at Cher and stare at her baby. It's ready to pounce and you can see the muscles. This was the biggest German Shepherd you'll ever see, man. One who would crush tennis balls in its mouth. Swear to God. They have hundreds and hundreds of pounds of pressure they can exert with their jaw. It'd take that baby's head off like that. Cher was so scared she broke out in hives from head to toe. By the time they got back to Bel Air. . . she was already erupting. . . she had to walk in the door and take off her clothes. They called the dermatologist. They called Sonny. He got pissed off. He called a lawyer. He was going to sue Mike. . . just because they went up there to see Phyllis and say hello and see the baby."[39]

---

[39] Gary Strobl's interview with Keith Allison 9-89.

Sunny Girlfriend

The fans were so happy about the birth that they started sending bags of diapers to Screen Gems for Michael. Everything should have been perfect at the Nesmith house, but things were not as rosy as the teen magazines were reporting. Some of the magazines started reporting that Michael and Phyllis had separated for a time. They would say that Phyllis and the kids went down to Texas for a while. These sources were guessing that Michael had probably let success go to his head and was being unbearable to live with. Perhaps it was because Phyllis found out that Michael had fathered another child while she was pregnant. On August 7, 1968, Michael Jason Nesmith Wilde was born to Nurit Wilde, a photographer, who was a friend of Peter's and had a cameo in The Monkees episode, *Monkees In Texas*.

The press, who would have loved the scoop that a teen idol had an out of wedlock child while his wife was already pregnant, apparently did not discover Jason's birth. The news would have destroyed Michael's career, as well as destroy The Monkees, which was something the press was well on the way towards doing anyway. Phyllis did return to Michael after a few months, much to the relief of the fans who had read about the separation in the pages of *16* Magazine and were waiting with baited breath for their favorite teen idol couple to reunite.

February 29 was Grammy night once again and The Monkees' song *I'm A Believer* was nominated for Best Performance by a Vocal Group as well as Best Contemporary Group Performance, Vocal or Instrumental. In both categories, The Monkees were up against the Beatles' *Sgt. Pepper* album, The Association and The Box Tops, but they all would lose to the 5th Dimension's *Up, Up and Away*. It would be the final time that The Monkees would be nominated as a group.

In early 1968, the single *Different Drum* reached number 13 on the Billboard charts. Written by Michael and performed by the Stone Poneys, the song received airplay because it had been written by one of The Monkees. The Stone Poneys' lead singer, Linda Ronstadt, had heard the song performed by a group called The Greenbriars and liked it so much that her group recorded it.

The record that it appeared on, *The Stone Poneys: Evergreen Volume II* had been released in June of 1967, and the group had broken up by the time the single had hit the charts. The group did reunite briefly to capitalize on the single's success, which eventually launched a superstar career for Linda. Of their version of the song, Michael has said many times, "Linda will always sing that song better than I ever could and I'm glad she did it, because it never would have been a hit if I'd recorded it back then." Michael finally had a glimmer of hope that he would be taken seriously as a songwriter and musician in the future if he could just stop 'monkeeing around.'

In mid-1968, Phyllis was in a serious car accident when she ran her Lamborgini sports car down Mulholland Drive and off a cliff. The car rolled and was completely totaled. Phyllis was almost totaled as well. She broke her hip, and her mouth was torn open on one side all the way to her left ear. After the ambulance took her to the hospital, they called Michael to say that they needed his permission for certain procedures. He refused. He said, "You put her in an ambulance and take her home." That afternoon a Christian Science practitioner came and sat with her for two or three days. There were no visitors allowed until the fifth day after the accident, as Keith Allison, a friend of Michael's from his San Antonio days remembered her remarkable recovery, "We waited down in the living room. She came down the stairs and walked on her own. Very slowly and had a blank stare about her. Just vacant. And there's just this pink line. And I talked to people that saw her. They said her mouth, her jaw was torn open. Her cheek was torn open. Cut. She hooked it on to something. They X-rayed her and she had broken bones. She had never been in a cast. And a week later she walked down and said hello. She says [straining], 'I can't talk with you, and I thank you for coming by. Maybe by next week we can talk.' She was like in a trance. She turned, walked back up the stairs. We hugged her and left. Amazing."[40]

---

[40] Gary Strobl's interview with Keith Allison 9-89.

"It Looks Like We've Made It Once Again"

The Monkees had been anxious to translate their popularity from the small screen to the big screen. The Monkees' movie had been announced for some time, but there was never enough time to film a motion picture due to the recording of the albums, the concert tours and the filming of the television show. Columbia allowed $750,000 for the budget of a movie they thought would be a ninety-minute version of The Monkees' popular television show. Little did the studio executives know that it was the guys' idea, along with Schneider and Rafelson, to totally

With actress Carol Doda on the set of Head

destroy The Monkees' manufactured image, in order for all of them to move along creatively. The guys figured this movie to be the first of a series of offbeat Monkee movies. As for Schneider and Rafelson, while they might have wanted to destroy The Monkees altogether so that they could move along in their own careers, they could not turn down the offer of a Columbia movie with their name on the credits.

Jack Nicholson was a B movie actor and screenplay writer whose best acting credentials seemed to be in an obscure Boris Karloff movie called *The Terror*. He was also a friend of both Rafelson and Schneider and they wanted Nicholson to write the screenplay for the Monkee movie. Nicholson, who had four produced screenplays; *Thunder Island*, *Flight to Fury*, *Ride in the Whirlwind* and *The Trip*, was infinitely more qualified for the job than Rafelson or Schneider.

Nicholson, Rafelson, Schneider and the four Monkees went to Ojai, California, for a weekend where, according to Davy, they smoked lots of marijuana and rambled ideas into a tape recorder. With the tapes, Rafelson and Nicholson went to the desert and wrote the script long hand while tripping on acid and then had the scribbling typed up by their production secretary.

When The Monkees found out that Rafelson and Schneider would be sharing screenplay credit, effectively leaving out The Monkees names, a major conflict erupted. Michael got so angry about the decision that he locked up the tapes in the trunk of his car. His manager, Jerry Perenschio, conducted the negotiations.

Micky and Davy followed Nesmith's lead in protest and the three of them went on strike. Peter was the only Monkee who showed up for the first day of the filming. Ironically the director didn't need him as he'd planned to use only stand-ins to test the color and lighting. After everything settled, the guys went back to work. They still didn't receive credit, but The Monkees would receive the paltry amount of $1,000 each

for their work in the film. The only exception was Davy, who, thinking he would outsmart the others, agreed to get a piece of the profits for this movie, which the teen magazines predicted would be a surefire hit.

The movie featured a cast that included Frank Zappa, large-breasted topless dancer Carol Doda, Annette Funicello, and a then unknown actress named Teri Garr, who was billed as Terry Garr. Also written into the script was a part that was written especially for 40's movie star Victor Mature to play the Big Victor, who represented the public, who ultimately controls The Monkees fate. As Bob Rafelson recalled, the screenwriters had no idea if they would even be able to get Mature to be in the movie until, "Mike Nesmith picked up the telephone and called Victor Mature and he actually got him on the telephone and said something about 'have you heard of The Monkees?' and 'well, we're doing a movie and would you like to be in it?' and whoever it was presumably slammed the phone. Now, we couldn't testify to the fact that that conversation was taking place. Mike could have been faking? We didn't hear the other end. So, then I picked up the phone and, by this time, we had an irritated Victor Mature. And finally an appointment was made to see him. I was convinced when we did he see him. He said, 'Why should I be in this movie?' I said, 'Well, it just seems to be for the whimsy.' And he said, 'For whimsy, I'll do it for whimsy.' And that's how we got him for the movie."

Filming was a rocky affair, as everyone's tempers would flare from time to time. Michael had a scene in which he, Micky and Peter are sucked into a vacuum cleaner, where Michael discovers a marijuana cigarette. In the final print of the film Michael says, "This is not one of your standard brands." According to Peter, Michael really wanted to say, "Look, a marijuana cigarette," in the style of W.C. Fields; however, Rafelson felt that that was just too outrageous to be in the film. Not being able to get his way, Michael stormed to his dressing room for about an hour and then came back and did the scene as it was originally written.

A few months later the film crew finished up the filming at the Valley Auditorium in Salt Lake City, Utah, where The Monkees filmed an in concert performance for the Nesmith song *Circle Sky*. They performed the song several times for the filming and afterwards took requests from the very cooperative audience that was filled mostly with pretty teenage girls.

Peter loved the live version of the song and was very upset when Michael had it recorded again with his own band for the soundtrack album. In an interview in the late '70s Peter said, "I don't think Mike has any community spirit whatsoever. Not that it's so strange, it's the way he was raised. He wanted to do everything himself. It was he who got the other two guys together to strike. He was gonna be the boss at any price, essentially."[41] Davy's reaction to the re-recording was, "He was very selfish in that respect. He didn't want The Monkees

---

[41] Gary Strobl's interview with Peter Tork 1-14-87.

to be a band."[42] Yet Michael maintains to this day that it was not his
decision to replace the live version of *Circle Sky* with his studio version.
As he said a few years ago, "I just don't have any idea how that
happened. I think that The Monkees always played it better. I can't
remember a studio version being better than the way we played it live,
because live it was just pure unbridled energy."

The film, originally called *Untitled* and then *Changes* and then
finally named *Head*, a term meaning "drug user", was a bizarre mixture
of comedy, drama, westerns and musicals and if you paid close attention
to The Monkees and their history, you could tell that *Head* was the story
of their rebellion against being Screen Gems puppets. The movie had
the boys fighting in Vietnam and going into a cave, and running
through a wall of fire emerging unscathed (unharmed by the scrutiny of
the press, the studio and their fans) ending up in a concert arena where
they are attacked by their fans who tear off their clothes and rip their
heads off (The boys are represented by mannequins that represent their
puppet image). Micky is then seen blowing up a broken Coke Machine
(commercialism) in the middle of the desert (the desertion by the
studio). All through the movie the boys keep getting trapped in a black
box (the endless life of jumping into a car to get into a hotel, then
jumping into a car to get to the concert arena and repeating this exercise
for months on end in the job of touring), the boys end up being dandruff
in Victor Mature's hair (being exploited by the studio for commercial
purposes and then disposed when finished) and a host of non-Monkee
images.

During the filming of the Monkee movie, their fifth record was
released. *The Birds, The Bees & The Monkees* was an album filled with
songs pulled from the archives as well as a few original songs.
Michael's songs no longer had the playfulness that his earlier songs did.
One of his tracks on the album, *Magnolia Simms* seemed as if he had
listened to way too many songs from the twenties. One of the other
Nesmith contributions on the album is the tedious *Writing Wrongs* that
appears to be an exercise in torture with a piano that won't quit, and
lyrics that seem to be drug influenced with a stream of consciousness
style.

The album spawned one single. The A side was *Valleri* an old
TV series track, which Michael deemed in an interview, "The worst
song I've ever heard in my life." Side B of the single was Michael's
song *Tapioca Tundra*, which earned him a hefty royalty check as *Valleri*
rose to number three on the charts.

---

[42] Gary Strobl's interview with David Jones 10-9-87.

Michael was still unhappy as a Monkee even saying to a reporter, "I've always told them that I won't go do my thing at the expense of being a Monkee, but I won't play their stupid Monkees games anymore. I won't play no more games. They can do what they want."

As soon as he could get out of town, Michael took off to Nashville to cut at least six tracks for a proposed Monkees double album project that would feature one album side for each of their musical tastes. When asked why he was recording in Nashville, Michael replied, "I like the studio, but the musicians are the greatest," for yet another slam on his simian brethren.

Among the musicians used for the recording were Buddy Spicher, David Briggs, Jerry Carrigan, Bobby Dyson, Kenneth Buttrey, Sonny Osborne, Lloyd Green, Wayne Moss, Charlie McCoy, Norbert Putnam and Harold Bradley. All had been out of work until Nesmith

hired them, and shortly thereafter the group named themselves Area Code 615 and became staples in Nashville session work. Six songs were recorded at the RCA Victor studios under the guidance of Felton Jarvis, who described the music to *Billboard* magazine as "folk-rock-country." Michael described the music as "weird". While in Nashville, Michael stopped by the Sho-Bud pedal steel guitar factory, where he ordered the most expensive model they produced and had his name inlayed in mother of pearl on the neck of the instrument.

Michael at the premiere of Head wearing his custom made western suit from the Nudie company. A hooded Phyllis can be seen to his left.

Head was sneak previewed at the Vogue Theater in Los Angeles. The Monkees attended along with about 100 guests. The audience just didn't know what to make of the film, and Rafelson and Schneider edited the film feverishly until the release date.

The official premiere of the movie was November 6, in New York, while in Los Angeles the premiere date was November 19. *Head* was not the success that all of its participants and Columbia Pictures thought it would be. The prospective audiences were confused by an odd advertising campaign for the movie, in which the television commercials featured no sound, but showed only Columbia advertising consultant John Brockman's balding head. There were hardly any mentions of The Monkees in the advertising, and there was no mention of the movie being a musical comedy. By looking at the advertising, one would think that this was some sort of psychedelic drug movie, and certainly not directed at The Monkees once substantial teenage audience, and it was figured that the adult public would stay away from a movie that featured The Monkees in it.

Reviews were mixed. *New York Times* reviewer Renata Adler, stated that *"Head* might be a film to see if you have been smoking grass or if you like to scream at The Monkees, or if you are interested in what interests drifting heads and hysterical school girls." On the less critical side, William Wolf from *Cue* magazine said *"Head* is an inventive and creative first film for The Monkees."

The film died a swift death at the box office, ending all possibilities of another Monkee movie. As Michael said in 1989, "We thought that this was the beginning of our film career, and that this was really going to be a tremendous hit movie. Boy, did we get that one wrong." Davy said about the movie, "We couldn't throw a thing like *Head* at the audience that we had, which was the 16-year old and unders. It was not an entertaining movie. It was an ego trip for Bob Rafelson."

The soundtrack for *Head* was not released concurrent with the film and it didn't appear in stores until December. It had posed a production problem for the record company. The front of the cover was a silver reflective material that would enable the buyer to look at the cover and see his own head.

The album featured the most songs by Peter to ever appear on a Monkee album with *Can You Dig It?* and *Long Title: Do I Have to Do This All Over Again?* Also on the album was Michael's studio version of *Circle Sky*, the Goffin & King penned *Porpoise Song*, and Harry Nilsson's *Daddy's Song*. A novelty on the album was the addition of dialogue from the film. Monkee fans didn't rush to buy the soundtrack, and the album peaked at #45 on the charts. The Monkees were definitely losing their touch on the buying public.

Keys To The Car

Whenever he could, Michael, a car-racing enthusiast, would travel to the Baja desert in Mexico to compete in the Baja 1000, racing a dune buggy or one of his trucks whenever he could. Dean Jeffries remembered his trip to Baja with Michael in November of 1968, "I built up a couple of dune buggies to go race in Baja and the two of us went down there. Either me or Mike was driving one of the buggies and one of us went flying over a cliff and we broke it before the race. I came back and started to repair it. He got madder than hell. He just jumped in his

truck which his buddy brought down. He'd rode down with me. And he took off with his buddies in a truck and headed back home and just left me out there in the middle of the desert trying to get my buggy fixed. That was the end of our relationship."[43]

Back in Monkeeland following the release of their movie, The Monkees started work on their television special called *33 1/3 Revolutions Per Monkee* for NBC. For some odd reason, The Monkees chose to redo the concept that didn't work in the movies. Filmed in two weeks, it was the story of the made for TV manufactured puppets trying to gain control of everything, which of course was also happening in real life. Although everyone creatively involved with The

---

[43] Gary Strobl's interview with Dean Jeffries 10-18-84.

Monkees series had moved on to other projects, the actors did not gain any creative control because they were shifted to new executives who dictated the same old orders.

The special featured Brian Auger as the maniacal music director (i.e. Kirshner) trying to brainwash The Monkees, with Julie Driscoll as his assistant. Also featured were Jerry Lee Lewis, Fats Domino and Little Richard as "the favors" because The Monkees liked them.

The musical numbers ranged from the ridiculous *I Go Ape* sung in monkey suits, to solo spots showcasing each Monkee's talent. The highlight was Michael's composition *Naked Persimmon,* where two Michaels, one clad in a gaudy western suit designed by gaudy western suit maker Nudie, and the other Michael wearing contemporary clothes, performed the song in front of a gigantic "Wanted for Fraud" poster. The ending of the special featured the fantastic but overdone "freak out" version of the song *Listen To The Band,* that resembled *American Bandstand* on acid. The bizarre special ended with Southern California being the victim of an atomic bomb.

When the taping of the special was finished, Peter Tork officially left the group. Peter had been unhappy in his role as the dummy of the group, and this was his first opportunity to buy out his contract, even though he had no other job lined up. He wanted to be taken more seriously in the rock community, which shunned such creations as The Monkees. According to Peter, it had been fun during the group effort recording of *Headquarters,* but he knew it would never happen again, at least while Michael was around. As Davy said in an interview, "Peter didn't hang around long after the show was canceled, which I think was due in part to the way Mike would always put him down offstage. He's got a real mean streak in him."[44]

---

[44] Gary Strobl's interview with David Jones 10-9-87.

The three Monkees chipped in two dollars each and presented Peter with a cheap watch with the inscription, "To Peter. Good luck for the future. From the boys down at work." Peter would soon run out of money, go bankrupt, and drop into an oblivion of drugs and alcohol. He would not recover for at least a decade. The other Monkees were not so lucky.

What Am I Doing Hangin' 'Round

The Monkees started out in 1969 as a trio. It was a surprise to many that Michael did not quit The Monkees first. Instead, as the cash cow lay dying, Michael thought that he would finally have control over everything. As Davy said in an interview, "Mike knew that he could never make it on his own, so he kept Micky and me close to him so that he could keep The Monkees name and popularity going as long as possible."[45] Michael said, "I could understand why he (Peter) wanted to go, 'cause I did too. But I felt like we hadn't quite finished, and that there were still a few things that we should try to do. There were some things The Monkees were and represented that hadn't been said or done. I was also keen on not just leaving it a loose end."

Monkees cut up on Laugh-In.

Screen Gems and Colgems could not have cared less what The Monkees did now as they were no longer a money making venture. All the studio wanted was to keep expenses low while the contracts expired. They didn't even care that The Monkees' new managers were their former gophers, David Pearl and Brendan Cahill. The guys knew it would be a hard climb back to the top but they were ready. For his part,

---

[45] Gary Strobl's interview with David Jones 10-9-87.

Michael thought he could raise a brand new group from the Monkee ashes and rebuild them as a popular music group, but their image had been far too damaged by now, mostly due to Nesmith himself.

Further undermining his goal was the unfortunate fact that most of the fans that had previously vowed to love The Monkees forever had gone on to the next teen idol, Bobby Sherman. Sherman, who had previously guest starred on an episode of The Monkees' television show, was now appearing in the fans' living rooms weekly starring in the Screen Gems TV show *Here Come the Brides*. As Sherman's photos grew larger on the teen magazine covers, Davy's face grew smaller, indicative of their declining popularity, until there was no photo on the cover and rarely more than one page devoted to the latest Monkees happenings. Without the TV exposure, their fans quickly forgot about them.

As Michael's career sputtered and fizzled, he found more time to socialize with people whom he had worked with on The Monkees' TV show. Monkees episode writer Dave Evans remembers, "I got to know him much better after the show was over. There was a period when we just hung out a lot, at his house and my house. Mike was married to Phyllis. Lovely lady. She's charming. We've spent many times together. But, it was lovely because after dinner, Mike would get his guitar out and he'd sing and play. So, we'd be sitting around the table and Mike would sing *Mr. Bojangles*, *Tumbling Tumbleweeds*, and *Beyond The Blue Horizon*. Those are old, old standards, but, those are ones I remember right off."

Micky, Michael, Johnny Cash and Davy on the set of The Johnny Cash Show.

The Monkees released a new album, *Instant Replay*, that was filled with rejected tunes from the seemingly bottomless barrel of Monkee TV show tunes. The most interesting song on the album is a song that Micky wrote from the viewpoint of his cat called *Shorty*

107

Blackwell. Michael is in a somber mood on this album as he sings about love lost from *I Won't Be The Same Without Her* to *While I Cry*. The highlights on the album are Davy's tunes *Me Without You* and his own composition about what was happening with himself and the other Monkees, as they were now in the role of discarded teen idols, called *You and I*. The album peaked at 32 on the charts and slid downhill fast.

The trio tried to make up for the loss of their television show by appearing on almost every variety show on TV, often with mixed results. On *The Glen Campbell Goodtime Hour*, a show that featured the talents of the former Monkees session musician, Michael lost his temper on camera as Davy flubbed a line. In an embarrassingly long appearance on *The Tonight Show with Johnny Carson*, Micky dominated the conversation talking about a *TV Guide* article called "How To Hog The Camera Without Seeming Pushy On The Talk Shows." He went on to discuss such things as holograms, even presenting one to Johnny, who barely got to say hello to Michael or Davy.

But not even appearances on *The Johnny Cash Show* and the extremely popular *Rowan and Martin's Laugh-In* could repair the damage that had been done. The Monkees even filmed a couple of episodes of a series that was ABC's answer to *Laugh-In* called *Turn On*. Unfortunately, the public couldn't handle a racier version of *Laugh-In* yet, and ABC turned off the series immediately after the first episode, leaving the other completed episodes unaired.

The Monkees television special *33 1/3 Revolutions Per Monkee* was finally aired several months after being completed. The delay in airing the special was due to the trouble NBC had in finding a sponsor for the show. Eventually they decided to air the special opposite the Academy Awards on the west coast, and it received terrible ratings. All plans for additional Monkees specials were scrapped.

The three Monkees decided to go on tour with a back up band called Sam and the Goodtimers, who were an R & B band in the same vein as Ike and Tina Turner. In an interview with Harold Bronson for *Hit Parader* magazine, Michael states that Davy and Micky found Sam and the Goodtimers at a club called The Red Velvet. It is still wondered among music historians why two groups that were total musical opposites would team together. Maybe The Monkees felt they had nothing to lose. Michael now seemed to be retreating from his desire to control the project.

The live shows featured The Monkees doing their greatest hits as well as their newest songs. Along with their usual repertoire, Davy would perform a version of *For Once in My Life* as well as *Show Me,* while Micky would perform a version of *Summertime.* Afterwards, Michael would come out of his self-imposed shell and perform songs such as *Tapioca Tundra* and *Listen To The Band.* Then he would retreat back to his spot of the stage where he stayed during most of the show, leaving the spotlight on Davy and Micky, who were doing tired comedy

On the set of Hollywood Squares; Micky, Davy, Joanne Worley, Judy Carne, Peter Marshall, Henry Gibson, Michael. Photo from the Duane Dimock collection.

routines that seemed like vaudeville rejects. Behind the stage on a large screen were small films that were directed by budding directors Micky and Michael.

The sparse audiences were at a loss as how to describe the new Monkees sound, since it now had a distinct R&B flavor. Unfortunately, the tour was not the success The Monkees had hoped for, as several dates across the country were canceled due to poor ticket sales. The concerts that were held were to low attendance houses. At one sparsely attended concert, Micky held up a sign that a fan handed him, and he showed the audience that it said "We Still Love You!"

Michael on the set of a Kool-Aid commercial. Photo by Henry Diltz.

In August all hopes for Monkeemania to return were dashed as the teen magazines announced that Davy had been secretly married since 1967. The fans saw this as betrayal from their hero and responded by rejecting them further. They didn't mind the fact that Micky had gotten married, as he had shared his courtship of Samantha Juste with the fans.

Ironically, while nobody wanted to see The Monkees in concert or listen to their latest records, the guys were breaking TV ratings records for *The Monkees* television show now in re-runs on Saturday mornings on CBS. There were reports that The Monkees, with Michael being the main person in control, were re-dubbing the music used in the episodes to reflect the current Monkees sound. There were also plans for The Monkees to sing songs written by other artists, such as Donovan and The Beatles among others and use those in the episodes as well.

To add to the further humiliation, Michael and the other Monkees were forced to appear in a series of Kool-Aid commercials opposite Bugs Bunny, which was about the last thing an artist who was trying to be taken seriously would be caught doing.

In October, The Monkees' eighth album, *The Monkees Present* was released. This album was originally going to be a three-record set, with each Monkee having his own record to display his musical style. Unfortunately, with sales of Monkees albums dwindling, Colgems refused to take such an expensive gamble. The highlights of the album were the Nesmith tracks, two of which were from his Nashville sessions. *Good Clean Fun* was the smartass title Michael gave to this mid tempo ditty, which was in response to the executive who told him to write songs about good clean fun. The other song was *Listen to The Band*, a well-liked song about Michael's experiences on tour with Jimi Hendrix. *Listen to the Band* peaked as a single at #63 and died immediately, proving that quality had no effect in reversing the slide that The Monkees were on.

Michael continued to make the most of his time off and would attend the Baja 1000 whenever he could. As a photographer of the event, Allen Daviau remembered getting on the plane to go back home, and seeing a familiar face, "Lo and behold, who's in the back of the plane but Mike Nesmith? He hitchhiked a flight back. One of the pilots was Paul Talman of Talman's Aviation. He was one of the famous movie pilots of all time. Michael was riding up in the front that day. I remembered Mike was a real white-knuckle flier from the tour with The Monkees. He did not enjoy being on airplanes. And here we were in a single engine craft trying to make Rosarito Beach before sunset. It was getting darker and darker and darker. By the time we circled Rosarito Beach it was nighttime. They had dug a little trench at each end of the beach and put gasoline in and lit it so that you could see the beginning and the end of the landing strip. I looked over at Mike and he was keeping his cool. The younger pilot landed it and made the most perfect landing. As the plane stopped, all these people came running out of the shadows cheering. The minute the door opened, Mike Nesmith said,

111

'I'm buying margaritas for everybody!' We went to the hotel and we had a real party that night."[46]

Michael may have been in a partying mood then, but on the whole he was unhappy with the Monkee project and wanted to branch out on his own. For Michael to achieve the musical freedom he so desired, he would have to buy out his contract for $160,000. It was widely reported that it completely wiped him out financially. Michael was quoted as saying, "There was some money that was due to me, and some other things that in order for me to go on to a solo career I had to abandon, and so I did that. So the idea sprang up, 'Oh, Nesmith made this move where he bought his contract out.' Basically, I didn't. I made this move where I gave up the contract, the monies that were due to me, in order to get a solo career going."

He announced his departure from The Monkees after their final concert as a trio on November 30 in Oakland California. As Lester Sill observed, "I always felt that Nesmith wanted control of the group creatively. And when he got control of the group, to an extent, the group was destroyed."[47] It had seemed that once the band could no longer serve a purpose for him, he would now bail out. As Davy observed, "When he realized the well was dry, he blew us off in an instant."[48]

After Michael left, Micky and Davy would fulfill their contracts by doing commercials and would record one more album as The Monkees called *Changes*. The industry joke at this time was that one more member would leave and there would be an album called "The Monkee." They then went their separate ways, each saddled with a teen idol image, which made it hard to find work, leaving their careers to fade. Davy made countless variety show appearances, appeared as himself on *The Brady Bunch*, and recorded an album for Bell Records, a subsidiary of Columbia, that went hardly anywhere. Micky made a few TV appearances, and made a few movies such as *Linda Lovelace For President*, *Night Of the Strangler*, and *Don't Walk On My Grass*. He would release a number of singles, none of them successful, and later headed to England to work as a TV director.

---

[46] Gary Strobl's interview with Allan Daviau 4-1-88.
[47] Gary Strobl's interview with Lester Sill 12-6-84.
[48] Gary Strobl's interview with David Jones 10-9-87.

Here I Am

As of March 1, 1970, Michael was no longer a Monkee; at least *he* thought he wasn't a Monkee anymore. He also was broke from the contract buyout, and to make matters worse, Uncle Sam was knocking at his door wanting $330,000 in back taxes. Michael thought that maybe they had made some kind of mistake, hoping that they would realize who he was. When he realized the situation was definitely real and that Screen Gems was refusing to advance him any royalties, he and the family packed up what the tax man would let them keep and drove away in a Volkswagen from their mansion to Palm Springs, to try to build a new life and revive his career.

Even though he was living in the house he had bought for his chauffeur Alfie Weaver, Michael described this period as the happiest time of his life. In an interview in *Forbes* magazine, Michael said that he felt that subconsciously he was trying to get rid of the money. "I flat wanted out of the whole insane deal. The money was proof that I was trapped. At one point I had nearly $1 million in my checking account. I said, 'Goddamn I'm going to run out of squares.'"[49]

In retrospect Michael said, "I couldn't keep myself or my family together (during The Monkees). This time

Michael circa 1970. No longer a Monkee, now a member of The First National Band. Photo by Henry Diltz.

around, God willing, the only thing I'll screw up is the money." It was this time that Michael wanted to reinvent his image from teen idol to

---

[49] *Forbes*, April 15, 1973.

serious musician, and he needed something that would set him apart from the other Monkees. Michael had been using the Monkee resources for years to rehearse, perform, produce and write for his eventual solo

The First National Band taking a break. From left to right: John London, Michael, Red Rhodes & John Ware, 1971. Photo by Henry Diltz.

career, and he wasted no time in kicking it off. As for his new band, Michael recalled, "Well, I didn't form the First National Band, I was asked to join. The bass player for Linda Ronstadt, John London, and drummer, Johnny Ware, gave me a call. I'd known them both for a long time and they asked me if I'd like to join their band. Then we asked Red Rhodes to join. I'd always known Red when he used to play at the Palomino Club in Los Angeles with his group, Red Rhodes and the Detours. I was a regular hot rodder and every weekend we used to go to the Palomino to have a good time. We had a regular table there and soon met Red. I did the last tour with The Monkees and then decided to join this band."

Regardless of how they came together, Michael was in total control of the group. It would feature his name in the band title, and he would produce the majority of the records, and sing all of his own songs, mostly culled from writings during his Monkee years.

On March 22, 1970, Michael Nesmith and The First National Band debuted their act at the Troubadour Club in Los Angeles. A couple of The Monkees, as well as most of the crew from *The Monkees* TV show were there to cheer on Michael, who seemed to be a bundle of nerves. The music in his new act was completely different from his

114

music as a Monkee, much to the surprise of the fans in the audience. He now performed country music with the greatest of ease. His repertoire included Hank Williams songs such as *I'm So Lonesome I Could Cry,* along with many Nesmith originals that would be recorded for the group's upcoming record on RCA.

As Michael said about the beginning of his solo career, "As it worked out, just kind of the ironies of the business, I had a record deal with RCA because I was a member of The Monkees. But there wasn't any way to deliver on that record contract without The Monkees being together. So, I said, 'Would you be interested in me as a solo artist?' And they pondered over this and thought about it and didn't know and everything, and Felton Jarvis was in Nashville, and there was a man

Photo by Henry Diltz.

named Harry Jenkins in New York. And the two of them got talking to each other and they said, 'You know, we ought to give this a try.' I said, 'Well, Felton can produce this album if you want.' And I put together The First National Band. And Felton came out. The reason I'm talking about Felton is because he was Elvis Presley's producer."

The First National Band's debut album *Magnetic South,* produced by Felton Jarvis, was released in July of 1970. The dedications on the album were numerous. The entire album was dedicated to Davy, Micky and Peter, Bert Schneider and Lester Sill. The song *Joanne* was dedicated to Jack Nicholson and Mimi Machu, whom Michael claims

115

the song is written about. The song *Beyond the Blue Horizon* was dedicated to the "Tomorrow" man, Don Kirshner, who was working at the time with a group called Tomorrow, which featured a lovely Australian singer named Olivia Newton John.

 Magnetic South opens up with the upbeat *Calico Girlfriend.* Next is the beautiful *Nine Times Blue,* which then fades into the fantastic *Little Red Rider.* After that is the beautiful song *The Crippled Lion* with the romantic *Joanne* right after it. Ending side A is a track called *The First National Rag,* where Michael tells the listeners that it is time to turn the album over to its B side. Starting the second side is the yodeling classic *Mama Nantucket.* After that upbeat ditty, Michael goes deep within himself for *Keys to the Car.* The overly long *Hollywood* is followed by the romantic *One Rose* and the classic *Beyond the Blue Horizon,* which is complete with the sound of alarm clocks, a rooster crowing and Michael yawning and whistling.

 The first single released from *Magnetic South* was *Little Red Rider* with *Rose City Chimes* as the B-side. The single had been RCA's choice since they didn't know what to make out of Michael's music, so they just picked the most upbeat song and they released it. Unfortunately the single never appeared on the charts, and the instrumental piece *Rose City Chimes* has never appeared on any Nesmith compilation until 2001.

 Luckily for Michael, a Philadelphia radio station started playing a different cut on the album called *Joanne.* With demand growing from radio stations, RCA

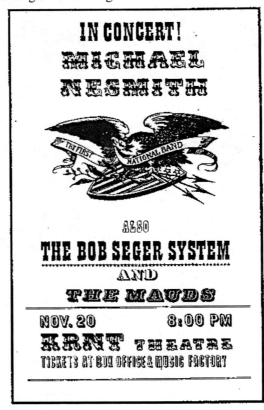

IN CONCERT!

MICHAEL
NESMITH

ALSO

THE BOB SEGER SYSTEM
AND
THE MAUDS

NOV. 20 8:00 PM
KRNT THEATRE
TICKETS AT BOX OFFICE & MUSIC FACTORY

116

released *Joanne* as the second single from the album. This single fared much better on the charts, peaking at number 21 and was thought to be a million selling single. As Michael said, "It should have been, but it wasn't. I have some sales reports from various distributors who say that the record sold 1,200,000 copies. But RCA's figures say that it only sold 325,000 so we didn't receive a gold record for it."

While Michael's song was climbing the charts, he was able to talk to the press about how The Monkees were dead, and how they never really got along anyway, "I don't like Peter Tork, never have liked him. I don't like him as a man. I have to qualify that now: me not liking someone doesn't mean that they're bad people-he could do a lot of wonderful things to and for me. Not liking someone to me is a very gut reaction-a very visceral attitude. The first reaction of Peter was one of dislike. I don't like him, I have never liked him, and I probably will never like him. I didn't enjoy playing in a band with Peter, and I still don't."[50]

In another interview in his outspoken anti-Monkee era, Michael said, "David and Peter and Micky were very heavy cats. They were no dummies. There wasn't a dummy among them. I didn't get along with them, none of us got along, because we were all very different, but they weren't fools." When asked if he sees anyone from The Monkees, Michael was quick to say, "I've seen no-one from The Monkees. I have nothing to do with anyone from The Monkees. I never talk to anyone from The Monkees."[51]

One reporter asked the whereabouts of his famous wool hat and Michael answered, "I was in Indianapolis playing at a club with The First National Band a couple of years after The Monkees. A girl walked up to me afterwards and she said, 'Do you remember this?' And she had the original green hat. The one. I said, 'Where in the world did you get that?' She said, 'You threw it to me at a concert one time.' And she still had it. She said, 'Would you like it back?' I said, 'No. You've kept it all these years. You can have it.'"

While the First National Band was touring England, Michael received word that Phyllis had given birth on September 10, 1970 to their third and last child together, a baby girl named Jessica Buffler Nesmith.

In November, *Loose Salute* was released. Produced by Michael, this second album from the First National Band sold poorly, despite yet another minor hit single which opened the album and charted at number 42, the falsetto-classic *Silver Moon.* The album was certainly more

---

[50] Hit Parader, February, 1972.
[51] Interview with Michael Nesmith from Zig Zag #39, 1973.

upbeat than its predecessor, with the rock side of his sound leading the way. Included is the classic *I Fall to Pieces,* which was a hit for country singer Patsy Cline back in the early '60s. *Thanx For the Ride* was about Michael turning his back on the Hollywood industry. *Dedicated Friend* was an ode to his car, which quite possibly could have been repossessed by the IRS. The song *Conversations* had gone under several titles, and was called *Carlisle Wheeling Effervescent Popsicle* at one point, and Michael was never satisfied that the song was complete. An upbeat rock remake of *Listen to the Band* is included, which is perfect save for the odd combination of a fade-in at the start, and a fade-out at the end. *Bye, Bye, Bye* is a rocking truck driver song illustrating Michael's dream of running away from everything, leaving all of his possessions behind, and living off of the land in Mexico. Always eager to experiment with his music, Michael and Red Rhodes went into the recording studio and mixed a quadraphonic extended version of *Silver Moon* for the 8-track release of *Loose Salute.*

In retaining the same great qualities of the first album, Michael continued to earn critical acclaim. Charlie Burton reviewed the album in the anti-Monkees magazine *Rolling Stone,* saying, "Mike Nesmith? Well, hang onto your 'wool hat,' cats and kitties, because this album is good. Mike Nesmith, you will remember, was one of the plastic Beatles, The Monkees, who can still be seen on Saturday morning TV, somewhere between *The Archies* and *Lancelot Link, Secret Chimp.* Mike's straightforward, no-bullshit vocals are a welcome change from the usual Byrds-y singing style generally preferred by country hippie bands, and the nine Nesmith originals on *Loose Salute* radiate, if not genius, then a good, solid versatility. I have never considered myself a Monkees fan, but I think *Loose Salute* by Mike Nesmith and the First National Band is one of the hippest country rock albums in some time, certainly the most listenable. Mike Nesmith? Why the hell not?"

To promote the album and the band,

Michael with Ringo Starr during a press party for The First National Band. Circa 1970 photo from The RLM Archives.

118

Michael and the First National Band performed at a press party in London. In the audience were members of The Beatles and other rock stars including Jimi Hendrix. In an interview, Michael gave details of his talk with Jimi, "I was surprised to see him in somewhat of a funk. He was not happy with the way his music had developed. He felt stultified somehow. He felt that what he was doing didn't have the substance it once had. I'm not sure he even realized how much substance it ever had. We were standing outside alone in a lobby and I felt a great deal of compassion for him. As he stood there, his eyes kind of drifted off, and I could see him trying to come to terms with some devil or something in his head. And he said, 'You know, I think I'm gonna start an R&B band. I gotta do something. I think I'm gonna work with some horns and put together something like Otis Redding does cause that's really where it's at.' I put my arm around him, and I said, 'Jimi, don't you understand, man, you invented psychedelic music. You invented it. Nobody ever played this before you came along. Why are you going through this crisis of self-confidence right now?' He didn't say anything, he didn't respond to that at all, but it was a very extraordinary moment in my life, and I think in him as well. He nodded kind of in agreement to that, but in a very humble way." A couple of days later, Jimi Hendrix was dead of a drug overdose.

Hear Me Calling

While The First National Band was suffering low attendance at their concerts, they started recording their third album. Midway through the project though, the band broke up reportedly due to a disagreement over the arrangement of a song *Propinquity*. To finish the album, Michael was forced to bring in other musicians.

On May 8, 1971, Michael appeared on *American Bandstand* where he performed *Joanne*. Red Rhodes accompanied Michael to the taping but he stayed backstage in the dressing room. When asked by Dick Clark where the other band members were, he explained, "Everybody just sorta went fishin'." Michael also stated that he really didn't like country music, although that was what he was recording. Dick Clark ended the segment by having the young people on the show dance to the title cut of the *Nevada Fighter* album. The album had not been released yet, so they showed a mock cover for the album.

Nevada Fighter was released to the same lack of attention as the other Nesmith albums. The album begins with *Grand Ennui* which has Michael running away from the boredom by buying everything in sight. The great romantic Nesmith compositions dominate most of the first side with *Propinquity (I've Just Begun To Care)*, *Here I Am* and *Only Bound*. The last upbeat song on the entire album is the title cut *Nevada Fighter*, which charted at number 70 on the singles charts. Included also is a remake of the Sons of the Pioneers cowpoke classic *Tumbling Tumbleweeds*, and *I Looked Away*, written by Eric Clapton. The record was a poor seller while it gathered critical acclaim. *Rolling Stone* reviewed the album and said, "Mike Nesmith and the First National Band have released three albums, wham-bam-thank-you-ma'am, in the time it takes most groups to recover from their first. Crass commercialism on the part of Mr. Wool Hat, wanting to glut the market with Nesmith product, right? Well, no. The reason that Mike keeps churnin' them out, I suspect, is that he knows his already good thing is getting progressively mellower. The next time you find yourself in a record store and happen to come across a Mike Nesmith/First National Band album, don't laugh or chuck your friend in the ribs and say, 'Mike Nesmith!?' Buy it instead. You're in for a pleasant surprise."

One critic created a timeless comment when he called Michael's music "the best music never heard." In an effort to let the public hear the music, RCA placed lengthy ads in music industry magazines stating "One Michael Nesmith Album for the Price of Three." The ads went on to explain that the first three albums were part of a trilogy. Side B of the albums, when played consecutively, told the story of the old west, while Michael's Top 40 hits were on side A of the albums. At the end of the ads, Michael was touted by RCA as "a cowboy for today's America."

In late 1971, RCA sponsored a series of free concerts at Southern California colleges. Among the acts were Michael and two obscure groups called String Cheese and Swampwater. The acts would travel in a bus and tour 12 colleges around California.

An issue of *Rolling Stone* from 1971 reported that Michael had been recently released from a Jefferson County, Colorado jail on $2,000 bond after being charged with marijuana possession. No other details have been found on this particular incident.[52]

After the First National Band had broken up, Michael naturally proceeded to start the Second National Band. The band members included Rhodes, Michael Cohen, Jack Ranelli (not Panelli as on the liner notes), Johnny Meeks and Jose Feliciano. The first album for the Second National Band was called *Tantamount To Treason Volume One* and it featured a harder rock sound not heard in the previous Nesmith albums.

Tantamount is a disappointing album compared to the previous three. Most of the songs on the album are too long with unnecessary and badly done musical bridges. The album's most enjoyable feature is the back cover that features the artists credits inside a recipe for homemade beer. Needless to say the album was not a big seller. The ever supportive *Rolling Stone* magazine said about the album, "...The newest Nesmith album harkens back to the serenity and tranquillity of that bygone western era, the country setting we've all been dreaming about. It rocks, it socks, it soothes, and it erases the tensions of modern rock country's frenetic ennui. This is an album you can wear the way Roy Rogers wore his spangled fringe shirts. If there is one drawback to Nesmith's work, however, it is perhaps his overuse (reliance) upon just that 'sound effect' quality of his music, the steel to evoke the wind, the Moog to evoke that desert quality; Nesmith uses these devices with consistency, and thus his music sounds repetitious to many people. That sound, however, is Nesmith's style, and I find the sound evocative enough that I think it's a strength rather than a weakness. It seems a matter of 'getting into it.' So if you have any romantic western inclinations at all, and if we're all lucky, we'll meet again around that campfire somewhere out where the 'doggies all roam.' And remember, wear your white hat."

RCA was not exactly overjoyed with the album, as Michael put it, "*Tantamount To Treason* just absolutely totally and thoroughly

---

[52] Rolling Stone, December 23, 1971.

freaked everybody out at RCA. They didn't want to know about it. They didn't understand it. They weren't interested in it." It's hard to understand how RCA could not be interested in an album that featured a recipe for homemade beer among the liner notes.

Only Bound

In an *LA Times* article, Michael's career was evaluated by a friend who said, "If only he hadn't been a Monkee. That really didn't help him. He's doing good work now, but no one is willing to listen to him." Michael performed at the Ice House for a week and joked in front of the audience that totaled 60 people. "Good Tuesday night," he said. Then trying to block the glare from the spotlight, Michael did a mock head count. "Twelve. Well, that's about right. That's what I'm used to playing for these days."

The article was accurate in stating that Michael was performing great music to half empty houses and recording albums that were not selling. Years later Michael would confide to a reporter, "A lot of people tell me those albums were influential. But the biggest album I ever had saleswise was 20,000 units. I don't know how influential you can say that was. They usually give away more albums than that."

RCA, stumped by the failure of the Nesmith albums, figured that it had to be the songs that were keeping the albums from being successful. RCA then approached Michael about writing another hit song like *Joanne*. As Michael said, "I couldn't write another *Joanne* anymore than the man on the moon could." In reply to this strange request, Michael released an album of new songs facetiously titled *And the Hits Just Keep On Comin.'*

Dedicated to Annalee Huffaker, Michael's former choir teacher, the album contained only Michael playing guitar and Red Rhodes playing the steel guitar, as RCA wouldn't pay for any other musicians. The album was as usual a low seller, but is regarded as one of Michael's finest albums. Moving away from his country sound towards a pop sound, Michael's songs were no longer western prairie songs but genuine love songs.

Included on the album was Michael's version of *Different Drum*, plus other songs written during his Monkee years but never recorded, such as *Two Different Roads*, *Harmony Constant*, and *Roll With the Flow*. One song on the album, *The Upside of Good-bye*, contains the word enrichening. It was revealed that there is no such word as enrichening and nobody bothered to correct Michael, and he would continue to sing the song with the incorrect word for years.

Two Different Roads

Michael, making use of the critical acclaim he had been earning, decided to branch out and become an entrepreneur. It didn't matter that he was still in debt, Michael was anxious to work in different mediums. It was around this time that Michael was offered a new project in a new direction. There are two versions of how the project began. The first version Michael recalled in an interview, "I'd finished addressing a communications seminar in Philadelphia, and Jack Holzman (president of Elektra Records) walked up to me and said, 'You know, you and I ought to be in business together,' and recognizing opportunity when it knocked, I said, 'I'm not clear what that alliance would be, but give me a minute, I'll think of something.' So I went back to my hotel and really just kind of took an overview of what the need was. I mean, I didn't need another record company. I'm not interested in making any more money. I don't have any money, but I'm not interested in making a lot. I thought, if there's something I can do to fulfill a need, that would be cool, then I'll do it, and it became apparent to me that the need was for the otherwise stifled music in Los Angeles to have an outlet. I don't know how it came about in terms of its specifics. We just began to talk for a while, and I said, 'This needs a home, I'm a producer, I can make records.' He said, 'How about if I build you a studio?' I said, 'Well, if you build me a studio, I'd put together a staff band around the Stax-Volt formula, because I've had good success in putting together bands."[53]

The more plausible second version has Michael approaching Holzman with an idea for a country label for "people who drive '72 Galaxies, punch cards in IBM computers and ride Boeing 747's back to Oklahoma for Christmas." Whatever story you believe, the label was partially financed by Art Luxinger, a Texas hamburger baron. After the Countryside ranch recording studio was built in California, Michael was named president of Countryside Records, he and Phyllis practically moved in to the ranch, and Countryside Records was born. Not all was well with Michael financially, as he was still broke, and he still owed $60,000 to the IRS.

Michael hand-picked the musicians for the Countryside house band: Red Rhodes (steel guitar), David Barry (piano), Jay Lacy (lead guitar), Danny Lane (drums), J.G. O'Rafferty (steel guitar), Marvin Cave (bass guitar) and Dr. R.K. Warnford (Rhythm guitar). The staff band appeared on all of the label's recordings. Countryside artists

---

[53] Interview with Michael Nesmith from Zig Zag #39, 1973.

included Red Rhodes, Garland Frady and Steve Fromholz, among others. When asked if he would ever release his own music through Countryside, Michael was adamant when he answered, "No, it's not going to occur. I don't think it's good, you see. As long as I'm running it, I can't be on this label because it wouldn't be fair to the other people on this label."[54]

While at Countryside, Michael was approached by a filmmaker named William Dear. Dear had directed a movie called *The Northville Cemetery Massacre* and wanted Michael to compose the music for it. As Michael said, "I was seriously becoming a contemplative holy man. A lot of pinched forehead. And these dudes show up wanting me to score a biker flick with a lot of sex and blood and everything else." The catch was they wanted Michael to score the movie for free because they didn't have any money. Michael agreed to score the music and *The Northville Cemetery Massacre* played at a few theaters and has pretty much been forgotten by everyone except for the diehard Nesmith fans. No soundtrack album was released, but the movie has been released onto video under its original title as well as other titles such as *Freedom R.I.P.* and *Harley's Angels.*

The Countryside label was launched at a party at the Palomino Club on January 31, 1973. Unfortunately, the party was short lived as Holzman stepped down as president and Elektra was taken over by David Geffen, who didn't seem to share or understand the same ideas as Nesmith. Michael wanted to leave Elektra since Holzman was gone. Michael said, "You would think he (Geffen) would have a sympathy for Countryside because of his historic bent, you know, The Eagles, Linda Ronstadt, things like that, and these were all people that I had been with in a talent circle for a long time in Los Angeles. But David and I just never got on. Whenever I get involved with anybody, one of the prime questions I will ask them is, 'What about my wife and kid?' and David's reply was, 'I can't be concerned about your wife and kid.' Now, of course, he can, it's not his business to be concerned but it separates the sharks from the men. And so rather than, 'What about your wife and kid?' or 'Do you need help?' It's just a real good question because not only is it loaded but it drives out a phony real fast. And that was the first conversation I ever had with him, because I had to find that out quick and it was just a shambles."[55]

Countryside shut down, but not before releasing two albums: Red Rhodes' *Velvet Hammer In A Cowboy Band* and Garland Frady's *Pure Country,* as well as numerous singles. There were several more

---

[54] Interview with Michael Nesmith from Zig Zag #39, 1973.
[55] Interview with Michael Nesmith from Zig Zag #39, 1973.

albums worth of material recorded by Ian Matthews, Spanky MacFarlane and others, but in the end Michael returned all unreleased material to their respective artists. Peter Tork even stopped by the Countryside Ranch to do some recording, but those tapes were reportedly not very good and none have surfaced through the collectors. The Countryside house band remained together long enough to record Michael's final album for RCA called *Pretty Much Your Standard Ranch Stash.*

Pretty Much Your Standard Ranch Stash could be considered Michael's most country sounding record. Its only flaw is that there are only seven tracks on the entire record, which clocks in at a paltry 31 minutes. The *Ranch Stash* album is great to listen to if you are in a bar and you are drinking up a storm, with the heartbreak songs of lost love and youth *Some of Shelly's Blues* and *Winonah*, which Michael co-wrote with Linda Hargrove. The B-side contains no Nesmith compositions, but instead Michael tackles some country western and bluegrass classics. *Born to Love You* has Michael doing quite well with remaking a Bob Wills song, and he does a good version of *Prairie Lullaby,* which years later would make its way onto a Rhino Records compilation called *The Cowboy Album.*

It also has what could be the first subliminal suggestion album cover, with a close up of Michael sporting long hair and a cowboy hat winking at the camera with the small words next to his winking eye saying in very tiny letters, "Buy this record." The photo inside the gatefold cover for the *Ranch Stash* album has Nesmith being tended to by naked water nymphs. The photo was based on John William Waterhouse's painting "Hylas and the Water Nymphs." As Michael recalled, "It's very nouveau art. But we just got cuckoo with it. We shot the whole thing in a swimming pool. RCA then said, 'Paint out the tits! Don't show their nipples.' Well that's OK with me. I'm not interested in appealing to anyone's prurient interests, even if I could."[56]

Michael's contract with RCA had finally expired, much to his relief. As he said at the time, "For the life of me, I don't know why they let me make records. I've asked them for a release from my contract four or five times and they just simply say, 'No.' I can't imagine why, I don't make them any money. I don't sell any records."

As Michael was having his own problems concerning his career and his finances, business was never better for his mother. Bette was having her Liquid Paper product manufactured overseas for the European market, and introducing the product to the business industry in Australia.

---

[56] Interview with Michael Nesmith from Zig Zag #39, 1973.

I Won't Be The Same Without Her

Michael filed for divorce from Phyllis on February 1, 1974, citing unhappy differences. The divorce was finalized March 21, 1975, but all agreements and such were not finalized until early 1976. In the divorce papers, Michael claimed his income was $20,000 a year in his occupation as "entertainer," whereas Phyllis listed her income as zero in her occupation as "housewife."

In the divorce agreement, Phyllis would receive the household furnishings, her clothes and jewelry, their place of residence in Van Nuys (plus the mortgage payments and a home improvement loan), a 1973 GMC truck (plus paying the loan for the truck), one half interest in BMI accrued royalties as of October 14, 1973, not exceeding a $625 total. Michael would receive the copyrights to all of his compositions created during the marriage, his clothing and jewelry, sole proprietorship of the publishing companies; Countryside Music and Pampas Music, and 100% stock ownership in two corporations; American Chemical Research and The National Smelting Corporation. There was no spousal support paid on either side, but Michael did pay $200 monthly as child support for each of the three children.[57]

Phyllis said about the divorce and her life post-Michael, "I heard some horror stories about the things that went on during the tours. Some horror stories that Bruce didn't tell me for years and years. And then finally he said, 'Aw. I think I can, I can tell you about this time in. . .' And I think to myself, 'It's not so surprising.' Oh, how it would have wounded me to hear those things then. How threatened I would have been. And I now hear them and I think about what a star, a teen idol is subjected to and the warping of perspective and the erosion of values, and it doesn't surprise me a bit. I'm not surprised that from this distance that I can feel the compassion that I feel for what they had to go through and what they had to handle. I guess I regret that I didn't have that perspective then. I think it probably might have saved my marriage. It might have. I'm not sure. You never can tell about these things. But it certainly would have allowed me to feel better about myself and better about Michael rather than feeling like it was a runaway train headed for a cliff and that I was powerless to stop the tide of events. I think it's interesting. If someone said, 'Wanna go back in time? You wanna erase this slate? You wanna have a chance not to go through that again? You wanna rewrite the script?,' I wouldn't do it. I wouldn't do it for a million

---

[57] Nesmith vs. Nesmith, Civil Case #D841 136.

127

dollars or for any other thing in the world. Because, how do you negate the things that bring you to the present? How do you say they were for nothing? It's not all easy. It's not all a slick ride. I feel so grateful at having had such a variety of worldly experience thrown at me and somehow making it through, somehow feeling today that my own values are reasonably intact, that I have had some successes in communicating those values to my kids, that I continue to grow."[58]

---

[58] Gary Strobl's interview with Phyllis Nesmith 2-13-85.

Different Drum

Now out of work, and with financial help from his mother Bette, who was about to resign from the Liquid Paper Corporation, Michael created The Pacific Arts Corporation in hope of distributing his music as well as others' music. The company was founded in the small town of Carmel, California, and was at first staffed only by Michael and his then girlfriend Kathryn, who would act as vice-president. When asked why he based his new company in Carmel instead of a major city such as Los Angeles, Michael replied, "I moved out of that center of L.A. reasoning in the following way, that in L.A. I'm in L.A. It's a remarkably small city. If you're in New York you're in New York, you're in a remarkably small city, but if you're in Carmel, you're in a place on the planet, and from there you can see New York, L.A., Tokyo, London and all of the places around. So I wasn't dropping out of the mainstream, I was really dropping into the center of a global consciousness so that I could deal effectively with Portugal and Hamburg and all of those other places. You see much more that easily past the miasma of inner-industry hype that happens so much in L.A. or the Big Apple."

While starting up Pacific Arts in the middle of nowhere, Michael was asked to produce some tracks for a group called Chilli Willi and The Red Hot Peppers. The recording sessions didn't go as planned, as only four tracks were cut and then only the backing tracks were used from two of the songs. When interviewed about his involvement with the band, Michael said, "I got halfway through and ready to do some more mixing and fixing up with them, I felt they had real potential. They just needed a lot of work and suddenly I asked about doing re-mixes and they just weren't interested. Not the band but the powers that be at Mooncrest (Chili Willi's record company). It could be that they weren't satisfied with what I had done."

In launching Pacific Arts in the press, and trying to improve his image, Michael would now claim that he was not broke at the end of The Monkees. He also claimed that he did not leave Hollywood in a Volkswagen with the last of his belongings. "That's pretty good press, but it's not exactly true. At the end of The Monkees I moved to a lovely home in Palm Springs. I wasn't running from any debts or because things had gotten bad; it was just that our work in L.A. had finished. The mistake comes in that I made so much money during The Monkees that I created a big tax liability, but I didn't owe anybody; I didn't go bankrupt or have any of those financial problems."

The first work released on the Pacific Arts Records label was a concept album by Michael called *The Prison*, which was a record that acted as a soundtrack for a book. The set was issued in a deluxe box and sold through mail order only. Nesmith toured through England and Ireland to promote *The Prison*, and he set up distribution rights with Island Records to distribute Pacific Arts Records throughout the world.

The Prison album runs all of the songs together as a single song to accompany the book, and the music is neither country nor rock, more like a form of easy listening lounge music. The sound is based around a simple guitar part with Michael singing alone, adding lots of percussion, conga drums, synthesizer parts, extended musical solos, occasional pianos going crazy, sound effects and occasional sweeping orchestral type sounds with great stereo effects. The song *Marie's Theme* ends with Michael repeating the hypnotic last line of the song at least a million times just so the reader of the book can catch up.

Some found the act of reading while listening to the record a bit distracting, while others had no problem since they completely ignored the book and concentrated only on the music. They suggested that perhaps Michael should have had instrumental music instead of vocal accompaniment. The book was a full 12-inch square size like the record, included the story in both French and English, and featured color paintings from the Kindergarten class from La Mesa School in Monterey, California. This is also the first time Michael would credit a machine as a musician on one of his albums, crediting the drum work to Roland Rhythm 77.

As to the concept of a book with a soundtrack, in several interviews, Michael talked of the phenomenon that occurs when one reads a book. He described how there is a movie that plays in your mind when you read, in which you hear the characters speak, as well as hearing the sounds of certain things such as cars racing by or explosions and such. Michael decided to write a book, and then record music to act as the soundtrack to accompany the movie that runs in your mind. The story of *The Prison* is about one man's struggle to break down the walls of his self imposed prison of despair, and once he does, to try to convince others to do the same once he has gained the wisdom.

Reviews for it were mixed to say the least, as one reviewer for the *L.A. Times* noted, "Were he to have deleted the record's lyrics and focused more on the book to supply the necessary words, Nesmith might have realized a less distracting work. Still, this first attempt at a most interesting concept ranks as an overall success."

The reviews for his concerts were mixed as well, as one reporter noted in England, "There was little Monkee business when Mike Nesmith played. He seemed more intent on putting his present philosophical stance over to the audience than displaying his musical talent. The concert had promised much: Nesmith is one of the few musicians to successfully come through the rock machine and re-establish himself as a cult figure. In the final analysis he was a disappointment. The early section of his performance was rewarding. His guitar work was immaculate and his vocals were restrained and distinctive. But his attempt to strike up a rapport with the audience didn't come off. And his quasi-intellectual raps were lost on the crowd. He played a large slice of his new concept album *The Prison*, which is accompanied by a 64-page booklet, and spent long periods explaining the mechanics and philosophy of the album. A classic case of ego trip."

While Michael was busy promoting *The Prison*, his former band members, Micky and Davy, called him to a meeting. They approached Michael and Peter with the idea of getting back together again. There was the possibility of the group doing a commercial for McDonalds, but Michael said he would do the commercial only if there was going to be another Monkee movie. That pretty much killed the idea for a Monkee reunion for the time being. Regardless, Micky and Davy got Monkee songwriters Tommy Boyce and Bobby Hart to fill in for the missing simians and they went on a successful tour and recorded an album as Dolenz, Jones, Boyce and Hart, as they were not allowed to use the Monkee name or logo.

Never Tell A Woman Yes

Michael married his girlfriend of two years, Kathryn Marie Bild, on February 29, 1976. While acting as the vice president of Pacific Arts, Kathryn also served as Michael's concert tour coordinator and his bodyguard. At some concerts Michael would be at the mercy of a female fan who would rush the stage and hold on to him, and Kathryn would go out on the stage and grab the fan and drag her off the stage.

Meanwhile Michael's mother Bette was divorcing Robert Graham. She resigned from the Liquid Paper Corporation after Robert and a friend of his gained control of the multi-million dollar company. The friend became the C.E.O. and the two men changed the formula in order to deprive Bette of her royalties.[59]

A friend of Michael's, Ajathan Gero, suggested that Michael perform a concert at Sonoma State University. It was this suggestion that prompted Michael to have the inspiration of putting together a stage production of *The Prison* instead of a standard concert. Nesmith would provide narration while ballet dancers performed to the music. The performances took place in June of 1976 at Sonoma State University and The Palace of Fine Arts in San Francisco. The shows were not sellouts, but one of the performances was aired on KCBS-TV in San Francisco.

I've Never Loved Anyone More, a song that was written by Michael and Linda Hargrove was given an award from BMI as one of the most performed songs of 1976. The song has been recorded by at least 30 artists including Hargrove, Eddy Arnold, Charly McClain, Billie Jo Spears, Tammy Wynette and Lynn Anderson. Anderson's version became a country hit, peaking at #14. Oddly enough, Michael has never recorded the song.

In England, Michael's albums had been faring a little better in the sales department, so RCA released *The Best of Michael Nesmith*. Michael was not pleased with this, as he planned to release his own album of hits. He raised some objections and the *Best of* album was halted in production. However, a limited number of copies of *The Best of Michael Nesmith* were manufactured only for the England and Australia markets. Nevertheless, a few copies did find their way to some U.S. import record stores where they were sold alongside Michael's own 'Best of album' called *Compilation*. In a deal with RCA, Michael bought up all of his albums that had been sent back by record stores after surviving the cutout bins, and sold them through his own company.

---

[59] *Fortune*, November 5, 1979.

In 1977 Michael went back to recording normal albums that did not require books to be read with them. One of the first to be released was an album of mostly new material called *From A Radio Engine to the Photon Wing*. The only non-Nesmith composition was Marjorie Elliot's *Along the Navajo Trail*, which had been recorded previously by Bob Wills & the Texas Playboys and The Sons of the Pioneers. The album, which Michael dedicated to God, features some of the most upbeat songs of his solo recordings, very different from his usual unrequited love, lost love, never loved, love forever type of songs. The songs, which were longer than typical Nesmith compositions, contained less country music and more pop as well as containing hints of calypso.

I'm Hearing The Light From The Window

One day Michael received a call from the powers that be at Island Records. It seemed that they needed a promotional clip of a song from the new album to show on television in Europe. Michael decided to make the promo clip of *Rio*, a song inspired by a Busby Berkeley musical called *The Gang's All Here* (1943) with Alice Faye and Carmen Miranda. Michael stated that the name of the song came from the street that ran right in front of his house at the time.

Michael looking dapper in a scene from his innovative music video "Rio", 1977. Photo from The RLM Archives.

Refusing to make a standard clip of a band playing, Michael spent $23,000 of his own money, recruited Bill Dear as the director, and much to everyone's surprise, they wound up making a musical film that could rival Fred Astaire and Ginger Rogers any day. The video was very colorful and filled with special effects such as Michael flying over the earth with women on his back. It was something totally original that had never been done before as a promotional tool.

When showing the executives at Island what he had filmed, the executives started screaming and cheering. They had expected to see Michael lip-synch while playing his guitar and instead got a mini-musical. With the aid of the promotional clip on TV music shows, *Rio* became a top 10 hit in Australia, as well as hitting the charts in England. In the U.S., where there was no popular TV show featuring music, the album barely made the top 200 on the charts and the single fared just as badly. Incidentally there was another song called *Rio* on the charts at the same time in Australia, that version performed by Peter Allen.

After *Rio*, Pacific Arts had plans for a second clip from the album called *Along the Navajo Trail*, even stating that they were a third of the way through the production of it. This project never saw the light of day. Michael also made plans to extend his musical book concept and make a video record out of the entire '*Radio Engine*' album, but this was not to be, yet.

Again the past reared its ugly head, as Micky Dolenz announced to the press in England that The Monkees would be reuniting to record an album for Arista Records. Michael was very quick to deny the story to the press, saying that he didn't know what in the world Micky was talking about, even though he and Micky were friends now and talked on a regular basis. While interviewing Michael, reporters constantly asked about this possible reunion, and finally Michael began having some fun with his answers as he told one reporter with his tongue firmly in cheek, "Well, we've been planning this for six months now, and we've signed a deal with a New Zealand record company, Kiwi Records. We are planning to put out some short 8mm films. Most of Davy's feet, and some of

Photo by Henry Diltz

Micky's hands, I think I may contribute an elbow. It's being scripted by two Japanese cleaning women who have consented to get together. And so far we've got 14 tracks recorded for the LP and all of them are the same song."

In a telephone interview with a publication in England, Michael again played the jokester when the reporter asked about the song *Joanne*, he rambled, "It's actually about Mimi. The only Fifi I ever knew was a poodle. No, I've never plucked a banjo. I plucked a chicken

135

once. No, I've no live concerts set until the fall. I've got a few dead ones coming up, though. I'm sorry you brought that up too." About The Monkees, Michael said, "They get together sometimes and throw potato salad at each other. Yes, I live in California. I also maintain a closet in New York State and I also live under a rock in Brighton, England."

Michael knew about the small packs of fans that would attend as many of his concerts as possible. He was considered to be a cult hero by these people, but he was uneasy in this role. Commenting on his status as a cult hero, Michael said, "Cultism. Well, someone told me that I was destined, this sounds terribly immodest, I don't mean it to be, I hope you read the ingenuousness in this, that I was destined to be a cult hero, and I always thought, 'How does a cult hero act?'"

Pacific Arts was gaining vast exposure in music industry magazines for its unique business dealings. Instead of an artist roster, Pacific Arts had a product roster. The artists had the choice of owning their master tape upon completion of recording or they could receive an advance, enabling them to receive royalties in the future. No one had ever really seen a record company such as Pacific Arts, and they didn't know if that was a good thing or a bad thing.

The records on the Pacific Arts label were categorized by label color. The crossover albums such as The Pacific Steel Co. and the Nesmith re-issues of *And the Hits Just Keep On Comin'* and *Pretty Much Your Standard Ranch Stash*, and others were on the white and gray label, of the "popular" series. The red label was the "collectors" series. The blue label was the "jazz" series that featured the *"Wichita Train Whistle Sings"* re-release. Then there was the gold label scheduled for the "classical" series, and there were also plans for Pacific Arts to start a book publishing division as well as a film division.

Michael wanted to put out his first live concert album, but he was never satisfied with the tapes he had made in the past. He finally decided to pick a random date and just release whatever he came up with. The date was November 10, 1977, in Melbourne, Australia, at The Palais. The album *Live at the Palais* was released on the Pacific Arts label in late 1978. It features longer and slower versions of most of his well-known songs including *Joanne, Silver Moon, Grand Ennui* and *Propinquity*. It also includes a Lynyrd Skynyrd type hot and classic remake of the song *Roll With the Flow*, as well as Michael's encore of the Chuck Berry classic *Nadine*, where the usually subdued Nesmith actually showed that he can rock and roll with the best of them. However the record is an edited concert with all of Michael's philosophies and on stage banter deleted. In the studio he changed a few guitar parts and he completely re-recorded the vocals for the final section of *Some of Shelly's Blues*. Still, with the repairs, Michael did not like the album, although the US fans liked it.

Now that the record company was doing well, things were moving up for Michael and Pacific Arts, and it was just a matter of time before something big would happen. As the film division was being developed, Michael wrote three screenplays as he continued to develop more visual art projects. One of these stories, entitled *Lydia*, was described by Michael as, "A delightful musical comedy with a lot of good fun in it, with a lot of nice music. At the same time it deals with some really fundamental problems and resolves them in the way I would resolve them, without being ponderous." Another title was *Overturn*, a "straight dramatic narrative" or for those who speak English, *a drama*, and then there was *Alligator Man*, a "suspense, action packed, old time, good conquers evil film."

In 1978 Michael ended his record distribution arrangement with Island Records. It seemed that Island refused to distribute the *entire* Pacific Arts catalog, and in return Michael terminated his contract with them and filed a lawsuit against Island Records claiming $2.5 million in damages.[60] Michael was forced to find distributors all over the globe to carry the Pacific Arts titles. These included Festival Records in Australia, Attic Records in Canada, Virgin Records in England and Stetson Records in New Zealand.

The record division of Pacific Arts was doing just fine financially. Michael was the only major artist on the label, even though he was quick to point out that, 'It's not a Mike Nesmith record company. It's not Michael Nesmith's monument to himself."

To satisfy his own musical tastes, Michael was looking forward to an album he wanted to release of some of L.A.'s finest cocktail lounge pianists, which reflected his own love for elevator music and cocktail music. He also went so far as to voice his distaste for most of the Pacific Arts releases. In an interview Michael said, "Some of the stuff we put out is garbage to my ears, but it might be important. Indian music doesn't interest me in the slightest, but I think it should be heard. To me, Bhagavan Das (who released an album on Pacific Arts) sounds like an epileptic trying to talk, but he is important and there are people who desperately want to hear that sort of thing. Shouldn't those people be able to?"[61]

---

[60] Record World, October 15, 1977.
[61] BAM Magazine, August 3, 1979.

I Am Not That

In 1979 an individual was going around Australia posing as Michael Nesmith. His real name was Barry Faulkner, and he was a con man who loved to swindle money out of innocent people. He was also adept at impersonating anyone from a doctor to a pilot, but his biggest scam was yet to come. Faulkner checked into numerous hotels in Australia posing as Michael and left without paying his hotel bills. He was also invited to all of the celebrity parties, and was given the best

Photo by Henry Diltz

seats in restaurants. Two fans in Sydney invited him to their house, but he fled when he was discovered indecently assaulting their 8 and 10 year old daughters.

The scam started to fail in Melbourne, as Faulkner, still posing as Michael, called a television station that was presenting a telethon to aid deaf children. Claiming to be Michael, he explained that his daughter was deaf, and he offered to appear on the telethon. He went by the station and pleaded with the audience to give generously. He promised that he would return to perform that night but, sitting in his hotel room, Faulkner started getting cold feet. He then called the producer of the telethon to say that he couldn't appear after all, as his daughter had been killed in a car crash.

Meanwhile a Festival Records executive who was watching the telethon, became very suspicious of this person, and called Michael in California to confirm his whereabouts. The fake tragedy made the news in Australia, and soon flowers and sympathy cards poured into the American home of the real Michael Nesmith, who quickly called Festival Records. Together they issued the following statement to the press: "(This fraud) has caused Michael a lot of personal grief. He wants to reassure everyone that all of his family is in perfect health, and that he is terribly upset about this cruel trick." Faulkner was in Sydney when he was finally arrested, but he was released in October 1979 and has not impersonated Michael since.[62]

---

[62] Who, June 14, 1993.

More Than We Imagine

In 1979 the real Michael Nesmith released his first highly commercial album, *Infinite Rider on the Big Dogma*. The entire album was designed as a video record, and all of the songs have very visual narratives. This was his first full rock and roll record, with Michael tearing into the first song, *Dance*. There is also some hard driving rock in *Factions*, which is a jab at rock culture. *Capsule*, which Michael said he wrote in case it would be discovered hundreds of years later, talks about everything from phony evangelists to disco music ("the current mating theme"). The song even includes a reference to the three hottest women singers of the time: Marie, Linda and Bonnie, and for those not wanting to find a music book to figure out who they are, the answers are: Osmond, Ronstadt and Raitt. The album even included what could be considered one of the earliest rap songs, *Cruisin'*.

Furthering his abuse of song titling conventions, Michael titles every song on the *Infinite Rider* album with a single word, followed by a lengthy extension to the title in parenthesis.

Michael Nesmith, the Infinite Rider, with wife Kathryn on her way out the door, 1979. Photo by Charles William Bush.

Wanting to see if the video success of *Rio* had been a fluke, Michael made the first video for *Cruisin'*. The video was shot around L.A., and was also directed by Bill Dear. It featured two roller disco girls, Lucy and Ramona, and Sunset Sam, played by a muscular young

man named Steve Strong.[63] He said that a crewmember had found
Strong in a bar and asked him to be in a music video. When Strong
asked what he would be doing the answer was simple, he would be
walking down Hollywood Boulevard in only a tiny red bikini.

When shown on HBO as filler at the end of movies, the video
proved to be just as popular as *Rio*. Michael had found his cause and
immediately started hailing video music as the next wave, predicting
that audio-only records would be obsolete. He said, "The record industry
is moribund, has been for some time. The sucker hit an iceberg about a
year ago and Pacific Arts is a lifeboat." He proclaimed proudly that he
had made his last "audio only" album, and that all future releases would
be on video disc.

Michael performing at Compton
Terrace in Phoenix, Arizona 1979.
Photo By Brad Waddell

To promote the now
obsolete *Infinite Rider* album,
Pacific Arts launched a
promotional campaign with
posters, T-shirts, postcards and
even life size and miniature stand
ups of Nesmith. Pacific Arts also
sent records to the radio stations
of *The Michael Nesmith Radio
Special*, which featured Michael
being interviewed by KSAN
deejay Steve Seaweed. The radio
special featured all of the tracks
from the *Infinite Rider* album, as
well as dry anecdotes in-between
each song told by Michael.
Overall, the album received many
good reviews from publications
such as the *Chicago Sun Times*
and *Rolling Stone*. The album
though, needed to be promoted
through a tour.

Unfortunately, the tour for *Infinite Rider* would be marred one
way or another. The main cause of trouble was Nesmith's Monkee past,
which continued to haunt him. At one concert in San Francisco an
audience member requested that Michael perform *Last Train To*

---

[63] In an interview with WLUP radio on May 10, 1989, Michael
identified the man as Hulk Hogan, which he corrected on the
commentary to Elephant Parts in 2003.

Clarksville, prompting him to reply, "Oh man! Where have you been for the last twelve years?"

In L.A. during Michael's encore, he succumbed to the audience's pleas to perform a Monkees song. Rolling his eyes, Michael launched into *Listen to The Band,* after which he said a curt "thank you" and left the stage.[64]

On October 28, 1979, Michael performed before his largest solo audience of 7000 people in Phoenix, Arizona. He was, however, the opening act for a heavy metal group called Point Blank, who in turn was an opening act for Robert Palmer. The crowd that day was not interested in listening to Michael sing in his falsetto for the song *Magic*. They didn't care to hear his brand of rock and roll. They just wanted him to get off the stage. The audience would scream "You suck!" or "Get off the stage!" There were probably only ten Nesmith fans in the audience. As soon as the concert was over Michael left as fast as he could. A fan that went backstage in hopes of meeting Michael was told that he had gone to see a group that he was thinking about signing to his record label. One has to think that maybe the incident upset Michael too much, or maybe he all of a sudden felt like Jimi Hendrix in front of a Monkees audience.

---

[64] Los Angeles Times, August 31, 1979.

Roll With The Flow

In late 1979, the Gillette Company bought the Liquid Paper Company for $47.5 million. They also changed the formula of Liquid Paper, which now was sold in 84 countries, back to its original formulation so Bette was again receiving royalties. These days Bette was spending her time as a Christian Science Practitioner, with her office located inside the Republic National Bank Tower in Dallas.

In 1980 Michael was still shopping around his ideas about the future of music videos. He had been talking since 1978 about wanting to do a TV show which showed only music videos, and he wanted to call the show *Popclips*. Michael called upon his former manager Jerry Perenschio, who was now the head of Embassy Television, a TV syndication company, to see what he should do with his idea. Embassy showcased the idea for the show at the National Association of Television Program Executives annual convention. Unfortunately, there were not enough people interested in carrying the show.

Undaunted by the lack of enthusiasm, Michael and his friend Bill Dear created the pilot for the *Popclips* show anyway. Michael then sought the advice of his friend Jack Holzman, who was now an executive at Warner Brothers Records. Holzman suggested he contact a young executive named John Lack at Warner Cable. Warner Cable and American Express jointly owned a transponder in the sky that  was not doing anything and they needed ideas on how to put it to use. On the basis of seeing *Rio*, *Cruisin'*, and the *Popclips* pilot, Warner Amex asked Michael to put together a show of music shorts to be aired on their Nickelodeon children's cable channel.

Michael and Bill Dear put together 56 episodes of a show that would retain the *Popclips* title. Comedians hosted the show; among them was Howie Mandel, who would introduce each video. Out of the

56 episodes made, the first 28 episodes did not air, as Warner Amex did not like the tone of the show.

Michael was so excited about the concept of music videos that he told *Billboard* magazine, "To me it's the single most important event in the history of the rock and roll music industry, bigger than the Sun recordings of Elvis Presley. And there is only one segment of the entertainment business that will understand what a video record is, the

Photo by Henry Diltz

record business. The record business understands retail sales and that's where all this is going." Michael's idea was that video records would replace audio records soon, and although this never came to pass, his claim that music video was going to be important to the music business was very valid.

At the same time as *Popclips*, Michael and his partner Bill Dear were commissioned to make eight short films for an ABC late night comedy series called *Fridays*. The films, known as the "Nesmith/Dear Films," included *Bite the Bullet, Flying Lesson*, and *Police Doctor. Saturday Night Live* showed some of the "Nesmith/Dear Films" in the same year. These films included *Foreign Film, Have a Nice Day*, and *The Man in the Black Hat*. These films featured Michael, who returned to acting in roles that showcased his comedic talents in small doses.

On May 12, 1980, Bette Clair McMurray Nesmith Graham died of a heart attack in a Richardson, Texas sanitorium. She was 56 years old.[65] Michael, along with his wife Kathryn, returned to Dallas for the services. Michael inherited half of her estate as a trust fund, reported to be at least $24 million dollars, while the other half went to an organization called the Gihon Foundation. Also part of the inheritance was that Michael would collect a royalty on every bottle of Liquid Paper sold until October 31, 1996.

Michael was also put in charge of the foundations his mother had begun, The Bette Clair McMurray Foundation and The Gihon Foundation, which were based in Dallas, Texas. Bette had named the latter foundation after a river mentioned in the Old Testament (Genesis 2:10-14), which was said to symbolize the rights of women. Michael had already been on the board of directors for these foundations since their beginnings and once said in an interview, "A few years after my career with The Monkees was over, I was a struggling artist trying to make ends meet. And for me to sit on this board and be forced to think about contributing thousands of dollars to a women's shelter when I was worrying about how to make my car payments was extraordinary."

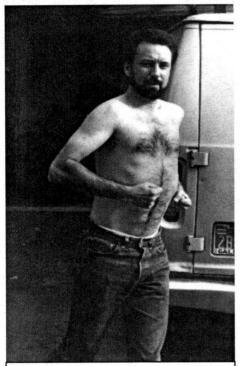

Photo by Henry Diltz

When asked yet again in an interview about the possibility of a Monkee reunion, the softening Michael said, "Well, there's always a chance. Never say never. It isn't anything I find abhorrent. You don't have to kick a dead dog too many times before you find out it's dead. The fact that it may rekindle some life, the flesh may come back on it's bones and it may pant and jump up in your lap and lick your face is not entirely out of the realm of possibility. But it is pretty far from the realm of possibility.

---

[65] Dallas Morning News, May 14, 1980.

And there's nothing in the past that has indicated that it's going to happen."

Just when he thought he wouldn't be hearing from the dead dog it jumped up in his lap again. Michael was asked by Micky, Peter and Davy to appear on the 1980 Emmy awards in September to present the award for Best Comedy Show. Michael agreed saying that he thought it was a good idea at the time. Unfortunately, fate wouldn't allow a Monkee reunion, as there was an actor's strike going on, and almost all of the celebrities were boycotting the event. Michael and Micky decided to honor the strike and not appear, much to the dismay of Peter and David who wanted to reunite. It would be the last attempt at a reunion for years.

Popclips was still airing, but the idea was blooming in Michael's mind that there should be a channel that ran music videos 24 hours a day like a radio station. In one interview Michael stated that he started approaching different companies, including one called Metromedia, where an executive told Michael, 'Music just won't work on television.' Not too discouraged, Michael then approached Warner Amex about such a channel. They were curious about how much material was out there for them to use. Michael told them, 'Put the thing on the air, they will start making videos.' Michael was then asked to be in charge of it. He turned down the offer because he was too involved with Pacific Arts and he also disagreed with John Lack on their vision for the channel. Lack saw the channel as a showcase for running commercials for records, whereas Michael saw music videos as an art form.

In another interview, Bill Dear said, "Warner Cable wanted to buy the name and the idea of the show from us and develop it into what has now become MTV. When Mike Nesmith and I heard what they wanted to do with it, we nearly had heart attacks, from disgust and laughter. So they watered down the idea and came up with MTV."

145

In yet another interview, John Lack said, "We didn't go back to Michael anymore. We parted company, not terribly amicably, but he has a lot to do with being the father of the (American) music video." Draw your own conclusion of how MTV was born. Michael supposedly got quite a few million for his idea, but he is legally bound from saying the amount. Michael wasn't too heartbroken about selling his idea, as he was about to start work on a project that would be a breakthrough in the home video industry.

Living Inside Of A Little Glass Room

Filmed in Monterey, California in a former mechanic's garage, *Elephant Parts* was Michael's first full-length video album and the first original entertainment program created specifically for home video. *Elephant Parts* was released on the VHS and Beta formats, with a laser disc version to be released a few months later. The title of *Elephant Parts* comes from the tale of the group of blind men, who are asked to touch parts of an elephant and describe what they "see," and in doing so each man describes a different animal. In the same way, Michael was pointing out the many different facets of the new music video art form.

Michael said that video was the future and to prove it, he shut down the record division of his company, which was the only division making any money, and focused only on video productions. The people

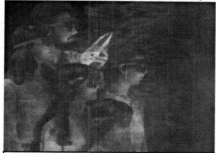

Michael and the NNS Family, featuring son Jonathan on far right.

who helped make *Elephant Parts* consisted of out of work actors and out of work crewmembers. The producer of *Elephant Parts*, Kathryn Nesmith said in an interview about the crew, "They're chomping at the bit for opportunities that they can't get in the movie business, but can get here."

Elephant Parts consisted of Michael's previously created music videos; *Rio* and *Cruisin'*, plus new music videos of *Light*, *Magic* and *Tonight* and short comedy films. The comedy bits include NNS: Neighborhood Nuclear Superiority, a commercial spoof, which features a family whose cookout is ruined by their neighbors. We then see the neighbors being wiped out in a puff of smoke by the NNS device while Michael gives his testimonial for the product. There is also a scene with Michael trying to translate a romantic Spanish song for his date and instead ends up

too Balloon balloon ballon, bla loo bah!

saying silly things such as, 'the fish eat my furniture' and 'small children calculate the deposit.' There is a bit of drug humor as Michael is a contestant on Name That Drug, which is a game show where the contestants sample the drug and they have to identify it's origin. Also in the drug genre there is a commercial spoof for Elvis Drugs that are

ART REMNANTS., INC.
361 Orange   434 Cheezwhiz Exwy.
Sand City, CA   Armslength, NV

shaped like teddy bears, guitars and hound dogs. This short clip would be among the first to exploit the drug problem Elvis had until his untimely death in 1977.

The total cost for *Elephant Parts* was $400,000 which Michael said he would recoup if he sold 25,000 copies of the video at $60 apiece, which was the going rate for movie video cassettes at the time. There was a publicity campaign for *Elephant Parts* with Michael granting interviews to everyone, so he could tell them about the end of the audio only record. There was even a gigantic billboard ad for *Elephant Parts* on Sunset Blvd. that featured a large picture of Michael that caused one fan to swerve off the road and nearly get into a wreck. Immediately the fan went to the nearest record store to get a copy of the video, and learned that Michael himself had been there just the day before dropping off the copies to sell. The video would be found on top of counters inside record stores, as the stores themselves did not usually carry videos for retail purposes, and they had no special shelving for them.

There were two premiere parties to launch *Elephant Parts*. The first was at Le Bistro in Beverly Hills, with guests such as Jack Nicholson, who by then was no longer a struggling actor. The other party was on June 17, 1981 at the Tavern on the Green in New York. Both of the parties were successes, with Michael receiving standing ovations after each screening.

Michael hired David Bean to oversee the syndication of *Elephant Parts* to cable TV and overseas broadcasters, as well as loaning prints to film classes. Bean made deals with ON-TV, SelecTV and others to air the video. Clips of *Elephant Parts* were shown on the first issue of the *Playboy* video magazine. *Rio* and *Cruisin'* were being shown on MTV, which was rapidly gaining ground in the new medium of cable TV and was on its way to becoming a big success, so much so that MTV was beginning to make new superstars in music based largely on the strength of their music videos.

As if Michael was not busy enough, he co-wrote a screenplay with his friend Bill Dear. The idea for a movie came about while he and Dear were waiting in line to see a movie. They were discussing what type of movie they would most like to see. By the time they reached the counter for popcorn they had thought up the concept, and Michael offered to co-write as well as finance. Costing $2.5 million dollars and filmed in Santa Fe, New Mexico, the completed *Timerider* would sit on the shelf for a while so a distributor could be found.

Michael was becoming well respected in the industry, even being called an innovator in the area of home video. He was so well known he was invited to participate in many industry panel discussions on home video and music videos, which were becoming popular at an amazing rate of speed. At a conference in Nashville on November 20, 1981, Michael said that Pacific Arts would probably sign a couple of video music producers in the next year to develop projects with artists and their managers. Unfortunately, due to the growth of Pacific Arts in the home video area, this was not to happen. Michael also stopped directing music videos, even though artists such as Paul McCartney, the Rolling Stones and others wanted his services and expertise. He said that he just didn't have the time, the interest or the need to make money.

He was also causing waves in the press and the industry by saying, "It's frustrating to talk to people in the entertainment business here who aren't aware of how potent music video is. I'm giving up talking to deaf ears. Moving some people into a position where

Michael Nesmith, the music video pioneer. Photo 1981 by Chester Simpson.

they understand is like pulling teeth. But I have no ax to grind. It's not hurting me. Let 'em sit by the side of the road as the bandwagon goes by."

While Michael was becoming well known for his video work, his past was catching up with him once again, but this time from Japan.

The Monkees song *Daydream Believer* was used in a Kodak commercial, and started a new wave of Monkeemania in Japan, spawning offers for all of The Monkees to tour. The TV show started airing in Japan as well, and most of the Monkee albums were reissued with Japanese lyric sheets. All of The Monkees would have their own solo tour of Japan except Michael, who said at the time that he was just too busy with his video work and expanding his Pacific Arts company in the fields of video, films and other forms of media. It was clear that being a Monkee was a part of Michael's career that would just not fade away.

In 1982, the National Association of Recording Artists established a category in their prestigious Grammy Awards for "Video of the Year." The nominees for the award included Blondie, Paul Simon and Michael Nesmith for *Elephant Parts*. On February 24, 1982, the award was presented in an awards ceremony before the live telecast. The first recipient of the video of the year award was Michael, who was presented the award by Gary Owens. His acceptance speech was very simple as all Michael said was, "Thank you. The music only phenomenon is now history."

Pacific Arts Productions (PAP) was a new company created by Michael to produce original works for cable television as well as home video and to find properties that could be exploited in as many mediums as possible. One of the first projects up PAP's sleeve was a 90 minute feature film created for home video called *Video Ranch*. Years later, Michael would describe *Video Ranch* as, "a magical land that doesn't really exist, like OZ. The tropical campfires are the magnetic south of that land, a navigational point. And the way you navigate is one of two ways, during the day, if you can find a flamingo, the flamingoes will always be flying toward the tropical campfires. And at night, when you can no longer see, the tropical campfires play Cole Porter tunes all night long, so you can navigate there acoustically. It is also kind of sweeps

150

together a lot of stuff from *Elephant Parts*. *Video Ranch* is a place where they raise television sets like cattle, and they feed them videotapes, and they go off to market as television sets do."

Also in the works over at Pacific Arts was a pilot for a half-hour show called *The Other News* that was never aired. PAP also acquired the Republic Pictures serials with the intention of remaking some, as well as developing spin-offs of some of the classic serials. PAP also was in negotiations for two books to be turned into cable series, but nothing was ever heard about them.

With the Japanese resurgence of Monkeemania came loads of fan mail into Pacific Arts, with fans filling the mailbox with Japanese dolls, kimonos and hundreds of other gifts, which Michael passed around to the office workers,

Michael Nesmith the home video pioneer, 1982. Photo by George Brich.

whom he hired because it was impossible for him to stay in the office since he needed to go out and promote his video products. But when Michael finally got around to reading some of the fan letters from Japan, he discovered much to his dismay, that many of his Japanese fans were talking about their admiration of the video *Elephant Parts* that they viewed at several public screenings, none of which had been approved by Pacific Arts. Michael contacted the FBI about the unauthorized public showings. After a three month battle in the Japanese court system, the matter ended with the company Japan All-Around Music agreeing to destroy the unauthorized 16mm print of *Elephant Parts*. The company would also turn over half of the receipts from the showings,

151

which would total only one tenth of how much Pacific Arts spent trying to solve the matter.[66]

After a long delay, Jensen/Farley distributed the film *Timerider: The Adventure of Lyle Swann* that was released on January 21, 1983. Michael was executive producer as well as composer of the music and he co-wrote the screenplay. The movie starts in the present, with a scientific experiment in which a monkey named Esther G. (named after Pacific Arts employee Esther Greif) is to be sent back in time. The experiment accidentally sends a motorcyclist back in time to the Old West, and he in turn runs into outlaws, causing comedy and chaos. How fitting that in his first film he would write a story where he put a monkey in danger.

Photo by Henry Diltz

Michael went out to promote the film on television shows such as *Late Night With David Letterman,* and Superstation WTBS's *People Now,* and he appeared on countless radio interview shows. During one interview when asked why he, was promoting the film instead of one of the stars, Michael replied, "It's easier for me to get into the newspaper offices, because I was once a Monkee and also won a video Grammy. And as the executive producer of the movie, it was really my creative vision and I also paid for the whole thing."

The reviews for *Timerider* were mostly negative, but it didn't matter as the film quickly made its money back at the theaters. Unfortunately, the movie was pulled from theaters as the distributor Jensen/Farley ran out of money.

It didn't matter where he was on the Timerider promotional tour, it seemed that Michael could still attract the fans, and he was gracious to all, as he happily signed Monkee records and everything else that the fans would give him to sign.

---

[66] *Variety*, May 26, 1982.

Michael had been the presenter when Paul McCartney was the first inductee into the American Video Awards Hall of Fame in 1983. The next year, Michael would be the second inductee into the Hall of Fame, and the presentation was televised in syndication in April of 1984. Lionel Richie introduced Michael, who proceeded to make waves in the industry by calling the award show a "thin disguise for a television show." Michael even went on to belittle the honor by saying, "It's a little silly for an awards television show which has been in existence for two years to even have a hall of fame!"

In May of 1984, Warren Nesmith died. Having patched up their differences years before, father and son were now close with Michael visiting Warren regularly in Brazoria, Texas. Michael had lost both of his parents now, with Bette passing away at the age of 56, and Warren now gone at the age of 65.

In his quest to make odd films, Michael had been sent the script for a movie called *Repo Man* by the director Alex Cox. The story of a repossession man's quest for a 1964 Chevy Malibu driven by a lobotomized nuclear scientist who is also pursued by the government because of the unseen object in the trunk. The story appealed to Michael. He helped finance the film, and he encouraged Alex Cox to use punk music in the movie.

Costing $1.5 million, *Repo Man* starring Emilio Estevez and Harry Dean Stanton, was released and bombed at the box office. A few midnight showings in Boston helped revitalize interest in the movie. To this day *Repo Man* remains a favorite cult film, as well as making millions of dollars for the distributor and main financier, Universal Pictures, and returning Michael's investment.

Years later, Michael would talk about the film with much adoration. On a television interview Michael said, "There's a great opening scene for *Repo Man* in which there's a long desert highway with a '64 Malibu swerving from side to side on the road. Finally a policeman pulls him over and asks, 'Watcha got in the trunk?' The driver says, 'You don't want to look in there.' The policeman goes to the trunk, opens it and there's a blinding flash of white light. There's nothing left of the policeman except for two smoking boots and the Malibu drives off. That all happens in the first two and a half minutes of *Repo Man*. That's a great opening scene. Do you want to see the rest of it? Sure you do! What is going on here? And, of course, the rest of the movie is just whacked, just hilarious."

This All Happened Once Before

Brandon Tartikoff was the president of NBC programming. He was considered the "Golden Boy," as he had raised NBC out of the Nielsen ratings basement in the early 1980s to make it the number one TV network. It seemed Tartikoff could do no wrong. He had seen *Elephant Parts* and he was curious if Nesmith could come up with a television show with the same idea of mixing music with comedy. Michael wanted the series to be successful so it would eclipse his success with The Monkees and hopefully ease any pain of letting MTV slip out of his fingers and watching it become a huge success.

Photo by Henry Diltz.

Armed with a couple of million dollars, Michael, along with his personal manager Ken Kragen, set up the Union Artworks, Inc. and started filming several episodes featuring Martin Mull, Jerry Lee Lewis, Sid Ceasar, Jim Stafford, and Laura Branigan. Micky Dolenz was even hired to direct some segments, although the segments filmed by him were never televised.

Nesmith and Kragen created an hour long pilot of *Television Parts* for NBC, who delayed the airing by more than a year and decided to edit the pilot down to 30 minutes. Brandon Tartikoff had high hopes for the series, although the rest of NBC was worried as the show was testing quite poorly.

154

For its debut in March of 1985, the show was given a perfect timeslot among the most popular shows on television, Thursday night right after *The Cosby Show* and *Cheers*. *Television Parts* just couldn't help but be a hit. The show didn't do as well in the ratings as Tartikoff had hoped, and the show was yanked off the air after one episode.

The filming of Eldorado to the Moon video from "Television Parts," 1984. Photo by Henry Diltz.

Most of the reviews were not as positive as Tartikoff had hoped. *People* magazine's reviewer Jeff Jarvis said about the show, "'I sort of don't even watch TV myself,' Michael Nesmith admits at the start of the show he produced and stars in. What gall from a man whose TV resume doesn't exactly include *Masterpiece Theater* or *M*A*S*H*. This guy was on *The Monkees*. Being a member of the Anglo-Saxon precursor to Menudo doesn't give him a right to be snotty about the medium you're watching and he's working in."

A little less critical was *The Washington Post's* Tom Shales, who said, "Nesmith attempts to do for, or to, comedy what videos did for, or to, pop music, and while one is inclined to wish him well for departing from traditional restrictive prime-time formulas, the fact is that *Television Parts* looks and feels like a late-night show. Nesmith is a little too precious in his host role, and is he really of such luminance that the official title of the program must be *Michael Nesmith in Television Parts?*"

Actually the show did get a few good reviews including *USA Today* who said, "This is *Laugh-In* for the music video age; it's a series pilot that keeps its feet on the ground while it sails into the wild blue yonder of possibility. *Television Parts* delivers state-of-the-art yuks. By grafting a with-it sense of humor and up-to-date video techniques onto the standard sketch format, the half-hour innovates without confusing. Here's the familiar barrage of rapid-fire comedy bits, but they look and sound new and now."

The show was put back on the NBC schedule on Friday nights in the summer months, and Nesmith and Tartikoff hoped it would find its audience.

To test the boundaries of television's influence on video sales, Michael released *Television Parts Home Companion* while waiting for *Television Parts* to return to TV. The video was a compilation of music videos and comedy

Filming the dance scenes from "Television Parts," 1984. Photo by Henry Diltz.

clips, some of which had been seen on *Television Parts*. Saying that he would be satisfied with selling 10,000 copies of the video, Michael said that the total demand for the video (with pirated copies included) might be 60,000-80,000 copies.

It's hard to say how well the television show could have promoted the video, as the ratings for the show, which aired during the summer of 1985, were way below expectations. The show ranked at the bottom of the Nielsen ratings list week after week. Tartikoff aired the last three episodes together in a 90-minute timeslot, preempting *Saturday Night Live*, prompting one reporter to say, "It may be time for Tartikoff to realize he is trying to get the baby to eat limburger cheese. The awful truth is that *TV Parts* is awful."

In an interview Michael said, "When I put the show on, the idea was that we'd find stand up comedians and see if we could make sort of comedy clips of some of their routines, but I couldn't get any stars to do the show. So I had to use unknown people like Jay Leno, Garry Shandling, Bobcat Goldthwait and Whoopi Goldberg.

"In order to get Bobcat Goldthwait on the air, I had to pay for it, the network wouldn't do it. And when the thing came out on network television during the summer, it absolutely died. It was the lowest rated television show in the last ten years of TV." As Michael recalled about its failure, "The important thing is that it was tried and that we made the effort. We know the shows are quite good. The ratings don't mean we were rejected by the watcher."

Photo by Henry Diltz

Waking Mystery

David Fishof, a high-powered concert promoter, was putting together a follow up to his successful Happy Together Tour, which featured reunions of popular music groups. Fishof already had Herman's Hermits (minus Peter Noone), The Grass Roots and Gary Puckett & the Union Gap signed for the upcoming tour and he set his sights upon one other group. To commemorate the 20th anniversary of The Monkees' television show and to headline the tour, Fishof set out to find the four Monkees and sign them up for the tour.

Peter Tork was the first Monkee who agreed to it, then Fishof and Tork got the other Monkees to agree, even Michael. Unfortunately, Michael then changed his mind when the tour started adding more dates. Unable to leave his office for such a long period of time, Michael had to bow out of the tour much to the frustration of the fans.

Unaware of the reunion plans, MTV celebrated the 20th anniversary of the series by airing a marathon of The Monkees episodes on February 23, 1986, little suspecting what it had unleashed. To everyone's surprise, millions of people, mostly young teenage girls, went crazy over The Monkees all over again, making most of the concerts sell out. Suddenly their small sixties reunion tour had moved up to stadium concerts, and the three Monkees became media darlings while Michael, the lone holdout from the tour, became fodder for the rumor mill with the fans and media alike.

Word spread quickly and inaccurately that Michael was indeed ashamed of his Monkee past and refused to tour with them. In every interview, Michael's disappearance would be brought up and the guys would make some funny remark about it. MTV even had promos running day and night asking America, "Where is Mike Nesmith?" It seemed that no one knew where he was until news spread that he was in Texas, watching over the production of the movie *Square Dance*.

Square Dance, based on the book by the same name written by Alan Hines, had been running into troubles getting financing. The story was of a 13-year-old girl who lives with her grandfather, leaves to find her estranged mother in Fort Worth, Texas, and falls in love with a developmentally disabled boy. The producers of the movie, Jane Alexander and Charles Haid, were having trouble securing money for the film. Their discussions with FilmDallas had broken down, and, just when the filmmakers didn't know where to turn, Michael was the one to get things in motion. Michael talked Brandon Tartikoff into financing half of the movie with NBC money, while Michael financed the other

158

half with Pacific Arts money, and *Square Dance* became the first film released by Pacific Arts Pictures, a company set up specifically for this movie.

Bombarded by the press about The Monkees, Michael would say, "There's a kind of continuing myth that The Monkees was an awful time for me, that I didn't like the people, all of which is totally false. I have no problems with it at all. I don't mind the association. I don't even care when people refer to me as an 'ex-Monkee,' though they don't do it as much anymore. I don't mind the recognition factor of someone asking if I was once a Monkee. A lot of people know me from *Elephant Parts* and *Television Parts*. Or as the guy who started MTV. The fact is, that was an important and valuable time of my life and I've never regretted a minute of it. I've always been very supportive. Because I'm pretty much on my own, and travel to my own drummer, a certain notion has developed in the minds of the press that I didn't like the experience and that I'm pretending it never existed. I won't do interviews about The Monkees not because I don't like them, but because I have nothing to say."

Given the media pressure over the Monkees tour, it is understandable that Michael's best recourse was to issue public statements that would not fan the fire. And if some of his words seemed to contradict what he once said in the past, so be it. That was then, this is now. The press still had their opinions, including, "On the one hand, it's been easy to sympathize over the years with Michael Nesmith's refusal to take part in any Monkee reunions. Here he is, trying to establish a serious filmmaking career and pass through middle age with a few shreds of dignity, while his erstwhile comrades in simianism head toward their golden years on the state-fair circuit, making funny faces and singing tunes about how 'Baby, you'll soon be 16.'[67]

"On the other hand, those with the slightest traces of mid-'60s nostalgia may have occasionally felt the urge to shake Nesmith by the lapels and demand: 'What's your problem, anyway, buddy? Ungrateful for all those royalties? Too artistic now to acknowledge your past and have a little fun, for criminy's sake? Loosen up, pal.'"

As The Monkees' tour went through America, it was wondered if Michael actually would make an appearance in concert. He did show up at The Monkees concert at Arlington Stadium in Arlington, Texas, on June 22, 1986, but in the audience, not on stage. He had been asked to attend a Monkees concert by the young star of *Square Dance*, Winona Ryder. When prodded by Ryder, Michael had the make up department make him a fat suit and disguise him well enough so that he and Nonie,

---

[67] David Jones song performed during the 1989 Monkees tour.

as he called the young star, could go see The Monkees without being mobbed. He said that none of the fans recognized him, but that is not true as he was discovered by a few fans. However, not wanting Michael to get trampled, the fans kept his presence to themselves.

Michael and Winona Ryder attending the premiere of "Pretty in Pink," 1986. Photo from The RLM Archives.

The Video Software Dealers Association convention was held in Las Vegas that year, and Michael was there, as he was every year, to promote his company. Holding a press conference to introduce his upcoming projects, he decided to begin the conference by answering questions that had not been asked yet but were inevitable. "Number one: No. Maybe in L.A. if we're there at the same time. Number two: I couldn't because my schedule wouldn't permit it. But I wish them the best. Number three: No, it's not entirely impossible but highly improbable. They're talking about a TV-movie and I might get in on that. And number four: Yes, I had a good time."

Columbia, trying to cash in on the current Monkee craze, held auditions for a new set of Monkees for a new television show. When asked why didn't they use the original Monkees for the series, Steve Blauner said flatly, "They're forty years old." Reportedly two sons of Michael's tried out for the series. Michael said in an interview, "He (Jonathan) went down. He said, 'Well, dad, they sort of like it, what do you think?' I said, 'You can go to Berkeley College of Music or you can do The Monkees.' He's in Berkeley." His other son Jason did not audition but was offered a role where he would basically play his father, he turned it down.

The lucky (or unlucky) four that were picked for the series were Larry Saltis, Jared Chandler, Marty Ross and Dino Kovas. The group and the series received a cold welcome from Monkee fans all over the world who were outraged that Columbia would do such a thing as try to replace the original Monkees. It turned out that by using the original Monkees real names in the series, that others couldn't play the same roles without being compared to the original actors, unlike most shows where the role and performer are separate. It seemed that the original four would be doomed to be The Monkees forever. The New Monkees' album bombed in sales and the series ran in syndication for only a few months before being canceled in December of 1986.

By sheer coincidence, Michael and company were back in L.A. just as The Monkees concert tour was coming into town. Michael called Micky and asked if he could join the guys for an encore at the Greek Theater on September 7. Micky was thrilled, it was unknown how Peter felt, but everyone knew that Davy was upset. He told a reporter, "I didn't

The Monkees reunited. September 7, 1986 at The Greek Theater in Los Angeles. Photo from The RLM Archives.

think it was a great idea. We've got a set show. There's three of us and we're on a sold out tour. And you just really don't need anyone coming and taking the limelight. Mike would have to obviously do a few work-outs in the gym if he wanted to go back out on the road with us. He's twenty years older and a lot fatter."[68]

The guys were trying to keep Michael's appearance a secret from the fans, who had their ways of finding out anything. One fan, Bonnie Rose, was sitting in a restaurant, where she overheard Davy say, "Well, he can't just stand there and sing 'Her name was Joanne.'" Then the rumors started spreading like wildfire. At The Monkees Convention in Los Angeles, Davy announced to the fans present that there would be a special guest at the Monkee concert that night. The fans had no doubt who the "special guest" would be.

---

[68] Eric Lefcowitz's The Monkees Tale, revised edition 1989.

Performing the encore of *Listen To the Band* and *Pleasant Valley Sunday* with the band, Michael did get the media out for his appearance. Most importantly, the fans all forgave him as he bowed arm in arm with his fellow Monkees and did the Monkee-walk with them. It helped that a pirated copy of MTV's film of the encore performance got around to most of the fans that didn't get to see the concert. Michael must have breathed a sigh of relief over his decision to not go on tour, as the tour ran from May to December with Davy, Micky and Peter playing over 200 shows. To spend that much time away from his business would have been impossible for Michael.

Backstage at the Greek Theatre, The Monkees meet their makers, Bob Rafelson, David Fishof, Bert Schneider. 1986. Photo by Henry Diltz.

In late 1986, Michael began negotiations to get Coca Cola to sponsor his upcoming project *OverView Magazine*, a brand new concept of a magazine distributed on videotape. The video magazine was scheduled for monthly release, starting with a test issue projected for January 1987.

In his dealings with Coca Cola, Michael had several meetings with Coke's financial analyst Scott Riklin. It was during these meetings that he stated he was looking for someone with financial experience to recapitalize Pacific Arts, as he didn't want to use any more of his own money to finance his company. Riklin said that he was interested in the job and soon after that, Riklin was offered the position of Chief Operating Officer of Pacific Arts. He accepted and his job would begin shortly after January of 1987 so he would have plenty of time to relocate from his residence in New York to his soon to be residence in L.A.[69]

---

[69] Riklin vs. Nesmith, Pacific Arts, etc... Civil Case # C659 943.

Thanx For The Ride

Michael separated from Kathryn in October. By November, Michael had moved to Los Angeles to be closer to the Pacific Arts office there. In doing so, he angered Kathryn by taking what she thought was her car, a 1986 Mercedes 560SL which was purchased along with another Mercedes, a 1986 560 SEC, in January of 1986. Kathryn was not without transportation though, as she did have a 1986 Dodge van which Michael had bought for her, but Kathryn said that it was for use on their six acre property in Carmel and that it was not practical for driving through the busy crowded streets of Los Angeles.

Kathryn then claimed that without her knowledge or consent Michael had canceled their joint accounts at the florist, the supermarket and other businesses in Carmel. The couple then worked on reconciliation with Kathryn keeping quiet about her car. Later she would say that she "did not want to rock the boat and unleash his anger while we were working towards more important objectives."[70]

On December 5, 1986, Michael joined The Monkees to film the annual MTV Christmas video. His cameo appearance at the end of the video as Santa, was the highlight of the video filled with Christmas songs and Davy romping with MTV V-J Martha Quinn, in a predictably jolly holiday style. After the filming, Michael joined the other Monkees for a post tour party at "Club 4D" in New York, where rumor had it that Davy was still miffed at Michael for getting the attention from the press and then leaving them again.

After a lengthy delay due to issues with the cover artwork, Michael's announced sequel to *Elephant Parts* was released on video in late 1986. *Dr. Duck's Super Secret All Purpose Sauce* was yet another compilation of comedy bits and music videos from the *Television Parts* show. The special guests on the tape included Jay Leno, Jerry Seinfeld, Whoopi Goldberg and Garry Shandling among others. The video was being promoted at selected college campuses around the country and was expected to be as big as *Elephant Parts*. It was not. Fans complained that it was not as wacky as *Elephant Parts* and that there was not enough of Michael and his unique sense of humor. There was only one original Nesmith song on the tape, the ending credits theme called *Dr. Duck's Super Secret All Purpose Sauce*, which contained some of Michael's offbeat humor, such as "How can something so

---

[70] Nesmith vs. Nesmith, Civil Case # D189 719.

delicious get my dishes so clean?" and "Does the champagne in your waterbed fizz too loud at night?"

The first public appearance of Michael in 1987 was on January 16 at the world premiere of *Square Dance* at the US Film Festival in Salt Lake City, Utah. Michael was seen at the event talking to the fans that had gathered, and talking to some of the press who had come to speak with him about his projects. The press would gladly talk to him, but they especially wanted to know about any possible reunions with The Monkees. Michael did not find this rediscovered celebrity too much of a burden now, as it provided him with a greater forum to talk about his future film projects, as well as the future of home video, still one of his favorite topics.

If it had been his decision though, he would have preferred to maintain his anonymous status as he said once, "I'm not comfortable with having fame attached to me or being recognized. I'd much rather have the fame attached to my work."

Rainmaker

Scott Riklin's first official day working at Pacific Arts was January 19, 1987. His main duty at the time was to raise at least three million dollars through investors to pay off a bank loan from Union Bank that was due in March. The loan had been acquired for the operational needs of Pacific Arts' involvement with *Square Dance*. Most importantly it was a loan that needed to be paid as future Liquid Paper royalties were being used as collateral.[71] If Michael was worried, he didn't let it show.

OverView Magazine was slated to be the '*TV Guide* of home video.' Michael spoke to anyone who would listen about his belief that magazines on video would be the next big thing. Spending hardly any promotion money for *OverView*, Pacific Arts stated that they preferred to let the product build the momentum of sales on its own. *OverView* startup costs were said to be about 15 million dollars, and was financed mostly by Coca Cola and NBC, as well as Michael. He also said that the magazine had enough sponsorship so that it could be sold for $4.95 on the newsstands, which was the same price as blank videotape.

The first issue of *OverView* was at least two hours long and contained movie reviews of past and current films by *Washington Post* critic Tom Shales, reviews of long form music videos by LA disc jockey Deidre O'Donoghue, and The Video Watchdog, a segment that focused on film continuity errors. There were also about 12 minutes worth of commercials ranging from chewing gum to the current Sylvester Stallone movie *Cobra*.

There were several innovative features of *OverView*, but they were hardly classified as entertaining. Among them were page numbers at the bottom of the screen for those who wanted to fast forward to a particular segment, a viewers' video letters segment, and a very annoying guy in a Tower Records store interviewing customers. The one redeeming feature of *OverView* was that you could erase the tape when you had finished watching it.

The first issue of *OverView* was test marketed in at least seven cities, including Phoenix, Denver, Sacramento and others, with disastrous results. NBC withdrew their financial support. They had wanted to air *OverView* on the network but Michael refused. Then Coke pulled the plug on their financial support as well. Video stores reported disappointing sales for a product that showed such promise. One store

---

[71] Riklin vs. Nesmith, Pacific Arts, etc... Civil Case # C659 943.

even returned their entire unopened case of *OverView*, which contained about 350 copies. Overall less than 1000 copies of the video were sold.[72]

Disappointed by the public's response, Michael kept mum about the project until a few years later when in a radio interview he said, "It was basic market research, but it turned out to be a moon-shot, because everybody was so interested in it. I had galleries of press lined up saying 'Well we hope this thing flies.' So it went up about three feet in the air and fell over sideways and blew up. Everyone said, 'Well, that will never work.'" Much to everybody's surprise, Michael has threatened to come out with another version of *OverView* someday.

---

[72] Dallas Morning News, March 16, 1987.

Nevermind the Furthermore, the Plea is Self Defense

Since *Dr. Duck* was not selling as well as hoped, Michael took advantage of his Monkees related popularity to promote *Dr. Duck* with a few in store appearances. One of the first was February 14, 1987, at a Sound Warehouse Record Store in Dallas. The line to meet Michael

Michael and Kathryn greet fans at a video signing. February 14, 1987. Photo by Tammy Bradshaw.

filled the store and extended around the building. He was late for the appearance, but no one seemed to mind. With Kathryn back at his side (reconciled for the moment), Michael entered the building to hundreds of almost orgasmic screams. Michael then got to meet all of the excited fans that were waiting hours for his appearance. Some of the fans grabbed at him, kissing and hugging him. Michael never looked agitated by the fans' enthusiasm, but one could tell it was making him slightly nervous. Some fans cried as they went up to meet him, while some gave gifts and had him sign everything they had brought. Some took the opportunity to talk to Kathryn, who was very gracious to the fans, but didn't hesitate to express some frank remarks about Michael when she had the chance. Later that same day the Nesmiths flew to New York.

On February 17, The Nesmiths were still in New York for the premiere of *Square Dance,* and they attended a reception afterwards that was organized in hopes of enticing investors to invest their money in Pacific Arts. Colleen Keegan, a friend of Riklin's who was hired to work at Pacific Arts, went up to Michael at the reception saying that she was able to get a million dollars for him. Unfortunately, no money came out of the reception and there was no end in sight for the financial troubles at Pacific Arts.[73]

Shortly after the New York trip, Kathryn was terminated from Pacific Arts. Obviously the reconciliation hadn't worked and Kathryn filed for divorce on April 17.[74] Michael would say years later, "My second marriage turned into a charade at its inception, but I lingered in the relationship in the misguided hope that it would correct itself. After many unpleasant years, I sought a divorce and was by myself now, more or less drifting from friend to friend."[75] The divorce that was sought by both of them was kept secret from the fans for years, as it was the standard policy of Michael to keep his personal life secret from the rest of the world. He might have thought the worst was over but it wasn't.

In April it was reported that the Pickwick Company, a record distributor located in Minneapolis Minnesota filed a lawsuit against Pacific Arts alleging that Pacific Arts owed them $120,000 for product that Pickwick returned to them in 1984. The complaint had been written in October of 1984, but Pickwick waited until February of 1987 to file the lawsuit. The final results of this particular complaint have not been located.[76]

In May, Michael went to the Cannes Film Festival in France to drum up interest in *Square Dance,* and in another movie he was just about to start work on called *Tapeheads.* While in Cannes, Michael received a call from Riklin stating that due to his error, Pacific Arts could not meet the payroll and that they were broke. Just as Michael came back and straightened up the payroll, escrow closed on the house in Carmel and Michael split the money with Kathryn, giving her $360,000.[77]

In great financial disarray, Pacific Arts laid off about six or seven employees on June 1, and Scott Riklin was fired on June 2. Riklin

---

[73] Riklin vs. Nesmith, Pacific Arts, etc... Civil Case # C659 943.

[74] Nesmith vs. Nesmith, Civil Case # D189 719.

[75] From Nesmith's The Long Sandy Hair of Neftoon Zamora.

[76] Minneapolis/St. Paul CityBusiness, April 8, 1987.

[77] Nesmith vs. Nesmith, Civil Case # D189 719.

was very upset that this happened, as he had moved from New York to L.A. where he purchased a home and now he didn't have a job. He also felt six months was too short a time and claimed that he had agreed with Michael to work at Pacific Arts for at least one year. In a meeting of the Pacific Arts Board of Directors, it was stated that a Chief Operations Officer was needed to replace Riklin, but the company couldn't afford to hire anyone.[78]

On June 23, Kathryn went to Pacific Arts and seeing "her" Mercedes in the parking garage, proceeded to drive off in it. She then telephoned Esther Grief informing her that she had taken the disputed car. In a court order wanting his car back, Michael explained that the Mercedes was his as he had traded in his mother's Mercedes 450SL that he had inherited for the more recent Mercedes. Michael claimed that the car was registered in his name, while Kathryn said, "Although the respondent may contend that the title to the automobile is in his name, and that it is therefore his separate property is not determinative of the issue, and is simply consistent with the manner in which he conducted business during our marriage and his insistence that he have his way concerning all financial matters." In the papers, he states that he considered the act of taking his car "nothing short of stealing." Michael was also upset by the fact that inside the car were the gate opener for his house, the gate opener for his office, the cover for his motorcycle, and various audiotapes. In court, Kathryn was forced to give the car back to Michael. After that incident, Michael filed a restraining order against Kathryn for her to stay at least 100 feet away from him, his house, his business, and the Pacific Arts warehouse.[79]

In 1987 The Monkees embarked on a second tour without Michael, that was promised to be just as big as the 1986 tour, but it was not to be. This time there were no other nostalgia acts on the tour. Instead, The Monkees used comedy performer "Weird Al" Yankovic as their opening act.

The major problem in the tour turned out to be the shunning of The Monkees by MTV, who had been their biggest backers. It seemed that The Monkees had been scheduled, without their knowledge, to appear on MTV's Superbowl party in January of '87. When nobody from The Monkees camp showed up, the MTV executives in charge were furious that The Monkees would stand them up. It seemed that Michael's own creation would ban The Monkees for life. This, of course, put a damper on the new Monkees' album *Pool It* that was released by Rhino Records during the tour. The album, as a result,

---

[78] Riklin vs. Nesmith, Pacific Arts, etc... Civil Case # C659 943.
[79] Nesmith vs. Nesmith, Civil Case # D189 719.

bombed on the Billboard charts. The two videos from the album, *Heart and Soul* and *Every Step of the Way*, were instead staples on Nickelodeon's *Nick Rocks* show.

In August, Scott Riklin filed a lawsuit against Michael for breach of contract and libel, saying that Michael stated "Riklin emptied the companies coffers while I was in Cannes." Riklin also alleged that Michael used the assets of the corporation for his own personal use, and withdrew funds from the corporation's bank accounts for his own use.

Michael responded in court by alleging that Riklin falsified sales reports and spent too much money. Michael stated that in 1986 Pacific Arts had a net loss of $269,440 whereas in 1987 the net loss was at least $1 million. Michael also claimed that Riklin borrowed $50,000 from the *Tapeheads* production loan and was about to borrow another $135,000 to fund the overhead costs that Pacific Arts Video was building.[80]

Meanwhile, the divorce proceedings were still going on with Kathryn, who was stating that she had 50% ownership in the company in the beginning. Through the years though, she alleges, that it was reduced to zero due to pressure from Michael. Kathryn listed her monthly expenses as $12,665, citing such items as a Christian Science Practitioner for $350 per month, and travel and vacations at $1,000. Her clothing per month was listed at $1,000, and food along with meals out were $1,250 per month. Kathryn also listed her income as zero, but started renting a home in Malibu for $4,000 a month. The court found that Michael's income per month averaged about $168,000, and he had to make one lump payment of $160,000 plus monthly payments of $20,000.

The same day that Michael was ordered to make the lump payment, he pleaded to the judge that he was unable to make the payments due to his inability to get the money from Bette's estate, since the Liquid Paper royalties were used as collateral for a loan, and due to the fact that he was now only making $10,000 monthly from Pacific Arts. The judge denied the request.

Kathryn claimed in the documents that Michael paid his personal expenses through his corporations, rather then being directly paid the large salary from which he would be able to make spousal payments. In retaliation, Michael refused to make payments and allegedly sold both of his Mercedes Benz and kept the proceeds.

Kathryn hired the accounting firm of Taylor & Liebman to audit Pacific Arts to show the court the true financial status of the company. Michael complained that Kathryn was wasting her money, as

---

[80] Riklin vs. Nesmith, Pacific Arts, etc... Civil Case # C659 943.

Pacific Arts was his sole property, and it was a money losing business that he said was "a moment short away from bankruptcy." Michael claimed in court papers that he was trying to find either a buyer or an investor for Pacific Arts to alleviate some of the debt that was growing in the company. The search for a buyer sent Michael to Australia for a meeting with Robert Ward of Filmpac Holding Ltd. While in Australia, Michael was able to earn some money by appearing in a commercial for Liquid Paper, which aired only in Australia and England.[81]

---

[81] Nesmith vs. Nesmith, Civil Case # D189 719.

You Just May Be The One

A single man, in spirit anyway, Michael started dating again. Going out on a double date with friends from the office, Michael couldn't keep his eyes off of the other guy's date, and she couldn't keep her eyes off of Michael. The other guy's date was a fashion model named Victoria Kennedy. She and Michael started dating and early in their courtship attended the movie premiere of *Roxanne* and were photographed extensively by the press. Michael has referred to her as his "partner in life" since 1987.

Michael and Victoria Kennedy at the premiere of "Roxanne," 1987. Photo from The RLM Archives.

On April 20, Michael took his deposition for the ongoing Scott Riklin trial. During the deposition, Michael was asked about Pacific Arts being different from Nesmith Enterprises, Inc. As Michael explained for the court, "My assumption is that if you open a hot dog stand and your last name is Funky and you don't want to do business under your own name, you can change the name of the stand to 'Delicious,' and it becomes the Funky Hot Dog Stand doing business as the Delicious Hot Dog Stand, but it's really Mr. Funky that owns it and operates it. That's my assumption. I don't know whether that's a legal definition or not."

Riklin's position was to claim that before he had been fired, he had been successful in obtaining potential investors, but Nesmith ran them off. He cited the facts that Chase Manhattan Bank had proposed extending Pacific Arts a $20 million line of credit, The First Bank of Minneapolis had expressed interest in extending a line of credit and undertaking a private placement to raise equity funds, Wescott Capital had agreed to commit $1 million contingent upon raising an additional $4 million from other sources and individuals David Comsky and actor Wayne Rogers had also been potential investors.

Photo by Henry Diltz

Riklin alleged that Michael would not discuss the financial problems of Pacific Arts during the entire time of Riklin's employment with Michael, stating that the company was "puttering along just fine." Riklin also claimed that Michael's behavior toward potential investors had been hardly professional insofar as during one meeting, Michael "stated that his main interest in life was playing golf." Riklin also claimed that Michael refused to fly to New York a day earlier than planned to meet with the Chase Manhattan Bank executive whose approval was required for the loan. There was no information on the outcome of the case and nobody has come forward with any information.[82]

On August 26, 1988, the marriage of Robert Michael Nesmith and Kathryn Marie Bild Nesmith was finally dissolved. The spousal

---

[82] Riklin vs. Nesmith, Pacific Arts, etc... Civil Case # 659 943.

payments were started June 1 at $8,500 monthly until June 1, 1990 when the support would go down to $8,000 a month for three years. On June 1, 1993, the support payments were $5,000 and the payments would continue until June 1, 1995.

As for property and possessions, Michael would keep any personal property of Bette Graham, his personal effects such as jewelry and clothing, his Walt Disney videos, his collection of Warner Brothers cartoons and his videos of Fred Astaire and Ginger Rogers's movies. He also was able to keep his audiocassettes of The Mills Brothers and Sons of the Pioneers. Michael was able to keep all of his companies including: Nesmith Enterprises d.b.a. Pacific Arts Video, Pacific Arts Video Records, El Paso Music and Peaceful Music. Also included were Pacific Arts Publishing, Pacific Arts Corporation, Pacific Arts Pictures, Union Software, United Art Works, Popclips and Zoomo Productions. Michael was also able to keep his membership in Pebble Beach Club in Carmel, California, as well as his house in Beverly Hills. Michael's other possessions included an Airstream motor home, the proceeds of the sale of the two Mercedes, a 1987 Jeep Cherokee, and 900 shares of Gulf Coast Development Corporation.

Kathryn would receive in the divorce her clothing and jewelry in her possession. She also received Pison Productions and Nesco Investments, a 1988 Jeep Wrangler in her possession, and any royalties owed her for *Elephant Parts*.[83]

---

[83] Nesmith vs. Nesmith, Civil Case # D189 719.

Release

Stressed out from his business problems and needing a break, Michael said that maybe he would now go back to performing music. He might have had the urge to get back into music, but he was not interested in being a celebrity, as he was enjoying his anonymity too much. As he said in an interview a few years later, "I really had all the taste of stardom that I wanted. It's an interesting life pattern but...I wanted to work in the arts unencumbered by the stardom. Fame tends to be a difficult piece of baggage."

Still wanting to hit it big into the movie business, Michael had several movies lined up for which he was going to serve as executive producer, but after time they vanished from the scene. One of the many was *Zippyvision*, a live action film based on the syndicated Zippy the Pinhead cartoon strip, with Randy Quaid set for the title role. The script was reportedly written and the film was ready to be filmed. As Bill Griffith, creator of Zippy The Pinhead recalled in 2000, "He (Michael) had a big sign over the wall behind his desk, a big circle with a slash through it that said 'No Monkee Jokes.' He was a very surreal character. He would speak only in metaphors: sports and military metaphors. His final parting words of advice to me were: 'Time to submerge, but never lose sight of the donut.' I knew what he meant. Sort of."

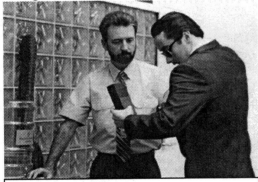

Michael and John Cusak on the set of Tapeheads. 1987 photo from The RLM Archives.

The other proposed movies were *Mopeds to Muleghe*, *Powerhouse*, and then *Motorama*, which were described in the *Hollywood Reporter* as "an absurd metaphoric drama about the human condition set in the future." Unfortunately none of the films were ever produced.

Michael did reveal that he had put in a bid for a particular movie and lost it, and the movie went on to become a cult classic. The movie was *This Is Spinal Tap*. Its director Rob Reiner took it to Michael, but when informed that Michael wanted to avoid releasing the movie to the theaters and wanted to release straight to video, Reiner kept shopping around the movie studios.

Then there was *Margaritaville*. When asked about the status of this never produced movie, Michael said, "Well, it crashed and burned just to cut to the chase. Jimmy Buffett and I kept trying to get this thing launched, and most of the major studios had other projects similar in development. That's the usual stuff that comes back. That can be true, or it can be a euphemism for 'We don't like this idea, go away.' I still talk to Jimmy from time to time. We had a couple of screenplays written on it and I don't know if it will ever come back. I thought it would be terrific. I think all of Buffet's fans would go see it. I've never seen any movie like it. Well, there was this one thing that we bumped up against. It was a Robin Williams movie called *Club Paradise*. When it bombed everybody got terrified of that kind of movie. It's not exactly the same thing. It has Jimmy's nice wacky sensibility about it, and it's full of his music, so it wasn't the same thing at all."

Tapeheads had been hailed at film festivals, but had terrible problems. The movie, financed by Michael as well as NBC cost $4 million. The initial distributor of the film, DEG, went bankrupt. After Avenue Pictures picked up the title, the movie was released into multiplex theaters where the public ignored it.

The promotional interviews done by the stars of the movie, Tim Robbins and John Cusak, were a shambles. The guys developed attitudes with the press even to the point of walking off the *Good Morning America* set before their segment. The damage was extensive and Michael took it upon himself to go out on the promo trail and spread the word about *Tapeheads*. Michael even went so far as to host a promo video for the films release on home video. The film did

Photo by Michael G. Bush

make a little bit of money and it did develop a small cult following. A few years after *Tapeheads*, Tim Robbins, now a major star, ran into Michael at a party and apologized for the trouble that he caused.

Michael has been known by many nicknames in the past, being called Nes, Papa Nes, Da Nez, The Nez, Papa Nez and then just plain Nez. Michael explains, "It was just a nickname that came up out of my motorcycle racing days. My old motorcycle racing buddies just started calling me Papa Nez. I think it had as much to do with the fact that whenever we'd go camping, and everybody was always looking for something, I was always the guy that either had remembered to pack it or brought it along. So everybody considered me sort of, you know, like when you go camping with your dad, he's always got the bases covered. So they started calling me Papa Nez. No one uses it anymore, now people just call me Nez."

Photo by Henry Diltz

Pacific Arts, also known in industry circles as 'The house that *Elephant Parts* built,' released a short compilation of Michael's music videos from the past ten years called *Nezmuzic*. He referred to this as an easy way for fans to watch all of the video clips featuring him without scanning through Elephant Parts and Television Parts Home Companion. He said also that this was his way of thanking his fans for their support throughout the years.

At the same time, Rhino Records released *The Newer Stuff*, which was a compilation of Nesmith's later hits such as *Rio* and *Cruisin'* as well as unreleased comedy songs such as *Tahiti Condo* and *Chow Mein and Bowling* which were produced for movies that were never released called *Neon Ruby* and *Video Ranch*. Other songs on the compilation were *I'll Remember You* and *Eldorado to the Moon*, which were featured on *Television Parts*. Michael also re-mixed some of the songs, smoothing out the song *Magic,* and totally changing the song *Carioca* from an upbeat dance song to a dark and eerie song for a back alley.

There were three versions of *The Newer Stuff.* The LP, which was an almost extinct format at this time, had 10 songs, the cassette featured 12 songs and the CD contained 14 songs. Fans were puzzled as to why there were so many different versions, but Rhino said that the different versions were made at Michael's request. Apparently he knew that the collectors would have to have all three versions. His girlfriend Victoria is pictured with him on the back cover of the album.

While promoting *Tapeheads* and his numerous projects, Michael mentioned doing a pilot called *Kitty Hoy: The Adventures of America's Sweetheart With An Attitude*. He said that he would not be starring and he did not specify if the pilot was for TV or home video. '*Kitty*' never saw the light of day.

Photo by Henry Diltz

179

Laugh Kills Lonesome

In the summer of 1989, The Monkees were on yet another tour, and as the show headed into LA, Michael let it be known that he was indeed going to reunite with them for a couple of days. It was a special occasion as The Monkees were going to be awarded a star on the Hollywood Walk of Fame, and Michael would be joining for several songs in a reunion concert.

Michael's entrance at the Universal Amphitheater concert on July 9, 1989. Photo by Michael G. Bush.

The 1989 Monkee tour had not fared as well as the 1986 tour, as the fans were staying away in droves, even though the quality of the show had improved greatly. Michael's appearance would insure that they would get some publicity and a boost to ticket sales. Called The 1989 Hollywood Star Celebration, the event began as Michael's fans gathered at the Roxy for a concert by Christian Nesmith's band OFF. In the audience that evening were Jonathan, Jessica, Phyllis and Michael who had attended the concert with Victoria. After the show, Michael happily signed autographs and posed for photos with the fans.

David Jones was not a happy Monkee at this point. The rehearsals for The Monkees reunion concert at the Universal Amphitheater were not going as smoothly as he would have liked. First of all he wanted the other Monkees there. Michael had already been to the rehearsal and after singing three songs, left David alone to work with the backup band. Peter arrived a little while later and got right down to work. Micky finally showed up, and while he explained that his wife Trina had a bad case of food poisoning and didn't want to leave her side, David didn't really want to hear it as he knew time was slipping away. Not very happy with Michael's brief appearance at the rehearsal, David complained to Micky "Mike wants to do *Joanne* and some obscure song (Cruisin'). I don't know about that." Micky just shrugged his shoulders and replied, "Let him do whatever he wants, we'll be doing our own new material, so what difference does it make?"[84]

The next evening all four Monkees gave a sold out concert at the Universal Amphitheater. It was the Monkee concert the fans had

The Monkees receiving a star on the Hollywood Walk of Fame on July 10, 1989. Photo from The RLM Archives.

been waiting for as Michael appeared from the wings midway through the show.

"Where've you been?" asked David.

"I've been lookin' for my hat."

With that, Michael jumped into his first song *What Am I Doin' Hangin' 'Round?* After that encouraging start, he went into versions of *Cruisin'*, *Joanne*, and *Papa Gene's Blues*. Afterwards, he went into the background-singing backup on the other Monkee songs. Michael made humor out of the fact that he did not know the show's comedy bits, and tried to keep up as best as he could.

---

[84] 16 Magazine, late 1989.

The next day was the unveiling of The Monkees' star on the Hollywood Walk of Fame, which is located in front of the Vogue Theatre, where the Monkee movie *Head* premiered. Michael showed up for the event, and seemed to be very appreciative of the honor, showing much more emotion about it then the other three guys as evident in his speech.

Photos by Henry Diltz

"The question I am most often asked is 'Where's Davy?' (audience laughs) No, the question I am most often asked is 'How does

182

it feel to be up with the guys after all this time?' Well, it's a mixture of feelings and all of them are good, but the one that pops to mind is a feeling of profound gratitude. There's such an outpouring of affection that I feel from you and for you, such a tremendous sense of support and love that's been with us over the years, that at a time like this almost anything I say seems trivial by comparison. But I can tell you on my behalf, and on the behalf of all of us, this has meant more than we can possibly ever say, and so from me to all of you and from all of us, God Bless, and thanks very much."

After the star ceremony The Monkees were given one plaque to commemorate the star presentation. Davy complained to a reporter, "We were given one plaque between the four of us and I suggested that we give it to Michael, but somehow it ended up in the hands of Bert Schneider which I could not stand. So that was kind of weird. He's not a Monkee." Peter was overheard the remark and said, "But he is The Monkees." "No, he's not. We're The Monkees,"[85] said a very angry David. A few years later, the always quotable David would say in an interview, "I hope I'm back here for my own star someday."

Later that day, a press conference was held for the media with the conference moving into another room so the fans could ask questions. The questions for Michael ranged from "Did you bronze the wool hat?" to "How do you like *Head* (the movie)?" At one point

Michael performing with The Monkees July 9, 1989 at the Universal Amphitheater. Photo by Michael G. Bush.

Michael was asked about the possibility of reissuing *The Prison* on compact disc format, which had replaced the record album in music stores. Michael revealed that he would release *The Prison* in a set with its sequels that had not been produced yet, *The Garden* and *The Magic Ball,* and that it would be a long time before they were released. After the conference, the guys were supposed to meet and discuss their future

---

[85] 16 Magazine, late 1989.

plans as The Monkees. There had been talk of a Monkees movie again but as Davy observed, "The whole thing was blown to pieces because of the other Monkees. Micky had to direct or he wouldn't do it, and Peter had to do the music or he wouldn't do it, and Mike, hell, he was never available to do anything anyway. It was always 'next week' with him."

Micky did not show up for the meeting, as he was definitely aware of the tension between him and the other two Monkees on the tour. The main cause of the tension was that Micky had asked Davy to postpone his solo career for the future of The Monkees, and then proceeded to announce *his* upcoming solo concerts and album. There was also tension among the group due to Micky having his manager Kevin Allyn manage the group instead of the guys managing themselves. The end result was that The Monkees again broke up as soon as the tour ended.

In the Summer of 1989, Michael was a judge for the CINETEX Comedy Awards, as he was an active member of the CINETEX Comedy Advisory Committee. Michael gave an interview to the CINETEX newsletter, and managed to lose a few people along the way with what he was talking about. In the interview Michael states, "Laughter is fundamental. It's the closest state you can find to the cosmic happiness spiritual masters talk about. There are levels of humor and we'll set some standards for them at CINETEX. First, a film should make you laugh. As simple as it seems, it is a very complicated act because it should suspend you in time and draw you into a separate world. There are high standards for comedy in film. The real players can pull you into a magic world and make you see things from a perspective you've never had, a perspective that will change the way you see those things in the future. If you're a dramatist, it's that profound moment that buckles your knees. If you're a comedian, it's that cosmic moment that elevates and makes you laugh at your world from a high place."

Michael was mentioned in a Dallas newspaper as contributing $1,000 to the election fund for the Republican representative for Texas Attorney General, Pat Hill.[86] This is out of character as Michael has made it clear he is a non-political person. As he said once, "I'm non-political. I don't care about it. I don't care who the president is. I don't care who the senators are. I don't pay attention to that stuff. When I say I don't care, I mean I don't pay attention to it."

The Gihon Foundation moved from its main offices in Dallas to Santa Fe, New Mexico, where Michael had set up his second home. The foundation's "Works by Women" art collection was deemed too fragile for travel and needed a permanent home. The foundation also changed

---

[86] Dallas Morning News, February 2, 1990.

its main goal from contributing grants to worthy causes to funding its own programs. The main program the Gihon Foundation funded was the Council on Ideas that cost $150,000 to produce. Every two years, a group of significant individuals meet and discuss the events of the time. The participants are paid $5000 each and set up with accommodations in an upper class hotel. The weekend ends with a press conference and a formal statement that is sent to all members of Congress as well as the White House. The non-political Nesmith serves as host for this event. His input was needed though after the 1990 Council on Ideas that ended abruptly when the members left after arguing about Fidel Castro. From then on, as Michael said in an interview, he gives them suggestions on how to start the proceedings. "It may be something as simple as 'be kind to animals' or 'ripe fruit is best.'"

Unwilling to give up on his idea of a magazine put out on a video cassette, Michael kept threatening, and sure enough the video magazine *Persona* was test marketed in Colorado, retaining the low price point set by *OverView* of $4.95. The film contained 90 minutes of interviews and news on Hollywood personalities, and was not really heard from again. Most of Michael's fans did not even know of its existence, as the video was not from Pacific Arts and did not feature Michael's name anywhere on the tape. It was not known how sales went, but Michael avoided the video magazine field from that point on.

Michael had always said that Pacific Arts was the PBS of home video, with its originality in programming and following the beat of a different drummer. Incredibly PBS itself was about to enter Michael's world. It was time for the mega-corporation to start thinking about marketing it's treasure trove of public broadcasting programs and something about the marketing record of Pacific arts caught the attention of PBS executives. The two companies came together and created PBS Home Video. Michael spoke of the possible financial rewards of joining forces with PBS by saying, "We could be talking about hundreds of millions of dollars. My feeling tells me this could be as big as PBS itself."

In another interview Michael said, "I think there'll be a time when PBS Home Video may be the largest revenue source for public broadcasting. They take it very seriously." PBS said that Pacific Arts was the best of the companies they had talked to, and they liked the fact that Michael was willing to pay the start up costs. In one interview he was asked how he would be able to persuade producers of major programs to jump aboard, he replied, "Money."

When launching the PBS Home Video label, Michael told reporters that he had spent $10 million dollars building Pacific Arts since it's beginning in the middle Seventies. Something to consider is how Michael is always ahead of his time. It was unique in 1990 to go to the video store and buy a video tape of a new TV show. There were already video tapes of single episodes of ancient TV programs but it was unusual to have brand new series, even entire series available for retail sale. Nowadays it is not uncommon for series with barely one season aired to already be available for sale in the DVD format.

Under the PBS Home Video line, Michael would release such titles as: *Ken Burns' The Civil War, The Dinosaurs, I Claudius, The Astronomers, LBJ, Eyes on the Prize,* and countless others. It was astounding to the completest Nesmith collectors, because there were so many videos coming out on the PBS label, as well as the Pacific Arts label, that it was difficult to keep up. Pacific Arts also joined forces with The Family Channel and Mystic Fire Video, but these projects did not last very long. The company also released a couple of audio books read by sports celebrities that were not widely distributed.

Michael and Victoria out on the town circa 1990. Photo from The RLM Archives.

Andy Ware had been a longtime fan of Michael's and was now the head of Awareness Records, a UK record company. He asked Michael about the possibility of reissuing all of his CDs. Michael approved and completely remixed and re-mastered *The Prison*, the first re-release planned. Some fans were shocked that this version of *The Prison* was almost completely different from the original. The remixed CD version is a lush full sounding soundtrack, which is possibly what Michael wanted in the first place. Gone was the simple arrangement as more modern synthesizers were added and new backup vocals were added. Red Rhodes steel guitar performance, which was barely audible on vinyl, is very apparent on the reissue. The book of The Prison, which was the centerpiece of the work, was now a tiny booklet that would fit inside of the CD case, losing all of the impact of reading the book and looking at the artwork, which was now thumbnail size.

The Prison received good reviews from critics who were not around when the original was released. Awareness then released the remaining Nesmith CD's three at a time every couple of months, except for *Live at the Palais*. There had been a discussion of releasing a different concert from the mid '70s instead, but nothing came out of it.

In 1991, The Monkees were eligible for induction into the Rock and Roll Hall of Fame, but when voting time came, the guys were ignored, much to the disappointment of the fans. Michael however said in an interview, "I would think it would be very strange to have a band in the Rock and Roll Hall of Fame that wasn't a rock and roll band. It was a television show about a rock and roll band. That's a little like nominating a movie about baseball to the Baseball Hall of Fame, or

Michael Nesmith, the CEO of Pacific Arts circa 1991. Photo courtesy of The Pacific Arts Corporation. Photo by Henry Diltz.

Gary Cooper because he played Lou Gehrig."[87] Nevertheless, the fans know what affect The Monkees music had on them and rock and roll.

Michael was about to enter the television field again with *Reel Life*, which was described in *The Hartford Courant* as a "non traditional series which zooms in on the unusual." The show was developed for the new Fox television network, but unfortunately was never picked up. Michael said, "In the same way that *Square Dance* is probably going to keep me out of dramatic movies, I think the failure of *Television Parts* is going to keep me off the networks."

---

[87] Goldmine, December 27, 1991.

Meanwhile, the titles on PBS Home Video were selling very well. An article in the public broadcasting newspaper *Current* reported that PBS Home Video sold $30 million in videos in its first year of operation, which was beyond the expectations of everyone in the video industry. A large percentage of sales came from the popular mini series *The Civil War*. PBS also went on to say that they expected to sell another $20 million in the next year.

Photo by Henry Diltz

Listen To The Band

In early 1992 Michael embarked on his first concert tour in 12 years, the Multi-Purpose Tour. The tour promoted a new Rhino

compilation of Nesmith's RCA work called *The Older Stuff*, as well as a collection of films that Michael had been involved with called "The Films of Michael Nesmith" even though neither was sold on the tour. Michael and his band, Luis Conte, John Hobbs, Billy Joe Walker Jr. and Joe Chemay would travel to the particular venues on the weekend and then fly back to L.A. for the week so Michael could get his work done at Pacific Arts. It was exhausting for him, but he had not garnered so much press for himself and his company in years. There was one catch with all of this publicity, though. Michael's publicists claimed that he wouldn't answer any Monkee questions.

The tour began in Nashville at the Bluebird Cafe and ended in Dallas at Poor David's Pub. The shows were all sellouts, but the funny thing was that most of the tickets were sold to Michael, who gave the majority of them to Pacific Arts employees and PBS employees, leaving hardly any for actual fans. Still it was a great experience for those who had never seen Michael perform live. The shows were comprised of songs mostly from his First National Band days, as well as a few cover songs such as *The Long Black Veil* and a new composition called *Moon Over the Rio Grande*.

Overall, the tour was a success, but that is not to say there weren't snags during the tour. First, while performing the concerts in bars and clubs, it was difficult for some of the audiences to listen to Michael sing while waitresses were taking orders for drinks. The second problem was the fact that the concerts were starting late into the evening, much to Michael's frustration.

On June 19 Michael gave a concert at the Peter Britt Music Festival in Jacksonville Oregon, which was filmed specifically for video release. The filming of the concert was grueling, as Michael had the flu and even passed out backstage and had to be revived with oxygen.[88] Although he was indeed ill, the concert was still one of his finest. The concert was released September 15 on video and on a double laserdisc of *Live at the Britt* and *Elephant Parts*. After the laserdisc's initial release, Michael decided that he didn't like the cover artwork and re-issued the laserdisc with a different cover. Inside the new package was an index card with his signature.

It was then announced that Michael was recording his first studio album in years. The name of the album was *"...tropical*

Michael performing at Poor David's Pub. February 29, 1992. Photo by Michael G. Bush.

campfire's..." and to the fans' delight, Michael would be going out on tour later that year to promote the new album. Initially there were at least ten dates planned for the tour, including dates in Houston, Salt Lake City, Boston and San Francisco. Tickets went on sale at all of the venues and they were selling quite well, but then Michael decided that

---

[88] Interview with Henry Diltz, July 11, 1992.

he didn't want to play in nightclubs. He told his booking agent he wanted to perform in theaters only. This meant that all of the shows were canceled except for about five, and then that list was shortened to about two, but an appearance on the PBS television show *Austin City*

Michael performing at the Peter Britt Pavilion in Jacksonville, Oregon. June 19, 1992. Photo by Henry Diltz

Limits was added.

The remaining concerts on the *"...tropical campfire's..."* tour were in Austin and San Francisco. For the concert at the Texas Union Ballroom at the University of Texas in Austin, the ballroom staff removed a few rows of seats and proceeded to spread out the remaining seats, as the tickets for the show did not sell out. In fact, the tickets did not sell well, with people staying away as they were afraid Michael would cancel the concert. There was also discontent in

George Steele, Ward Sylvester, and Michael at the Britt Festival. Photo by Henry Diltz.

the Nesmith camp, as some of the road crew was heard complaining to anyone who would listen that this "tour" was among the worst they had

191

ever been involved with in terms of budget and hostile managers and bodyguards.

The audience couldn't tell anything was wrong, as the show was outstanding. Michael performed his hits as well as songs off of the *"...tropical campfire's..."* album. He also appeared to be in a good mood, as he joked with the audience and the band. As Michael came out to do his encore he read a note from a fan club in Houston called The Monkees Connection. He announced that the presidents, Colleen Wright and Carolyn Thomas, had raised money through their club to name a star in outer space after Michael. He was very touched and pleased that his fans had done this for him.

Photo by Henry Diltz

"...tropical campfire's..." was released in October on the Pacific Arts Audio label. It seemed ironic that Michael was no longer making video records but was now back to making audio only records. The CD received mostly great reviews from all of the music reviewers who had always loved his music, as well as those discovering his music for the first time. One review stated, "Sheer joy was the feeling. Mike Nesmith is doing country music again. The ex-Monkee is a true Renaissance man. This new record sounds like it feels to wake up as the sun rises over a California desert; particularly songs such as *Moon Over the Rio Grande* and *Twilight on the Trail*, which should please Sons of the Pioneers fans. There's also a similar sandy feel given to the two Cole Porter songs (*Begin the Beguine* and *In the Still of the Night*). His sense of humor is still with us; *I Am Not That* could easily fit on one of those early '80s records. *One...* and *...For the Island* are two versions of the

192

same song, one instrumental and one vocal. This is a refreshingly cliché-free return to form from a very famous man who refuses to rest on his laurels."

In doing interviews to promote the album, there were the usual Monkee questions, and presumably after one Monkee question too many, Michael told a pesky reporter, "If I'm not going to tour for my own album, why would I tour with The Monkees?"[89]

---

[89] Toronto Sun, April 9, 1993.

Zilch

In June of 1993, it was reported that Pacific Arts had fallen behind in paying PBS royalties. PBS Home Video projected a net loss of $542,000 despite the sale of cassettes earning about $5 million for PBS and the producers since PBS Home Video began. Representatives for PBS said that they would hire consultants to find some ways of raising capital. They did specify that they would not end their agreement with Pacific Arts at that time, as it was scheduled to terminate anyway in either 1996 or 1995 depending on whichever video industry magazine you believe.

One night, Michael attended a show by the Hellecasters, a group featuring the unusual arrangement of three lead guitarists, John Jorgenson, Will Ray and Jerry Donahue. Michael liked the group, as Jorgenson explained, "Michael was starting his Pacific Arts Audio label and liked us because we had an odd sense of humor like he did, and we were eclectic enough for him to like it. So we went to the recording studio and we did a record mostly of stuff we'd done live."

The Hellecasters became extremely popular with the record buyers and guitar aficionados, to the point where The Hellecasters and their debut album *The Return of the Hellecasters* were voted "Album of the Year" and "Country Album of the Year" by the *Guitar Player's* readers' poll.

For Nesmith fans there were two releases from Pacific Arts to look forward to. The first release was a video box set of the *Television Parts* series. Michael had previously said that he couldn't release any more compilations of clips from the *Television Parts* TV show due to the Screen Actors Guild rules restricting re-editing of television shows. So finally, to eliminate this problem Michael planned to release all of the episodes uncut. The box set would include a book filled with photos on the making of the television show. Pacific Arts was so serious about the release, *Dr. Duck* and *Television Parts Home Companion* videos were put on moratorium, a term that means that they are no longer available. Unfortunately, despite all of these plans, the video box set was never manufactured.

The second release was the long planned sequel to *The Prison* called *The Garden*, which Michael started recording in August of 1993. In several interviews he joked that, "*The Prison* has been given several magazine's awards for the most dreadful concept album of all time. All the more reason to do a follow up."

The original release date for *The Garden* was to be in late March with a CD-ROM version of *The Garden* coming out the same day and at the same price. Unfortunately, the release of both versions were put on hold, as Pacific Arts was having problems with the Magic Eye artwork for the cover, a special effect where the person stares into the artwork and sees images in 3-D.

Confusing the fans, *Entertainment Weekly* magazine ran an article on Michael to promote *The Garden* with the title of the article being "Mike Nesmith's Chart Proof Music." The fans then started calling all of the record stores to no avail, as they were all told that there was no such record as *The Garden*. After many delays, the audio version of *The Garden* was finally released shortly after Labor Day without the Magic Eye artwork, replaced by paintings of Monet's garden.

The Garden is a continuation of *The Prison* story in which Jason is still uptight about everything going on around him. He is still questioning everyone about numerous changes that occur in front of him and it seems that he is never satisfied with the answer. The main premise of *The Garden* is that Jason, throughout the story, has to find this person named Jack and get him to turn the water on in the city to get the gardens to grow again. The music for *The Garden* was mostly instrumental as to not distract the reader. The final song on the CD, *Life Becoming* features Michael's vocals as well as background vocals from Christian, Jason and Jessica Nesmith.

There was also a plan for *Video Ranch* to be filmed, as it was announced that the script was finally ready. The movie would be made not for home video, or the movie theaters, but it would be made for CD-I computer systems, but was never completed.

Pacific Arts Audio released a 2 CD set called *Complete*, which featured the three First National Band albums. Inside the package was a catalog entitled "The Complete Works of Michael Nesmith." The order form had a sense of humor as it read, "Yes, I would like to order every last item that has absolutely anything to do with Michael Nesmith, don't care what it is, don't care what it costs, I want it all. Or, at least the items indicated inside. Thanks. (And please say hi to Nez for me.)"

Photo by Henry Diltz

I Need Help, I'm Falling Again

In October 1993, PBS abruptly ended their partnership with Michael and Pacific Arts. Through a spokesman Pacific Arts said, "We are unable to reach an agreement on a plan to assure PBS and the producers timely payments on royalties and licensee fees." In an article about the separation, there were unconfirmed reports that Pacific Arts would lose $500,000 in 1993 and owed more than $1 million in royalties to producers.

Photo by Henry Diltz

Because of the canceled projects, as well as the postponed projects, rumors started flying everywhere. Finally the May 6 issue of *Video Business* magazine ended all suspicions with one of the leading stories "Pacific Arts Video Calls It Quits." The article stated that the video division shut down and the relationship with UNI Distribution was terminated. The shutdown was blamed on PBS and the several problems Pacific Arts had involving the use of the PBS logo as well as the past payments of royalties. Wanting to completely sever ties to Michael's company, PBS wasted no time and signed with Turner Home Video to re-release some of the same videos as well as many others, leaving Pacific Arts in ashes. In a letter via e-mail to a fan, Michael stated "the PBS deal was very bad economically for Pacific Arts Video, and it made more sense to close the company rather than try to recover from the bad PBS deal."

197

This was an especially sad announcement for the older Nesmith fans that had seen the birth of Pacific Arts when the staff consisted of Michael and his then girlfriend Kathryn. They had seen the highs of *Elephant Parts* and the lows of recent times. Each time Michael would bounce back with something new. The Pacific Arts name would not even go on through Pacific Arts Audio. It was decided that the name could be confused with the video division, so the name of the audio company was changed to Rio Records.

March 17, 1994 Michael was scheduled to appear at the South by Southwest Film and Media Conference in Austin, Texas. The first appearance at the conference was to be a question and answer session between a screening of *Repo Man* and *Tapeheads*. The second appearance was to be on a panel at a discussion on the future of movies. It was also rumored that Michael would make a conference-related appearance at the Hellecasters concert at a club called La Zona Rosa. The Hellecasters were at the conference to promote their act, and their new CD on Michael's Rio Records label, *Escape From Hollywood*.

Much to everyone's disappointment, a few minutes before the screening of *Repo Man*, it was announced that Michael would not be appearing. It seemed that he had developed an upper respiratory infection and was home in California on his doctor's orders. A call to Michael's assistant Christine Giuliano confirmed this story, but fans were suspicious that maybe he was purposely staying in California due to the many business problems he was having. It was common knowledge that Michael adhered to the philosophy of Christian Science, so it seemed odd that he would following doctor's orders. One thing was certain; the organizers of the event were reportedly so upset that they said that Michael would not be invited to the conference again.

In May of 1994 it was announced in a major entertainment magazine that West Coast Video Duplicating Inc. had slapped Michael with a $4.8 million dollar lawsuit. The actual amount was $2.4 million according to court records. In the article, the West Coast Video Duplicating Inc. suit claims that Michael owed them a sizable sum due to unpaid bills for video duplication services. Since the invoices clearly show his company liable for these services, Michael and his lawyers had opted for a trial with a jury in order to try and delay the proceedings while he tried to win the PBS lawsuit.[90]

---

[90] West Coast Video Duplication vs. Nesmith, Civil Case # BC 102 155.

Dance and Have a Good Time

Michael gave a free concert on July 16, 1994 at an event called The Taste of Dallas in the popular West End section of Dallas, Texas. Fans came in for the show from all over the country, as it was now a rare occasion for a Nesmith concert, and the fans had no way of knowing which show would be his last.

Photo by Henry Diltz

As the show began it was obvious that there had been no rehearsal. Michael had flown in for the concert, arriving during the Hellecasters opening act, and was planning to leave immediately afterward for a press conference at the Gihon Foundation in New Mexico, where he was hosting the foundation's Council on Ideas meeting that weekend. The lack of a rehearsal was also obvious, as Michael did not even play guitar during the show. He also seemed to be a bit out of it as he performed. He seemed awkward without his guitar as during the show he would wave his arms around and dance around on the stage not too gracefully. He even fumbled words on some of his trademark songs and even forgot some words to *Cruisin'*.

The show was a shock for the fans that had always seen him dressed up in his cowboy clothes and being serious. Now they had a portly man on stage, wearing a yellow pineapple shirt and singing his old hits. Fans called this show "The Nesmith Lounge Act." A video of this concert has been floating around ever since, and it remains an embarrassment to the fans, who prefer their hero serious. The fans were hoping that his next shows in Oregon, a month later, would be more dignified. They would be in for a surprise.

There was a panic among the Montieth Riverpark staff in Albany, Oregon as the concerts featuring the Hellecasters and Michael were nearly canceled. The bass guitarist for the group had developed heart problems and had to go to the hospital. The musicians told the park director that would need to cancel the concert, as they would not be able to teach anyone all of the songs in such a short amount of time. Park director Dave Clark refused to cancel the concert saying that there had not been a cancellation in the entire 11 year history of the River Rhythm concert series. Luckily another bassist was found and was able to fill in, as he was accustomed to playing different music each day as a backup artist.

With a healthy band, Michael went ahead and performed at the park in Albany, Oregon, on August 18. The fans were surprised to find that security at the event was not allowing cameras. They said that Michael had insisted on it. The fans were outraged, but a few did sneak in with their cameras and they took photos when no one was looking.

The show began with *Laugh Kills Lonesome*. Michael appeared to be very relaxed on stage as he began to joke around with the audience. He asked the audience to pretend they were in Paris and then he exclaimed, "And my name is Armando, Armando the Newt!" After performing a few songs, Michael talked to the audience again.

He joked that through his life he had written two million songs, even giving examples as "There's Too Much Salt in This Salad" and "Look Out There Goes A Truck." After a few more songs, Michael ended the show by saying, "I am Armando, you are Albany. I love you this much, very big." Fans did not know what to make of Michael.

Some of the fans loved this wacky Michael as opposed to what they called the Michael with the robotic movements (i.e. Chuck E. Cheese). Most of the fans hoped this was just a passing phase Michael was going through, as they were traveling to Hood River, Oregon to see him perform a couple of days later.

The *Albany Democrat-Herald* reported that the park fund-raising collection during the intermission of the Hellecasters/Nesmith show at the Montieth Riverpark was only $550, hitting an all time low. The article also stated that the residents' tax dollars might have to be used if the park were going to continue the concert series. The park director was dumbfounded when trying to find the reason for the low amount. He questioned the number of basket passers and then went on to ask if the audience had liked the music.[91]

The night of the second Oregon concert, the band members took to the stage wearing black shirts with white lettering that said

---

[91] The Albany Democrat Herald, August 19, 1994.

"Armando The Newt." After performing a few songs, Michael started talking to the audience by saying, "I would like you to pretend we are all on ice skates. I have no idea why, but just pretend that this is the Ice Capades and we are brought to you by Disney! And while you are thinking that way, I want you to think about Chinese food. Think of a Lenny Bruce routine with Chinese people in it. And my name is Armando, Armando the Newt!" Michael then proceeded to sing a few songs including *Tanya*, which he forgot some of the words to. After he performed *Cruisin'*, Michael told the audience, "I was thinking of calling myself Drywall and making the sign of the Nautilus, but I don't know what that means!" For the fans it meant disappointment, as this was not the type of performance they had expected to see from Michael Nesmith. They had no idea what had gotten into him, but most of them hoped it would pass.

I Fall To Pieces

It was inevitable that PBS would file a lawsuit in 1994 against Pacific Arts over unpaid royalties. PBS, *The Civil War* producer Ken Burns, The Children's Television Workshop, WGBH, and WNET all combined their lawsuits, which totaled more than $2.3 million. PBS sought $1.4 million and claimed that they had given Pacific Arts the right to use the PBS logo. WGBH claimed to be owed $250,000 from seven *Mystery* and *Masterpiece Theatre* titles. Also claimed was at least $27,269 for an episode of *The American Experience*. WGBH also claimed that Pacific Arts distributed five episodes of *Frontline* and sublicensed seven episodes of *This Old House* without authorization, and that Pacific Arts threatened to release four more episodes. WNET alleged that Pacific Arts failed to pay more than $400,000 for 30 episodes of *Nature*. The Children's Television Workshop (home of Cookie Monster) stated that they expected to receive $250,000 from the royalties from *What Kids Want to Know About Sex and Growing Up* and expected Nesmith to reimburse the CTW for ads placed in periodicals to promote the title. The lawsuits name Michael personally as well as his companies; based on their claim that Michael had made an agreement to issue payment personally to the rights holders if his company was unable to pay. That agreement, PBS claims, was the factor for their decision to work with Pacific Arts. It seemed that a long legal entanglement like this would dominate Michael's time for all of 1995 and 1996.[92]

Tragic news occurred on November 23, 1994, Monkee songwriter Tommy Boyce was ill and getting progressively worse, and not wanting to burden his wife Caroline, got his gun out and shot himself. The news shocked Monkees fans around the world that wanted to understand this tragedy. Michael mentioned Tommy's passing by stating at the end of a post to The Monkees mailing list, "So long Tommy. See you on the other side."

During this time period, Michael continued to demonstrate his uncanny ability to seize upon the cutting edge of the newest technology. Michael started writing a book on the World Wide Web of the Internet. *The Long Sandy Hair of Neftoon Zamora* was a multi-media project where the reader could watch the work being created chapter by chapter, as well as look at photos, maps and a short video clip relating to the story. There were also sound clips explaining how to pronounce such

---

[92] Current, February 20, 1995.

nonsense words as *Ungerret*. The web page became the hot topic of the Internet mailing list and USENET newsgroup of The Monkees, now that the actual band members joined the fans on-line. Micky Dolenz was shown the Internet Web pages and other fan projects by Michael, and signed up for his own account to talk with the fans on-line.

The *Zamora* story deals with Michael's search for a blues singer named Neftoon Zamora in the New Mexico desert. Once Michael finds her, he falls in love with Neftoon even though she is a liar. The book switches back and forth between the story and autobiographical paragraphs in which Michael touches on subjects like his marriages to Phyllis and Kathryn, touring with Jimi Hendrix, his relationship with his mother and the Christian Science religion. Michael had completed six chapters of his on-

All four Monkees meet at the Rhino Records offices before their platinum awards ceremony. Photo by Henry Diltz.

line story before being convinced he could sell it as a traditional book, so the web project remains unfinished.

The Grammy nominations were announced on January 5th, 1995 and to everyone's surprise Nesmith received his first musical Grammy nomination for Best New Age Album for *The Garden*. The announcement came the same day as The Monkees were presented with long overdue platinum albums for *The Monkees, More of The Monkees, Headquarters, Pisces, Aquarius, Capricorn and Jones Ltd.* and *The Birds, The Bees and The Monkees.* The platinum awards came about due to Rhino, a media company that capitalized on the nostalgia market for baby boomer music. Rhino had recently purchased the entire Monkees music catalog, the Monkees logo, and everything else except for the television syndication rights, which were still owned by Sony/Columbia. Platinum awards did not exist in the 60's, and although The Monkees had received many gold records, Rhino was now able to certify that the Monkee records had sold more than one million copies. Rhino hoped the publicity generated by the ceremony would promote the new Rhino CD reissues of all of the Monkee albums, as well as the video release of Head.

The platinum awards ceremony was held in the Hard Rock Café in Beverly Hills, and the press gathered in full force. It was an odd ceremony as Rhino Records President Harold Bronson did almost all of the talking, announcing the plans Rhino had for The Monkees. Micky and Davy said a few words of thanks and Peter joked with the photographers. Michael, who arrived for the ceremony on his motorcycle, stood in the background and didn't say a single word.

Back at Michael's own Rio Records, there was a flurry of small activity. Lewis Storey, a singer/songwriter from Arizona, recorded an album called *Crazy Heart*. He went to Rio Records and was signed to a contract, making him the third act on the Rio Records artist roster. The record was released on February 14, 1995, and Rio Records had planned to send Storey out on a concert tour. Unfortunately, Rio did nothing with Storey and the record sank without a trace, practically unheard by the public, due to the growing litigation problems surrounding Michael and Pacific Arts.

The Grammy Awards were televised on March 1st. The New Age award was not televised live, but it was one of the awards given out earlier in the evening. Paul Winters won the Best New Age award for his album *Prayer For the Wild Things*. Michael didn't even know that he had lost, as he was late to the ceremony, which he attended with Victoria, singer Dwight Yoakam and Yoakam's date, MTV personality Karen Duffy.

The Monkees receiving their platinum records at The Hard Rock Café in Los Angeles, CA. Photo by Brad Waddell.

Michael was pleased that he had at least been recognized for his music, even though he felt out of place in the New Age category. As Michael told a reporter, "When I recorded *The Garden*, I certainly didn't think of it as being

New Age. At a certain point, I guess you really just have to be happy that they're willing to get you on the ballot."

In the way of litigation, Michael filed a countersuit against PBS on February 28, seeking $35 million in damages. Michael alleged in his lawsuit that PBS failed to live up to their promises in their deal with Pacific Arts. He claimed that PBS sold the home video rights of *The Civil War* to Time-Life after Pacific Arts was already distributing the title. Other claims include PBS failing to help sell the tape, as well as PBS developing titles for video release too quickly for Pacific Arts, who found it impossible to raise the capital to pay the producer's royalties as well as buy the rights for new titles.

Michael with his son Jason Nesmith and Jason's mother Nurit Wilde, 1995. By Henry Diltz

Instead of releasing the usual 12-24 titles a year, Pacific Arts was forced to release 143 titles before the label ceased operation during the third year of the agreement. Michael also claimed that PBS required Pacific Arts to pay unreasonably high advances as well as paying producers' royalties for titles that were poor sellers. Michael also claimed that the network realized the situation and agreed to make changes in the deal so Pacific Arts could make payments to the producers. Unfortunately, Michael claims in the suit that the producers were falsely informed by PBS that Pacific Arts would be filing for bankruptcy and with this information the producers withdrew their payment deals.[93]

With *The Garden* finally released and the CD-ROM version put on the backburner permanently, despite three test pressings, and no more projects planned, Michael decided to hold a concert in early March. Rio Records called the event a marketing test for The Hellecasters, who would be opening the show with their full ninety minute set.

Michael announced on The Monkees mailing list on the Internet that tickets were not selling well and that it would probably be a small intimate concert. The fans on the Internet had the best seats in the house, since they were keeping each other informed daily as to when the tickets would go on sale. The other seats on the bottom level were filled with people such as Harold Bronson of Rhino Records, Bobby Sherman, and most of Michael's children.

Michael & his children, from left to right: Christian, Jessica, Michael, Jonathan and Jason, January 5, 1995. Photo by Henry Diltz

The concert overall was a success, as Michael pulled out all the stops to make this concert the finest he has ever given. The show began with an acoustic set with Michael alone on guitar followed by a set with his band, and then finishing up with the Hellecasters joining the band. This was his first show in ages performing with a steel-guitar player other than Red Rhodes, who was ailing. The songs ranged from *Joanne*

---

[93] Current, April 3, 1995.

to *Mama Nantucket* to *Listen To The Band,* which set the crowd screaming. Afterwards Michael signed autographs but left abruptly, reportedly in anger, when he discovered that his son Jason's group Nancy Boy had performed the night before and had not bothered to tell him.

Outside the theater, Michael was trying to pack up his Red Jeep Grand Cherokee, to no avail, when some autograph dealers approached him with several albums for him to sign. It was obvious he was tired and he really didn't want to sign everything they had. After prodding from the dealers to sign more, Michael left for his dressing room to escape the crowd. After a while he came back and signed autographs and tried to pack some more. As always, he signed on his terms, he wouldn't sign too many and then quit signing altogether when he saw that the dealers had shoved two genuine fans to the side so they could get his signatures. Glaring at the dealers, he allowed the two fans to go up and get a few autographs and even posed for photos with them. He does not appear happy in the photos, but at least the fans knew that he cared. After that Michael quit signing and finished packing everything that included gifts ranging from stuffed monkey dolls to a bouquet of flowers designed to appear as the cover of *The Garden,* that the Monkee Internet group had given him. After everything was packed, Michael and his lady Victoria drove off into the night.

Shortly after the Wadsworth concert, Jim Cowan quit his job as the head of Rio Records to work for UNI Distribution. It was the beginning of the end for Rio Records. Soon after that everyone was laid off, from Pacific Arts president George Steele to Michael's personal assistant Christine Giuliano. The only person left was Gretchen White, and one person in the shipping department. Gretchen didn't know what she had done to keep her job while even the president was laid off. Gretchen worked as hard as she could answering the phones and taking care of everything, but it was too much work for one person and Michael fired her, unhappy that she couldn't handle everything. Gretchen was followed by a woman named Wendy who was then dismissed a couple of weeks later. At one point, there were no people answering the phones over at Rio Records.

In August of 1995, Red Rhodes passed away from interstitial lung fibrosis resulting from rheumatoid arthritis. It was a sad time for the Nesmith fans, who respected and admired Red's steel guitar work on almost all of Michael's albums. The news of Red's death had started out as a rumor, with fans e-mailing Michael begging for the truth, but to the surprise of many, Michael would not say a word confirming or denying the passing of his longtime friend.

To help promote The Monkees for Rhino, Michael was asked to appear in a Pizza Hut commercial with his fellow simians. Michael backed out of the project, saying that his daughter Jessica was getting married that same day and that he was to give the bride away. Two weeks before the wedding, Michael reportedly backed out of the wedding, stating that he refused to give Jessica away because he did not believe in marriage. The decision shocked

everyone, further alienating him from his family and especially his daughter. The wedding took place on June 10 with everyone in attendance, except for Michael.

Estrangement from his children was nothing new for Michael. In an interview Michael joked, "Well, every once in a while I get my kids together and I say, 'Lets think of something really twisted and weird we can do. Would you guys like to spend a weekend in a closet? What would you like to do so you could have a book to write? Have you got a pet I could squash with a car on purpose? Just anything. Just horrible and reprehensible." In actuality, the child that he is closest to is Christian who was married once, and has at least two children from different relationships, making Michael the first Monkee to be a grandfather. Jonathan hears from his father only once every couple of months despite the fact that they lived near each other for years.

Photo by Henry Diltz

Hey, Hey, He's a Monkee

Rhino Records had been looking at setting up a big reunion tour of all four Monkees to celebrate the 30th Anniversary of The Monkees in 1996. All four Monkees, including Michael, who was uncharacteristically excited about it, had agreed to it. It was meant to be

the first tour to feature all four Monkees since 1968. After the press had been notified of the upcoming reunion, Michael then announced to the other guys that he just couldn't go on tour because of his future court

The Monkees are presented box sets of The Monkees' TV series on video by Rhino's Harold Bronson, 1995. Photo by Henry Diltz

dates that would more than likely occur during the tour.

The news spread quickly to the fans, who were all disappointed to say the least. Some of the fans understood, but some fans quickly said that Michael had never planned to go on tour, and that he had always intended to back out at the last minute. It was also said that Michael would join the other Monkees when they played Los Angeles, this immediately angered the fans on the East Coast. Later Michael stated that he would not make an appearance at any of the shows. There was no pleasing anyone this time.

To defend himself, Michael made his own statement about his disappearance from the tour via the Internet by stating that he could not go on tour due to his legal problems. He also talked about his possible appearance on a new Monkee record that Rhino was planning.

The 30th Anniversary tour did not revive Monkeemania as everyone had hoped. The cards had been stacked against The Monkees anyway since Columbia Television kept the cost of the syndication rights to The Monkees TV show incredibly high, apparently in retaliation for losing the Monkees copyrights. This insured that no TV station would air the show, which is essential for creating interest in the reunion. The TV Show is always the trigger for any significant Monkee excitement, and the fans and the media were unable to create the same hysteria as there was in 1986.

Michael sold his house in Beverly Hills, preferring to live just on his ranch in Santa Fe, New Mexico, and reportedly sold Pacific Arts Publishing, a very profitable catalog mail order company which sold mostly PBS titles. The closing of all of his many companies coincides with his decision that he is finished with distributing his own products, as he stated in a recent e-mail message. The PBS lawsuit has apparently caused Michael to decide to close down all of his related projects down in order to have less outstanding assets for the lawsuit to target.

Michael is also embarking on a career as an author. St. Martins Press is now publishing his first book, The Long Sandy Hair of Neftoon Zamora. Still enamored with his soundtrack concept, the book will have a CD soundtrack with music designed for the book, however, it will be sold in bookstores as opposed to record stores. He also started working on his second book called *Tiffany, Shooting Her Father's Gun* which has yet to be published.

As for his budding film career as an executive producer, it has stalled indefinitely. Michael had bought the film rights to Douglas Adams' *The Hitchhikers Guide to the Galaxy,* only to have the film delayed by rewrites from Adams as he finished writing a novel. Other delays in the film would have to include Michael's numerous litigation problems. The film is finally being made but Michael is longer involved in the production. KTVT channel 11 in Fort Worth, Texas announced at one time that there were plans for a *Dr. Who* feature film with Michael as executive producer and Steven Spielberg as director but those plans never materialized.

Still, as before, The Monkees were never totally out of the picture for Michael Nesmith. Although Michael had made it clear that he was not going on the tour, the *San Jose Mercury News* reported from old news that he would appear at The Monkees concert at the Reno Hilton on June 19. This misinformation made it necessary for Michael to break his silence about the touring. Using the internet, he stated that he was not going to do any cameos on the tour, he would not do any in-store appearances with the guys, television appearances nor any other related appearances with the other Monkees. On the tour, Micky would tell each different city that he "just got off the phone with Mike" and that Mike was in Nashville "mixing the new record." He told the fans that Mike sends his love and that he did not like touring so "get over it."

210

Even though Michael could not or would not tour with The Monkees, he did work with them on the first new original Monkees album featuring the entire group since 1968. On June 2, 1996, there was a listening party where the four Monkees listened to the final product and were very humble but proud about the project. The four guys played all of the instruments and wrote all of the music on the album titled *Justus*. It seemed that all four guys had finally reconciled their fate as being Monkees forever, and returned to their musical roots, making at least one more full group effort for the fans.

As for being a Monkee for the rest of his life, Michael stated in an interview that, "I realize that if I were ever fortunate to win the Nobel Peace Prize, it will be reported that, 'Monkee Mike Nesmith Won the Nobel Peace Prize.'" In another interview, Michael was quoted as saying, "In my own mind, I've always been a part of that (The Monkees). If I win the Nobel Peace Prize, I'll probably thank David, Micky and Peter. It was a very important and happy time of my life, so I'm comfortable with it in whatever incarnation."

Justus was released in the record stores on October 15, 1996 to mixed reviews, which ranged from a great review from *The Los Angeles Times* to *The Miami Herald* who deemed it, "Justjunk." Fans were disappointed in the promotion that Rhino gave the album. One fan even started a "Campaign for *Justus*" web page on the World Wide Web, which featured phone numbers for radio stations around the country as well as addresses for several talk shows on television such as Rosie O' Donnell and Jay Leno.

The album has some great moments, but the vocals on some of the album tracks appear to be mixed to the background, especially the one song that Michael sings vocal on, a remake of *Circle Sky*. Michael's other song on the album, *Admiral Mike* is an attack at irresponsible journalists, mainly those responsible for the suicide of Admiral "Mike" Jeremy Boorda, who shot himself in 1995 when the press revealed that he was wearing medals that he had not earned. *Admiral Mike* is an angry song that could have used someone with a strong angry voice (i.e. Nesmith) to sing it. It is impossible to take Micky Dolenz seriously when he sings the phrase "You slimy toads."

Micky redeems himself though when he sings his other songs on the album, which were written mostly after a painful divorce in the early '90s. *Regional Girl* is a well crafted rocker about aspiring actors serving food in Hollywood, and *Dyin' Of A Broken Heart* features some exciting Nesmith lead guitar playing. Peter's song *I Believe You* has a slow jazz sound to it, and his other contribution, *Run Away From Life* is sung by Davy and takes, as Michael said, "a Bowie-seque approach." The fans were divided on their opinions of the album. One fan said it best when he said, "Its not your mothers' Monkees anymore."

The Monkees with Brandon Tartikoff backstage at Billboard Live. Photo by Henry Diltz.

When asked why he provided lead vocals for only one song on *Justus*, Michael said, "We decided to stick with doing what we did best as a band. Davy and Micky are our lead vocalists. I was never really the singer in the band. I like Micky's singing and if I had a choice, I would have him sing the songs."

On November 20, The Monkees gave an invitation only concert for loyal fans and the disloyal press in a trendy Los Angeles nightclub, Billboard Live. The upstairs portion of Billboard Live was the VIP section where celebrities such as Dwight Yoakam, Kevin Costner, Little Richard and Brandon Tartikoff could see the show as well as all of Michael's children except for Jason, who was busy with his band, Nancy Boy. The excitement in the club was overwhelming waiting for the first entire concert with all four Monkees in 28 years.

After a wait that seemed an eternity, The Monkees took to the stage to enthusiastic applause and screams. The first song performed of the evening was *Circle Sky*, which sounded as if Michael was purposely trying to drown out his voice with the music. After the song was finished, he put on a pair of sunglasses and a baseball cap that read,

The Monkees perform their first complete reunion concert in 28 years at Billboard Live in Los Angeles, CA. Photo by Brad Waddell.

"Dwight Yoakam's Bakersfield Biscuits," much to the disappointment of the fans who were taking photos. After seven more songs that were performed with great enthusiasm from the entire band, The Monkees left the stage with the crowd wanting more. The Monkees were back; even it was for one night.

There are plans for all four Monkees to tour England and the rest of the world. Some fans are excited while most are taking a "wait and see if Nesmith shows up for even one concert" attitude. They also were planning a one-hour prime-time special for ABC revisiting the Monkees original TV show format with music from the new album. One thing is certain, Michael finally seems happy in his role as a Monkee.

Michael will undoubtedly continue dabbling in multi-media projects, as he is an unstoppable visionary, and he is not afraid of failure because he knows what is required to succeed. Although he could have sat back and retired with his vast fortune, he consistently gambled on new technology experiments that he could learn from and that he hoped his fans would continue to enjoy. As Michael himself wrote to the fans on the Internet, "Thank you all for your kind letters, e-mail, etc. I cannot tell you how much they mean to me, how much I value your support. I am sorry not to answer you all, but time and the volume of mail make it practically impossible. I hope you will take the sentiment of this message to heart and know that there have been times I have continued in my work only because of the tremendous support and encouragement you have given me over the years."

Photo by Craig Sjodin

Hills Of Time: 2005 Update

The Monkees reunion didn't go quite the way it was planned or hoped. Initially, there was some optimism held by Rhino Records, The Monkees, and their fans too, who thought that perhaps MonkeeMania could be revived with the upcoming projects, products and the involvement of Michael Nesmith. The Disney Channel aired a documentary "Hey, Hey We're The Monkees" in January of 1997 that featured lengthy interviews with all four Monkees. To further cash in on the MonkeeMania, Rhino records released a Monkees coffee table book with quotes from the extended interviews, assorted t-shirts, lunchboxes, jigsaw puzzles, greatest hits compilations, pajamas, boxer shorts, director chairs, throw blankets, and a CD-ROM.

Photo by Henry Diltz

A thirty-minute infomercial had been filmed to promote the *Justus* CD, with the plan being to sell the infomercial to TV channels and cable channels across the US, but instead, Rhino released it on home video for the fans. The

Photo by Henry Diltz

'infomercial' contained music videos for some of the songs off of the *Justus* CD as well as several small comedic bits.

The Monkees' made-for-TV special (originally titled "A Lizard Sunning Itself on a Rock" before being changed to the more commercial "Hey, Hey,

It's the Monkees") aired on ABC on February 17, 1997. Filmed with a budget of $1 million dollars, it was written and directed by Michael and featured songs from the *Justus* CD. The fans were mixed in their reactions. Some fans thought it was a weak reunion show that needed a plot and many claimed that the fault was with Michael who, they said, badly needed co-writers on this project as they felt he worked better in a mutual relationship.

Other fans felt it was a nice update with the main premise being that the show was still being produced for the last 29 years, just never aired.

Photo by Henry Diltz

According to the script for this TV movie, the Monkees still were struggling to pay the rent and perform at country clubs but Monkee Mike kept insisting that this episode not have a plot and that the group probably owned that beach house by now. For updating purposes, the Monkeemobile was turned into a low-rider by the ever-mechanical Monkee Mike. Still, whatever critical debate it generated among the fans, the special ranked a disappointing 73 out of 106 shows for that viewing week.

Photo by Henry Diltz

Around this time, Michael was updating the fans on an inconsistent basis on the Internet and one of his messages included this paragraph: "I have agreed to a short Summer American tour after July.

Probably fifteen or twenty dates. No cities have been set. It will probably be a repeat of the show we are putting together for the UK, a forty or fifty minute set of the four of us playing, then a solo section with each one of us taking one number, then an augmented section where we will play as a quartet but with horns and other keys, then a finale. We are experimenting with big screen video; both pre recorded and live, and will bring that as well.[94]

Photo by Henry Diltz

In March of 1997 Michael did go on tour with The Monkees in the United Kingdom. The British press was unkind to The Monkees with headlines such as 'Just Too Old to Monkee Around' and 'Last Train to Nowhere,' and those were the milder headlines. The four Monkees were on several TV shows such as Noel's House Party as well as The Clive James Show promoting the concerts, and Michael would alternately be taciturn and then animated, even joking with the other Monkees. The concerts were successful and had sold out at nearly every venue. Still, there was a dark cloud hanging over The Monkees, despite the adoration of the fans and the booming box office receipts.

One problem with the tour was that Michael was not

Photo by Henry Diltz

socializing with his band mates. As Davy recalled, without bitterness, "I remember when we checked into the hotel in London, he checked out

---

[94] Statement on Internet newsgroup Alt.Music.Monkees, February 8, 1997

the next day. He moved into a 400 pound (US$600) a night hotel. 'It's all about the quality of life' he said. The quality of life comes secondary when you could be around your buddies you ain't seen in 25 years. At least socialize and get to know them a little bit better. We should've known the writing was on the wall at that particular time."[95]

The tour included the four Monkees as well as the regular Monkees touring band. Their opening act was Nancy Boy, which featured Jason Nesmith (who was billed in the tour books as Mike Jason Nesmith Jr.) The Monkees played as a quartet at first, and

Photo by Henry Diltz

then were joined by the touring band later on in the show. Each concert had each Monkee take a solo spot in the show. Michael's song in the beginning of the tour was Laugh Kills Lonesome. During the tour, Jason reportedly informed his father that the audience wasn't reacting well to the song, so it was changed to feature Rio, which was well received by

Déjà vu with Rafelson and Schneider. Photo by Henry Diltz

the fans. The shows had the usual Monkees hits as well as songs from the *Justus* CD. During the brief breaks between the songs, clips from the ABC special were shown that were met with mixed results from the audience, for example references to US figures such as Martha Stewart. Fans noticed a lack of movement from Michael during some of the

---

[95] Monkee Business Fanzine, June 1998

shows this could have been related to Michael reportedly contracting food poisoning during the tour.

The Monkees did go on a US Summer tour in 1997, only they went without Michael Nesmith. After the UK Tour, Michael didn't tell his band mates that his involvement with touring as a Monkee was over. As a result, the other three Monkees only found out about his decision when Michael didn't show up for the rehearsals. The official statement for Michael's absence was that "the producers of the (Monkees) movie have asked me to write the screenplay and I would stay home and do that in order to get the film out." Unfortunately, the truth slowly started emerging that the UK reunion tour had not been as rosy as it had appeared to be.

When asked why Michael wasn't touring. Davy replied, "When you find out, let me know. Actually, I'm still waiting for him to call to tell me he's not doing the US tour. I haven't heard from him since we left England. He never even called! He hasn't called any of us.

Photo by Henry Diltz

Nobody's spoken to him since we left England. He talked to Ward Sylvester, I'm sure, but that's it."

Photo by Henry Diltz

"But he was good at spending our money," Davy continued. "We spent $100,000 to rent Brixton Academy in England for a week to rehearse, and then he spent more money to build a set in the rehearsal hall, a set like the one that would be used onstage on the UK tour, so he could hear how it would sound. We spent a hundred grand learning how to play the songs all over again."[96]

----

[96] Monkee Business Fanzine, June 1998

Davy said, "He's all very self-opinionated, y'know?...He says yes yes yes and agrees with everyone, then goes off and does what he wants to do. You can only put up with that so long. I'll definitely welcome him back into the fold if he wants to come and do a movie and he's got some ideas, but he's got to realize his talents in that department are untried and untested. It's a different thing making an Elephant Parts, making a short or a video for Lionel Richie than it is making a feature."[97]

To another reporter he said, "Mike did 14 stadium shows with us in England. Mike's always been the odd man out. He's limited as a musician and doesn't have that much of his own stuff to perform on stage. Even when we were doing the show, Mike didn't contribute a lot. There could have been a broomstick wearing a wool hat and it would have been as exciting as him. He didn't do much, he really just filled up space on stage. Mike never blew the charts into chaos. He's not what you would call a team player. But he's definitely an interesting character."[98]

Peter said in a 2004 interview, "I don't know how he came to be

Photo by Henry Diltz

this way but the poor boy basically can't work with anybody else. He has learned over the years to allow other people into his orbit, which only means that he is now in control of a larger crew than he ever had before. He didn't want to work with the Monkees anymore. The reason he didn't come back to America with us was that when he joined the operation, he

---

[97] Arizona newspaper Get Out, July 17, 1997
[98] State News, Michigan State University, July 24, 1997

220

made sure it was his way or the highway. But even that wasn't enough for him. I don't think he had enough control."[99]

Micky stated, "I'm a bit disappointed. He (Michael) really hates touring, being out there subjected to the rigors of the road, the unpredictability and the discomfort. As you know, he never toured much by himself as a solo act. He's the type of person who likes to control all aspects, and that's why he writes and makes films. He had a great time on the TV special."[100]

Michael commented on the tour in 1999, "I have lost contact with them since the last time (we toured), which was a couple of years ago. We did some (concert) dates in England, not to my liking, or should I say, not terribly interesting to me. The creative return just wasn't there and I wanted to do other things." Michael said in relation to wondering why older rock and rollers sing the blues, "I've been on stage with people (Davy Jones) dressed up like Elvis impersonators and that's not a lot of fun, so being on stage with people playing the blues I guess is easier."[101]

Despite his saying that he was finished with self-distribution of his projects, Michael created Videoranch.com, a web site where fans could buy his products. One of the first things available was *The Prison* LP box set signed by Michael for $50. He also found some copies of his *Rio* 45 that was also selling for $100 a copy. Also available are his CDs, Videoranch T-shirts and his autograph inside expensive western themed frames. In April 2001, Videoranch offered vintage items from the 'Nesmith Archives' such as sealed copies of the *Infinite Rider* LP at $150, *Live at the Palais* on the defunct 8-track format was offered for $40 as well as copies of one of the Michael Blessing singles for $500.00 each.

Michael had written a full-length motion picture treatment for the Monkees movie, which was in development and had the interest of producers. Michael wrote it with the ideal actors he had in mind for the roles. It involved Jeff Goldblum and Lisa Kudrow in the town of Weekly, which is based on the World Weekly News tabloids. Goldblum has invited the Monkees to perform in the Ramada lounge to give the town credibility. After the show, the Monkeemobile has trouble starting and Goldblum recommends the services of a holistic mechanic who fixes cars by meditation. The Monkees stay in town and see a flying saucer. It is explained to them by Goldblum that there are daily UFO abductions in addition to other odd events, including a woman who is killed by her

---

[99] tcpalm.com interview March 26, 2004
[100] Monkee Business Fanzine June 1997
[101] To Jonathan Brandmeier on his radio show in 1999

fur coat. But the big problem seems to be that Bat Boy is held against his bat-will somewhere in Weekly. The Monkees also meet Elvis Presley who recently moved there just after getting married. While this is happening, Oliver Platt plays a talent manager-producer who is constantly pursuing the Monkees in hope of pitching ideas for a Monkees movie. Rosie O' Donnell plays Platt's former high school sweetheart who shows up after leaving her husband. Platt begins pitching a movie that is a description of this movie. The movie ends with The Monkees saving Bat Boy and everyone is happy at the end.[102]

Michael and his partner in life, Victoria Kennedy. Photo by Henry Diltz

The plans for a Monkee movie ended when Davy refused to sign an option for his services, which would pay him and the other three Monkees for not agreeing to make a Monkee movie for any other producer. Without his commitment to the project, it was cancelled. So, once the producers withdrew their financing, Michael abandoned his last project as a Monkee.[103]

During this time, fans were told of plans for a possible Videoranch Resort that Michael was interested in having built, and this place would be a working piece of art the general public could visit. This, it had been announced, had always been one of his dreams. Michael was serious enough about the idea to go so far as to scout different locations for it, and he had spoken to a management company for hotels.

---

[102] 3 page movie treatment, "The Monkees 'Weekly World News' Movie"
[103] Monkee Business Fanzine September 1998

Some of his ideas included a tropical campfire around a pond where people could have a campfire breakfast, which would resemble the *Laugh Kills Lonesome* painting. Another thought was to have some

New York Book Signing, Photo by Brad Waddell

of the rooms built inside of a canyon hidden from the outside world. Their restaurants were to be called the *Formosa Diner* (from the song on *The Newer Stuff*) and The Littlehorse Diner (from the *Neftoon Zamora* book). Michael had insisted that a drive-in movie theater be a part of the complex. There would be screens throughout the property that would show other places deemed Videoranch worthy. Michael had plans to have the first Videoranch Resort in New Mexico, with future locales in Portofino Italy and Costa Rica.[104] Unfortunately, a Videoranch Resort never materialized.

Michael was spending many hours on the Internet and sharing some limited time with the fans. Videoranch developed a mailing list of special fans they deemed 'A list' members. These fans were placed on a special mailing list for advance information and special sales regarding Videoranch. This new program had a mixed reaction. The fans that got in were extremely happy as they thought they had the inside track on Michael's every move. The fans that were excluded were offended as they were under the impression that only fans that spent money were good enough for Videoranch.

Michael added another feature to the Videoranch site called Active Worlds, which was a 3D

Los Angeles Book Signing, Photo by Pat Smith

[104] Videoranch online chat transcript October 7, 1998

virtual program for PC users. People could go into 'VRanch3D' and adopt an identity and walk around the environment, which had palm trees, swimming pools and sound clips of Michael's music around the various spots. On November 6, 1998, Michael gave a tour of the new place to A-Lister members where he helped people learn the program. Michael even entertained the idea of doing a virtual concert one day in the special world.

The A-Listers group impressed upon Videoranch how much they loved Michael by saying that they wanted an audio book of Michael reading his Neftoon Zamora book. Finally in 2002, the audio book was released and sold only through Videoranch. Both the VRanch3D and the A-List would eventually lose their novelty and would be abandoned.

Michael's novel "The Long Sandy Hair of Neftoon Zamora" was released in November of 1998 from St. Martin's Press. It was released without a previously planned soundtrack CD and also omitted a number of autobiographical references that he had made in the earlier drafts that were on the Internet. Reviews were mixed as Library Journal called it a "...rambling and largely incoherent first novel" while many fans loved it. Videoranch said that Michael was 100% behind doing a book tour and he did keep his word by appearing at two bookstores, the first in Los Angeles and the second in New York where he read excerpts from the book. Fans noticed that Michael was extremely nervous as he had trouble reading without gasping for air. It was in New York where he appeared on the Joan Hamburg radio show where he had casually referred to Victoria as his wife. Fans were speculating if Michael had indeed married again but Michael is still private and has never clarified this. Family members were also divided as some said he was married and others stated that he was not.

The PBS lawsuit case finally went to trial. The files are sealed so little is known except what was released to the press. The trial, which lasted four and a half weeks, ended on February 1, 1999 with the jury awarding Michael $47 million dollars. During the trial, the jury listened to charges that PBS had allegedly defrauded Michael. It

Texas Book Festival, Photo by Brad Waddell

was revealed in the testimony that when Michael wanted to sell off some of the titles to other video companies to alleviate the cash flow problems that Pacific Arts had at the time, PBS promised to work with him. But in fact, PBS was allegedly scheming to take the entire video label away

from Michael's company and sell it to another video company that could handle the large volume of sales, as well as paying the producers on time. Michael appeared on Court TV to discuss the verdict but the interviewer, who introduced him as the 'dreamy Monkee,' was more interested in finding out when he would be rejoining the group. PBS appealed the verdict and the two parties reached an undisclosed settlement on July 7, 1999.

With his newly gained third fortune, Michael bought a house in Carmel, moving Videoranch's headquarters to California, while still retaining his seven-acre New Mexico residence.

April of 1999 found Michael as a judge for the Taos Talking

George Stanchev, Aaron Lohr, Jeff Geddis and L.B. Fisher as The Monkees

Picture Festival. Consisting mainly of short independent films, the grand prize was five acres of land in Taos, New Mexico.

Michael appeared at the Texas Book Festival in Austin, Texas on November 6, 1999. He read an excerpt from *The Long Sandy Hair of*

Neftoon Zamora and he was much more relaxed while reading. Afterwards he conducted a question and answer session with the audience consisting mainly of questions about his past. He then went into the author's area and signed copies of his book and other memorabilia. As of July 2004, this is his last public appearance with his fans.

In June of 2000, the cable channel VH-1 premiered their original made for TV movie *Daydream Believers: The Monkees Story* starring Aaron Lohr as Micky Dolenz, George Stanchev as Davy Jones, L.B. Fisher as Peter Tork and Jeff Geddis as Michael Nesmith. Despite the fictional happy ending of the movie and the various character composites to save time & budget, the fans thought it was well done. Three of the Monkees viewed the movie and liked it. Michael's opinion was not known as Videoranch's statement was "He didn't watch it."

Jeff Geddis did an admirable job trying to fill Michael's wool cap but Peter noticed one thing as mentioned in an interview, "The actor who plays Mike looks like him, but his attitude and manner are very different. You don't get any of Michael's character from that. Michael was very steely-eyed."

Texas Book Festival, Photo by Brad Waddell

The Gihon Foundation hosted its biennial Council on Ideas on the weekend of July 22-23, 2000. Conducted at his New Mexico ranch, Michael invited the press and the event was covered more extensively than ever. Two New Mexico newspapers, Wired magazine and WFAA-TV in Dallas, Texas were among the media that covered the event. It was also the last Council on Ideas event held, as Michael preferred to lay low and work on projects that held his interest.

While Michael was in Carmel, he would listen to a favorite station of his KPIG, known for playing an eclectic mix of music. Michael started promoting their radio station on Videoranch, and the station was once offered for free on the Internet, so the fans around the world could listen. He recorded a Videoranch

226

commercial for broadcast on KPIG and he did a live interview in the studio on August 15, 2000.

For the holiday season of 2000/2001, Michael created a radio station on the Internet web service myplay.com that consisted of holiday music. "And I like the corny stuff," he said at the time. "I play it around my house starting the day after Thanksgiving." His myplay music set-list ranged from Gene Autry and Willie Nelson to Dean Martin and The Beach Boys. He even recorded a holiday greeting that would play when the station started.

In 2002, Michael was on TV again (in the audience) on the 1st American Film Institute award ceremony that aired on the CBS network

in the US. Michael was also shown in interview segments giving comments about the movies *Momento* and *Moulin Rouge*. Michael, a member of AFI's Board of Trustees since 1992, was on its film nominating committee, which would select the films nominated, but he was not on the jury of voters. However, the ratings for this awards show were not favorable so the future ceremonies would be conducted as unaired private ceremonies.

Photo from the American Film Institute

Michael started working on 'Rays', his latest CD, but he was undecided as to the path his music would go. He was reportedly finished with the work, but at odds with the distributor as of this writing as to whether it would be released as a standard music CD, as a download-only album, or both.

During the interviews he gave regarding the PBS verdict, he stated several times that he had written a screenplay called *Fried Pies*, a musical about 'going out to dinner;' which he wanted to direct and he hoped would be filmed soon. There was a 'Nez part' in the movie, but Michael's agent was trying to cast someone younger in the part.[105]

Michael was asked about his second novel project, *The America Gene* and said, "The germ of the idea came from "Zamora," where (the character) Nez realizes that he's been trying to avoid his own personal Las Vegas and that the life of all Americans comes with a potential arc from Tupelo, Mississippi to Las Vegas, Nevada, and that Elvis lived it out. So the book that I'm writing now is called *The America Gene*. It's a

---

[105] Videoranch employee 'Slim' from Videoranch chat transcript December 16, 1998

story about a man who is very successful, makes an attempt to avoid his own personal Las Vegas as he finds the gene awakening in him and pushing him into wearing stranger clothes and doing weirder things."[106]

Always eager to try new things, Michael was among the first artists to offer his music for downloading on the Internet for a fee. Videoranch offered all of his commercial recordings and two previously unreleased tracks from the *Infinite Rider* sessions: *Rollin'* and *Walkin' in the Sand,* as well as a few tracks from a concert from the late 70s.[107] He also was among the first artists to license all of his music to be downloadable through the new legal music downloading sites.

Photo by Henry Diltz.

Throughout his career Michael has seemed to cherish opportunities to produce music and images filtered through his personal creative viewpoints. In many cases, these projects have proven to redefine imaginative concepts as well as push ideas that were genuinely ahead of their time. Michael is a performer who respects input from his fans, but ultimately, he makes the decisions about which paths he chooses to follow and he now has the luxury of pursuing them without being subject to financial pressures generated by corporate demands. Michael Nesmith continues to be a songwriter and author whose energies still fascinate his devoted fans.

---

[106] Los Angeles Times, May 24, 1999
[107] Erroneously identified as a 1981 concert.

Appendix 1: 2005 Monkees Update

The Monkees went on their 1997 summer tour without Michael and filled the seats with the diehard fans that had always been loyal. The absence of Michael Nesmith had kept the curiosity seekers home and while The Monkees performed admirably as always, they had saturated the market for their show and were not getting as many bookings as they needed to sustain a touring career. So for the good of the group, they quit touring as The Monkees and went solo for a while. Davy announced to Billboard magazine in 1998 that The Monkees were 'over for now.' He added that if there would be any future reunion tours, 'It will be the four of us or nothing.' He went further to tell Monkee Business Fanzine, "I really don't want to work with those guys, not after what Peter and Micky did in regard to having Mike take over the operation. Ward Sylvester is still talking that in the year 2000 (The Monkees) will be out there. Peter Tork will be 58 years old then! You only get so many chances, and I think that was our chance."

Davy signed on to tour with Peter Noone from Herman's Hermits and Bobby Sherman,

Davy, Peter Noone and Bobby Sherman on the Teen Idols Tour.

another of Ward Sylvester's clients. The tour was billed as the Teen Idols Tour and the surprise highlight was Sherman who hadn't toured in decades. Davy wasn't the star of the show and it was starting to show in his performances. One of the things noticeable to the fans was that Sherman would sign autographs while he was performing while Davy would either ignore the fans at the stage edge with items to sign or state during the show into the microphone, "This isn't the Bobby Sherman show."

Davy promoted the tour the best to his ability except for when he cancelled an appearance on the morning program *The View* when they wanted him to sing *Daydream Believer* rather than one of his own compositions. Wanting a new career path, Davy told the *Los Angeles*

Times, "I have escaped the Monkees somewhat at this point, and hopefully forever. I have nothing to prove at this point, but everything to gain by being out there on the chance some smart young director might see me differently and change my life again."

Peter toured with his new group Shoe Suede Blues and seemed happier than ever. He also toured with his friend James Lee Stanley. Peter also found time to appear in two episodes of the TV series *Seventh Heaven* and one episode of *The King of Queens*.

At the same time, Micky was trying to boost his directing career rather than rest on his drum set by directing an episode of *Boy Meets World*. Micky was also performing on cruise ships singing old rock and roll songs rather than an all-Monkees repertoire. Micky was a guest star of the TV pilot his ex-wife Samantha Dolenz produced called *Who's For Dinner*.

Wanting to give his fans more than just Monkees songs, Davy left the Teen Idols Tour. He claimed that he felt pressure to remove his original material from the tour so he left. Immediately Ward Sylvester called in a replacement

Micky, Peter Noone and Bobby Sherman on the Teen Idols Tour.

teen idol by the name of Micky Dolenz, who had no trouble singing only Monkees hits. In case of any scheduling conflicts Micky may have had due to his directing career, the tour producers had Peter Tork on standby.

Because of the expanded choices of channels on cable TV as well as the insatiable need for pop culture shows, The Monkees' story was told several times on television. In 1998 *E! Entertainment Television* aired the Monkees' *True Hollywood Story* with interviews from Davy Jones, Peter Tork, Micky Dolenz and several others. Davy's first wife Linda Haines Jones and Micky's first wife Samantha Dolenz were interviewed and reportedly these women had asked Phyllis Nesmith to grant an interview as they had all stayed friendly throughout the years, but Phyllis refused. Michael Nesmith was the first Monkee to agree to be interviewed but the PBS judgment was in the process of resolution, and Videoranch turned down all interview requests for a time. The pitch given to some of the interviewees was that this was the story of how Michael Nesmith "destroyed the Monkees and how he tried to have total control over the entire project only to toss them aside when their purpose was served." One wonders if Michael received a different pitch to the project.

While E! was preparing their version of the Monkees story, VH-1 was working on an episode of *Behind the Music* that would tell The Monkees tale while focusing on their battle for music control. For the show, VH-1 was able to secure new interviews with Micky and Peter but had to use interview footage of Michael and Davy from the Disney documentary from a few years earlier. VH-1 also aired *Daydream Believers*, a movie featuring young unknown actors playing The Monkees. Due to this flood of Monkee business, interest started building regarding the current careers of The Monkees.

Davy spent his time touring as a solo act and trying to find the right path for his career to go on. He bought an old church in Beavertown, Pennsylvania in the hopes of turning it into a museum to house his incredible collection of career memorabilia as well as a rehearsal studio. He also released an updated version of his autobiography, which was filled with many more stories and a great number of additional photographs. As if he wasn't busy enough touring and promoting his book, he was taking care of horses at a stable in Beavertown with intent to race them or train them for others to ride. In addition, he hired David Fishof as his personal manager. This struck many older Monkees fans as surprising as Fishof, who had orchestrated the Monkees 1986 comeback, also had sued the Monkees back in the 80s for alleged monies owed to him.

With Fishof back in control, Davy and the other Monkees went on tour in early 2001 as a test to see if they should tour in the summer. Why? Peter told the *Chicago Sun-Times*, "They made me an offer I couldn't refuse." Davy said in a different interview that, "We're masters of this. We've done it so many times. We just have to show up sober. That's our only rule. Other than that, it's like a boys' holiday out. We'll do it again. We'll probably do it a hundred more times, too, before we die."

Fishof's involvement got them into the recording studio of Lou Pearlman, the manager who handled several boy-bands including the Backstreet Boys and 'N Sync. Joining the Monkees on their tour would be an up and coming boy band managed by Pearlman called Natural. Davy, Micky and Peter agreed to cut remakes of three Monkees hits that were recorded for Pearlman's label but the songs were never released.

231

Fishof also got the Monkees photographed for Vanity Fair magazine; unfortunately the photos and the accompanying article were never run due to a change in personnel at the magazine.

The 2001 summer tour was well received by fans and mixed reviews from the critics who loved to bash the Monkees for no good reason. This tour was different as there was more of an emphasis on comedy. As Micky explained to Monkee Business Fanzine, "Other tours where we didn't have comedy, that was probably because we weren't getting along. It's tough to do comedy when you're not getting along."

Everything looked good for the Monkees, as there was a projected UK tour for October of 2001. Peter then lowered the boom and gave notice in July that he would not be accompanying the other Monkees overseas. He was happy to finish the current US tour but, according to Peter who gave his reasons to Monkee Business Fanzine, Davy broke a pre-tour agreement by speaking abusively. It was suggested that Davy spoke rudely to both Peter and to Peter's driver, but as Peter said specifically, "I've become more protective of my serenity lately, and I wasn't finding much of it on the road on this tour. Davy's reaction was to say, "I'm flabbergasted." Micky's reaction was to harshly say, "Once a quitter, always a quitter" forgetting that he himself had quit from the Monkees back in the early 1990s.

The Monkees 2001 Tour Photo.

Fishof had scheduled one of the final concerts of the tour to be filmed for a DVD release. The concert in Anaheim, California, would be the final concert of the three Monkees. As soon as the contracts were signed and all T's were crossed and I's dotted, Peter was fired from the group. Even though there were two other US shows on the summer tour, Peter was told not to show up, as Micky & Davy didn't want him on stage and issued the ultimatum that if he showed up, they wouldn't perform.

The UK tour was rescheduled for March of the next year due to the September 11 attacks. Micky & Davy did tour the US in the Spring & Summer of 2002 as "The Stars of The Monkees Show featuring Micky Dolenz and Davy Jones." The show was originally to also include The Osmonds and Barry Williams, but The Osmonds dropped out, and then Williams appeared for only a few dates. The Monkees would break up again. Before 2002 ended, Micky got married to his longtime girlfriend Donna Quinter on September 20, 2002.

Micky went on the road in 2003 as Zoser in Aida. He would travel around the country performing the role before winding up in the Broadway version of Aida. Micky was so happy with big city life that in December of 2004 he accepted a job as a morning drive-time DJ on oldies radio station WCBS in New Jersey. Peter continues touring with either James Lee Stanley or Shoe Suede Blues. Davy performs around the country but he devotes most of his time to his horses, for as he said in concert recently that he performs 'to support my horse habit.'

Appendix 2: Michael Comments on 9/11

In the aftermath of the terror attacks of September 11, 2001, we had the tools of the Internet to learn within 24 hours that all of The Monkees were safe in California. Michael rarely comments on news events, but in this one case he did post the following item to his web site just a few days after the event.

September 11, 2001

Darkness.
Oh darkness.
Do not tread on me!
I am light and I will destroy you instantly and forever.
I have seen your face before, and you are nothing.
Do not come near my window or door.
Do not come near my heart.
I am intelligence, the light of Mind.
I am spirit, the light of Truth.
I am love, the light of Life.
Do not suppose you can withstand my gaze.
I live forever, even as you die.
Your deluded and perverted notions of afterlife, and martyrdom, suicide
     as sacrifice, obtain not here.
Here you die in vain, useless.
My brothers and sisters, children, wives and husbands, my family of
     mankind live on in spite of your terror, of your dream of death,
     for we live in Spirit and in Truth, while you, oh darkness, are
     never more than darkness.
I will shine into the farthest reach of life.
I will vanquish you to non existence, obliterate you by my righteous
     might.
Do you think to frighten me?
Do you think to kill me?
Think again, oh darkness.
For I am light.
In my light all are comforted.
In my light all can see.
By my light, darkness shall perish, so that all may live.

Appendix 3: The Prison Story

During one of Nesmith's concerts he attempted to describe to the audience the multi-layered story of *The Prison*:

"*The Prison* begins with the song *Life, the Unsuspecting Captive*. It is during that song that Jason the protagonist is introduced to you inside a prison that is just dark, cold and yuck. He is in there with a very strange assortment of inmates, in that the men and women are in there together, so that they are able to share some kind of love, but it's mostly a physical love that is not very deep. Prison life is prison life as it's generally keeping most of these inmates who would seek happiness locked into some shallow sense of mirth instead of real joy.

"One day Jason finds a hole in the west wall big enough for him to walk through and he asks his lady friend Marie, 'What is all of this?' She says, 'Oh, don't go through there. You go through there, you will never come back,' and he says, 'Well, I thought that was the point.' She says, 'No, you don't understand. If you go through there, you won't come back, because it's a trap designed to eliminate troublemakers.' And Jason says, 'Well, um, do you know what's out there?' She says, 'No, some people know what's out there but it's mostly just banana city. Everybody who has gone through and has come back is a squirrel by now and you can't even talk to them.' Jason goes to talk to one of them asking about going through and the guy says, 'Don't do it man whatever you do. It's crazeola. Crazeola weirdness.'

"So Jason, thinking about this odd reaction, says to himself in one of his introspective moments, 'Well, it seems to me that nobody in the prison is going to be able to describe accurately to me the nature of freedom, so what I'm gonna do is I'm gonna go through the hole in the wall, and I'll see you later, Marie, and thanks for the warning.'

"Well, he goes through the hole in the wall and he is immediately surrounded by darkness and mist, and, because it is so completely overwhelming to him, he loses his way and cannot find his way anywhere, even back to the prison, which looms now as a very secure haven to him, because it appears that the only thing that is on the outside of the prison walls is a very terrible and difficult state in which we exist. Now during this time there is a tune playing in the background called *Dance Between the Raindrops* and this takes place as Jason discovers a light dawning, as it's the morning coming on, and he finds a place where he can go lay down, because he has spent the night more or less standing in one spot frozen with fear. This song ends by the time it is full morning.

235

"The sun finally wakes Jason up, cause it's midday and it's kinda bright and he gets up and looks out at the day and he realizes that he's in paradise. Now I don't know what paradise is, I mean that was a very hard place to come to. Paradise, I mean, it goes all the way from hanging out at the sea shore to going to Las Vegas, I mean who knows what paradise is. It is mawkish and garish to some people, and it's sublime states of consciousness to others, and it goes on, but the place that Jason is in is paradise, it's a given.

"He meets a guy there named Tom who begins to explain to Jason what he's done by coming through the prison walls is move beyond the barriers of time and space, to which Jason replies, 'Did I die?' I mean, it's logical right? Beyond time and space, death instantly. 'No, no,' Tom says. 'You didn't die, it's just that you've begun to develop a larger sense of understanding things beyond finite bits of conceptual reasoning.' 'Far out,' Jason exclaims. Tom says, 'Yeah, you see because you're reasoning right now in little conceptual models made up of the tiniest little finite particles, and it doesn't make any difference how far you reason with these finite particles, they are finite particles.' Jason says, 'What does that have to do with anything?' Tom says, 'Because you have been logically drawing the conclusion that time stretches to eternity.' 'But how can it if it's finite?' asks Jason. 'It doesn't. Eternity encloses time. You've been believing that all of this stuff that you live in the middle of stretches on infinitely beyond the stars. But how can it? It's all finite. It's very clear it goes from there to there, it starts and stops. What you've begun to do is nibble a little bit at the edge of the infinite and the eternal,' answers Tom. Jason says, 'I'm hungry.' Tom says, 'Yeah, naturally. C'mon, I'll get you something to eat.'

"So they go back and Tom begins to explain some more things, and Jason meets Tom's old lady there named Janey, and he says, 'Well, I'd like to go back and see the prison.' So Tom says, 'Yeah, sure, come on back I think you will be surprised.' They go back to the prison and outside of the prison it's very extraordinary, because there are all of the beds lined up in the middle of the rows, and there's the kitchen table off to one side, and there's the solitary confinement cells with the men standing six feet apart from each other, but they are separated by absolutely nothing, because there are no walls. Tom says, 'You see, man, outside the prison there is no prison. It's on the inside that it looks like a prison.' Jason says, 'That's the greatest piece of information that I've ever had in my life. I'm gonna go get Marie quick and bring her out here.' So Tom says, 'O.K. go ahead if you want to.'

"Jason runs in to the prison and says, 'Hey Marie, you're free. C'mon with me.' She says, 'O.K. great I'm free, I don't have a clue what you're talking about, but I love you I will follow you anywhere. That's my role as a woman. You're the man and I'm the woman, whatever you do I will do, even if it's dumb.' Jason says, 'Well, I don't know that I like that. Come out with me because the minute you're outside you will instantly see that it's all these beautiful wonderful things that's happening. I've found paradise out there.' Marie says, 'Yeah, O.K. I mean eight paces to the left and behind that's me and I'll just do that thing.' She follows Jason outside, and Jason says, 'Well, you see?' Marie says, 'Uh uh.' Jason says, 'What?' She says, 'I don't see what you're talking about.' He says, 'No prison dummy, look no prison see? Outside there is no prison and inside looks like a prison, it makes perfect sense right?' Marie says, 'I still see a prison.' And Jason is not figuring on this, and at that point Marie and Jason part ways and she goes back into the prison and sits down behind one of the nonexistent walls and cries and cries, and Jason remarks to his own self, 'Isn't it a tragedy?,' but he feels no remorse for some strange reason.

"Jason goes back to the cabin and he sees Tom waiting there and Tom says, 'I'm glad you worked through the thing with Marie, because I knew she wouldn't come, and it's good you saw past that because now you're beginning to catch on to a different state of love, getting on past subject-object love, where you don't have to have love that you do to somebody. Love is a state of consciousness, a place where you are. That's the meaning of the phrase 'being in love,' it's like being in a sea or being in a pool of love, and you don't have to have all these, you know, you thought Marie turned you on to that place, but you don't now, right?' Jason says, 'Well, I don't know that I understand totally what you're talking about, but it sounds, you know, pretty cosmic. I don't know, yeah, whatever.'

"Tom then says, 'Well, then, good because I'm splitting, and you're now the new guide.' Jason says, 'Hold everything! I'm not ready to be anybody's guide, I mean, I just got here!' Tom says, 'No you're understanding everything that needs to be understood, man. You're thinking, aren't you?' Jason says, 'Yeah, but what does that have to do with anything?' Tom says, 'Every answer you need is always there, always arising in your own consciousness, and try to look at that.' Jason says, 'Well, when will I understand what you're saying to me?' Tom says, 'Well, that's a funny thing, you know we were talking about the infinite and infinity? One of the interesting things about infinity is that it's beyond time. You believe now that growth occurs through time, however, as you grow to the little understanding of the infinite, one of the first things you will see is that you have been there all along. It's just like the prison, you were free all the time you just didn't know it.' Tom at this point splits, and Jason turns and goes inside."

Appendix 4: Michael Nesmith as Musician

Singles

as Mike Nesmith

Highness	HN-13	Wanderin/Well, Well	1963
Edan	1001	Just A Little Love/Curson Terrace	1965

w/ Mike, John &Bill

Omnibus	239	How Can You Kiss Me/Just A Little Love	1965

as Michael Blessing

Colpix	CP-787	The New Recruit/A Journey With Michael Blessing	1965
Colpix	CP-792	Until It's Time For You To Go/What Seems To Be The Trouble Officer ?	1965

w/ The Monkees

Colgems	66-1001	Last Train to Clarksville/Take a Giant Step	1966
Colgems	66-1002	I'm a Believer/(I'm Not Your) Steppin' Stone	1966
Colgems	66-1004	A Little Bit Me, A Little Bit You/Girl I Knew Somewhere	1967
Colgems	66-1007	Pleasant Valley Sunday/Words	1967
Colgems	66-1012	Daydream Believer/Goin' Down	1967
Colgems	66-1019	Valleri/Tapioca Tundra	1968
Colgems	66-1023	D.W. Washburn/It's Nice to Be With You	1968
Colgems	66-1031	Porpoise Song/As We Go Along	1968
Colgems	66-5000	Tear Drop City/A Man Without A Dream	1969
Colgems	66-5004	Listen to the Band/Someday Man	1969
Colgems	66-5005	Good Clean Fun/Mommy and Daddy	1969

w/ The Wichita Train Whistle

Dot	17152	Don't Cry Now/Tapioca Tundra	1968

as Michael

238

Nesmith and The
First National
Band

RCA	47-9853	Little Red Rider/Rose City Chimes	1970
RCA	74-0368	Joanne/One Rose	1970
RCA	74-0399	Silver Moon/Lady Of the Valley	1970
RCA	74-0453	Nevada Fighter/Here I Am	1971
RCA	74-0540	I've Just Begun To Care(Propinquity)/Only Bound	1971
RCA	45-263	Texas Morning/Tumbling Tumbleweeds	1971

as Michael
Nesmith and The
Second National
Band

RCA	74-0629	Mama Rocker/Lazy Lady	1972

as Michael
Nesmith

RCA	74-8004	Roll With The Flow/Keep On	1973
RCA	447-0868	Joanne/Silver Moon (reissue)	1975
Pacific Arts	WIP 6373	Rio/Life, The Unsuspecting Captive	1976
Pacific Arts	SIP 6398	Navajo Trail/Love's First Kiss	1976
Pacific Arts	PAC-101	Roll With The Flow/I've Just Begun To Care	1978
Pacific Arts	PAC-104	Rio/Casablanca Moonlight	1979
Pacific Arts	PAC-106	Magic/Dance	1979
Pacific Arts	PAC-108	Cruisin'/Horserace	1979

Albums and Compact Discs (Reissues are included)

w/ The Monkees
*= Nesmith tracks (either sung by or written by)
**only on reissue

Colgems	COS-101	The Monkees	1966
Colgems	COM-101	The Monkees	1966
Rhino	R2-71790	The Monkees	1994

(Theme From) The Monkees
Saturday's Child
I Wanna Be Free
Tomorrow's Gonna Be Another Day
Papa Gene's Blues *
Take a Giant Step
Last Train to Clarksville
This Just Doesn't Seem to be My Day
Let's Dance on
I'll Be True to You
Sweet Young Thing *
Gonna Buy Me a Dog
I Can't Get Her Off My Mind **
I Don't Think You Know Me **
(Theme From) The Monkees **

Colgems	COS-102	More of the Monkees	1967
Colgems	COM-102	More of the Monkees	1967
Rhino	R2-71791	More of the Monkees	1994

She
When Love Comes Knockin' (At Your Door)
Mary, Mary *
Hold On Girl
Your Auntie Grizelda
(I'm Not Your) Steppin' Stone
Look Out (Here Comes Tomorrow)
The Kind of Girl I Could Love *
The Day We Fall in Love
Sometime in the Morning
Laugh
I'm a Believer
Don't Listen to Linda **
I'll Spend My Life with You **
I Don't Think You Know Me **
Look Out (Here Comes Tomorrow) **
I'm a Believer **

Colgems	COS-103	Headquarters	1967
Colgems	COM-103	Headquarters	1967
Rhino	R2-71792	Headquarters	1995

You Told Me *
I'll Spend My Life with You
Forget That Girl
Band 6 *
You Just May Be the One *
Shades of Gray
I Can't Get Her Off My Mind
For Pete's Sake
Mr. Webster
Sunny Girlfriend *
Zilch *
No Time
Early Morning Blues and Greens
Randy Scouse Git
All of You Toys **
The Girl I Knew Somewhere * **
Peter Gunn's Gun **
Jericho **
Nine Times Blue * **
Pillow Time **

Colgems	COS-104	Pisces, Aquarius, Capricorn and Jones Ltd.	1967
Colgems	COM-104	Pisces, Aquarius, Capricorn and Jones Ltd.	1967
Rhino	R2-71793	Pisces, Aquarius, Capricorn and Jones Ltd.	1995

Salesman *
She Hangs Out
The Door Into Summer *
Love Is Only Sleeping *
Cuddly Toy
Words
Hard to Believe

240

What Am I Doin' Hangin' 'Round? *
Peter Percival Patterson's Pet Pig Porky
Pleasant Valley Sunday
Daily Nightly *
Don't Call on Me *
Star Collector
Special Announcement **
Goin' Down * **
Salesman * **
The Door Into Summer * **
Love is Only Sleeping * **
Daily Nightly * **
Star Collector **

Colgems	COS-105 The Birds, The Bees and The Monkees	1968
Colgems	COM-105 The Birds, The Bees and The Monkees	1968
Rhino	R2-71794 The Birds, The Bees and The Monkees	1994

Dream World
Auntie's Municipal Court *
We Were Made For Each Other
Tapioca Tundra *
Daydream Believer
Writing Wrongs *
I'll Be Back Up On My Feet
The Poster
P.O. Box 9847
Magnolia Simms *
Valleri
Zor and Zam
Alvin **
I'm Gonna Try **
P.O. Box 9847 **
The Girl I Left Behind Me **

Colgems	COS-5008 Head (soundtrack)	1968
Rhino	R2-71795 Head (soundtrack)	1994

Opening Ceremony
Porpoise Song (Theme From "Head")
Ditty Diego- War Chant *
Circle Sky *
Supplicio
Can You Dig It
Gravy
Superstitious
As We Go Along
Dandruff?
Daddy's Song
Poll
Long Title: Do I Have to Do This All Over Again?
Swami- Plus Strings
Ditty Diego- War Chant * **
Circle Sky * **
Happy Birthday to You **
Can You Dig It **
Daddy's Song * **
Head Radio Spot **

Colgems	COS-113 Instant Replay	1969
Rhino	R2-71796 Instant Replay	1995

Through the Looking Glass
Don't Listen to Linda
I Won't Be the Same Without Her *
Just a Game
Me Without You
Don't Wait for Me *
You and I
While I Cry *
Tear Drop City
The Girl I Left Behind Me
A Man Without a Dream
Shorty Blackwell
Someday Man **
Carlisle Wheeling * **
Rosemarie **
Smile **
St. Matthew * **
Me Without You **
Through the Looking Glass **

Colgems	COS-117 The Monkees Present	1969
Rhino	R2-71797 The Monkees Present	1994

Little Girl
Good Clean Fun *
If I Knew
Bye Bye Baby Bye Bye
Never Tell a Woman Yes *
Looking for the Good Times
Ladies Aid Society
Listen to the Band *
French Song
Mommy and Daddy
Oklahoma Backroom Dancer *
Pillow Time
Calico Girlfriend Samba * **
The Good Earth **
Listen to the Band * **
Mommy and Daddy **
The Monkees Present Radio Promo **

Rhino	RNLP 70139 Live 1967	1987
Rhino	RNCD 70139 Live 1967	1987

Last Train to Clarksville
You Just May Be the One *
The Girl I Knew Somewhere *
I Wanna Be Free
Sunny Girlfriend *
Your Auntie Grizelda
Forget that Girl
Sweet Young Thing *
Mary, Mary *
Cripple Creek
You Can't Judge a Book By Looking at the Cover *

242

Gonna Build a Mountain
I Got a Woman
I'm a Believer
Randy Scouse Git
(I'm Not You) Steppin' Stone

Rhino	RNLP 70150 Missing Links	1987
Rhino	R2 70150 Missing Links	1987

Apples, Peaches, Bananas and Pears
If You Have the Time
I Don't Think You Know Me *
Party
Carlisle Wheeling *
Storybook of You
Rosemarie
My Share of the Sidewalk *
All of Your Toys
Nine Times Blue *
So Goes Love
Teeny Tiny Gnome
Of You *
War Games
Lady's Baby
Time and Time Again

Rhino	R2 70903 Missing Links Volume Two	1990

All the King's Horses *
Valleri
St. Matthew *
Words
Some of Shelly's Blues *
I Wanna Be Free
If I Ever Get to Saginaw Again *
Come On In
I'll Be Back Up On My Feet
Michigan Blackhawk *
Hold On Girl
The Crippled Lion *
Changes
Mr. Webster
You Just May Be the One *
Do Not Ask for Love
Circle Sky *
Seeger's Theme
Riu Chiu

Rhino	R2 72153 Missing Links Volume Three	1996

(Theme From) The Monkees (TV Version)
Kellogg's Jingle
We'll Be Back in a Minute
Through the Looking Glass
Propinquity *
Penny Music
Tear the Top Right Off My Head
Little Red Rider *
You're So Good

243

Look Down
Hollywood *
Midnight Train
She Hangs Out
Shake 'Em Up
Circle Sky *
Steam Engine
Love to Love
She'll Be There
How Insensitive *
Merry Go Round
Angel Band *
Zor and Zam
We'll Be Back in a Minute
Tema Dei Monkees

Rhino   R2 72542 Justus   1996
Circle Sky *
Never Enough
Oh, What a Night
You and I
Unlucky Stars
Admiral Mike *
Dyin' of a Broken Heart
Regional Girl
Run Away From Life
I Believe You
It's My Life
It's Not Too Late

Rhino Handmade RHM2 7715 Headquarters Sessions   2000
3 disc history of the making of The Monkees' third album. Instead of listing
each of the 84 tracks, listed are the ones involving Michael's vocals.
Nine Times Blue - demo vocal
Until It's Time for You to Go - demo vocal
Sunny Girlfriend - acoustic remix of master vocal
Sunny Girlfriend - tracking session take 7 with scratch vocal
You Told Me - take 15 with rough lead vocal
Zilch - Mike Nesmith vocal track
The Girl I Knew Somewhere - (first version) mono master
You Just May Be the One - mono master
Sunny Girlfriend - mono master
You Told Me - mono master

Rhino Handmade RHM2 7755 The Monkees Summer 1967   2001
4 disc set of 4 concerts from the 1967 Monkees tour.
Introduction
Last Train to Clarksville
You Just May Be the One *
The Girl I Knew Somewhere *
I Wanna Be Free
Sunny Girlfriend *
Your Auntie Grizelda
Forget That Girl
Sweet Young Thing
Mary, Mary *

244

Cripple Creek
You Can't Judge a Book By the Cover *
Gonna Build a Mountain
I Got a Woman
I'm a Believer
Randy Scouse Git
(I'm Not Your) Steppin' Stone

w/ The Wichita Train Whistle

Dot	DLP 25861 The Wichita Train Whistle Sings	1968
Pacific Arts PACB 7-113 The Wichita Train Whistle Sings		1978
Videoranch CD release (no number given)		2001

For musicians-- see separate appendix

Nine Times Blue
Carlisle Wheeling
Tapioca Tundra
Don't Call On Me
Don't Cry Now
While I Cried
Papa Gene's Blues
You Just May Be the One
Sweet Young Thing
You Told Me

as Michael Nesmith and The First National Band

RCA	LSP-4371 Magnetic South	1970
Awareness AWCD 1023 Magnetic South		1991

Michael Nesmith: Guitar & vocals
O.J. "Red" Rhodes: Pedal steel guitar
John Ware: Drums
John London: Bass
Earl P. Ball: Piano

Calico Girlfriend
Nine Times Blue
Little Red Rider
The Crippled Lion
Joanne
The First National Rag
Mama Nantucket
Keys to the Car
Hollywood
One Rose
Beyond the Blue Horizon

RCA	LSP-4415 Loose Salute	1970
Awareness AWCD 1024 Loose Salute		1991

Michael Nesmith: Guitar & vocals
O.J. "Red" Rhodes: Pedal steel guitar
John Ware: Drums
John London: Bass
Glen D. Hardin: Piano

Silver Moon
I Fall to Pieces

Thanx for the Ride
Dedicated Friend
Conversations
Tengo Amore
Listen to the Band
Bye, Bye, Bye
Lady of the Valley
Hello Lady

RCA	LSP-4497 Nevada Fighter	1971
Awareness	AWCD 1025 Nevada Fighter	1991

Michael Nesmith: Guitar & vocals
James Burton: Guitar
Al Casey: Guitar
O.J. "Red" Rhodes: Pedal steel guitar
John Ware: Drums
John London: Bass
Joe Osborne: Bass
Max Bennet: Bass
Glen D. Hardin:Piano
Michael Cohen: Piano

Grand Ennui
Propinquity (I've Just Begun to Care)
Here I Am
Only Bound
Nevada Fighter
Texas Morning
Tumbling Tumbleweeds
I Looked Away
Rainmaker
Rene

Pacific Arts Aud. PAAD2 5066 Complete	1993

Compilation of First National Band albums

as Michael Nesmith and The Second National Band

RCA	LSP-4563 Tantamount To Treason, Vol.1	1972
Awareness	AWCD 1026 Tantamount To Treason, Vol.1	1991

Michael Nesmith: Guitar & vocals
O.J. "Red" Rhodes: Pedal steel guitar
Michael Cohen: piano & moog synthesizer
Jack Ranelli: Drums
Johnny Meeks: Bass
Jose Feliciano: Congas

Mama Rocker
Lazy Lady
You Are My One
In the Afternoon
Highway 99 with Melange
Wax Minute
Bonaparte's Retreat
Talking to the Wall
She Thinks I Still Care

as Michael Nesmith

RCA	LSP-4695 And The Hits Just Keep On Comin'	1972
Pacific Arts PAC 7-116 And The Hits Just Keep On Comin'		1978
Awareness AWCD 1027 And The Hits Just Keep On Comin'		1991
Rio Records RIOD 2014 And The Hits Just Keep On Comin'		1995

       Michael Nesmith: Guitar & vocals
       O.J. "Red" Rhodes: Pedal steel guitar

       Tomorrow & Me
       The Upside of Goodbye
       Lady Love
       Listening
       Two Different Roads
       The Candidate
       Different Drum
       Harmony Constant
       Keep On
       Roll With the Flow

RCA	APL1-0164 Pretty Much Your Standard Ranch Stash	1973
Pacific Arts PAC 7-117 Pretty Much Your Standard Ranch Stash		1978
Awareness AWCD 1028 Pretty Much Your Standard Ranch Stash		1991
Rio Records RIOD 2007 Pretty Much Your Standard Ranch Stash		1995

       Michael Nesmith: Accoustic guitar & vocals
       O.J. "Red" Rhodes: Pedal steel guitar & dobro
       Jay Lacy: Guitar
       Dr. Robert K. Warford: Guitar & Banjo
       David Barry: Piano
       Billy Graham: Bass & fiddle
       Danny Lane: Drums & percussion

       Continuing
       Some of Shelly's Blues
       Release
       Winonah
       Born to Love You
       The Back Porch and a Fruit Jar Full of Iced Tea
         a. The F.F.V.
         b. Uncle Pen
       Prairie Lullaby

Pacific Arts PAC11-101A The Prison		1975
Awareness AWCD 1020 The Prison		1990
Rio Records RIOD 2009 The Prison		1995

       Michael Nesmith: Guitar & vocals
       O.J. "Red" Rhodes: Pedal steel guitar
       Michael Cohen: Keyboard
       David Kempton: ARP Odyssey
       Chura: Congas
       Roland Rhythm 77: Drums

       Opening Theme (Life, the Unsuspecting Captive)
       Dance Between the Raindrops
       Elusive Ragings
       Waking Mystery
       Hear Me Calling?

Marie's Theme
Closing Theme (Lampost)

RCA   RS 1064   The Best of Michael Nesmith (U.K. only)   1976
Silver Moon
Different Drum
Harmony Constant
Two Different Roads
Mama Nantucket
Conversations
Joanne
Bonaparte's Retreat
Some of Shelly's Blues
Rainmaker
Listen To The Band
Grand Ennui
I've Just Begun To Care (Propinquity)
Nevada Fighter

Pacific Arts PAC 7106 Compilation   1977
Pacific Arts ILPA 9425 Compilation   1977
Some of Shelly's Blues
I Fall To Pieces
Born To Love You
Different Drum
Harmony Constant
Prairie Lullaby
Joanne
Propinquity (I've Just Begun To Care)
Silver Moon
I Looked Away
Continuing
Roll With The Flow

Pacific Arts PAC 7107 From A Radio Engine To The Photon Wing   1977
Pacific Arts ILPA 9486 From A Radio Engine To The Photon Wing 1977
Awareness AWCD 1027 From A Radio Engine To The Photon Wing 1992
Pacific Arts PAAD 5063 From A Radio Engine To The Photon Wing
Rio Records RIOD 2008 From A Radio Engine To The Photon Wing 1995
Michael Nesmith: Guitar & vocals
Lonnie Mack: Guitar
David MacKay: Bass
Larrie Londin: Drums
Jerry Carrigan: Drums
David Briggs: Keyboard
John Shane Keister: Keyboard
Lisa Silver: Violin
Greg Taylor: Harmonica

Rio
Casablanca Moonlight
More Than We Imagine
Navajo Trail
We Are Awake
Wisdom Has It's Way
Love's First Kiss

248

The Other Room

Pacific Arts PAC 7118 Live At The Palais	1978
Awareness AWCD 1030 Live At The Palais (withdrawn)	1992
Videoranch CD (no number)	2001

        Michael Nesmith: Guitar & vocals
        John Ware: Drums
        David MacKay: Bass
        Al Perkins: Guitar
        James Trumbo: Keyboard

        Grand Ennui
        Calico Girlfriend
        Propinquity
        Joanne
        Roll with the Flow
        Some of Shelly's Blues
        Silver Moon
        Nadine Is It You?

(The Videoranch CD release contains 4 bonus tracks from two other concerts: 'Grand Ennui' & 'Capsule' from Armadillo World Headquarters late 70s, and 'The Crippled Lion' & 'Listen to the Band' The Gretsch concert, 1995)

Pacific Arts PAC 7130 Infinite Rider On The Big Dogma 1979	
Awareness AWCD 1031 Infinite Rider On The Big Dogma	1992
Rio Records RIOD 2006 Infinite Rider On The Big Dogma	

        Michael Nesmith: Guitar & vocals
        Paul Leim: Drums
        Lenny Castro: Percussion
        John Hobbs: Keyboards
        David MacKay: Bass
        Al Perkins: Lead guitar & slide guitar
        Tom Saviano: Saxophone

        Dance (Dance & Have a Good Time)
        Magic (This Night Is Magic)
        Tonite (The Television Song)
        Flying (Silks & Satins)
        Carioca (Blue Carioca)
        Cruisin' (Lucy and Ramona and Sunset Sam)
        Factions (The Daughter of Rock n' Roll)
        Light (The Eclectic Light)
        Horserace (Beauty and the Magnum Force)
        Capsule (Hello People a Hundred Years From Now)

Rhino	R1 70168 The Newer Stuff (L.P.)	1989

        Total Control
        Tanya
        I'll Remember You
        Formosa Diner
        Eldorado to the Moon
        Magic
        Cruisin
        Light
        Carioca
        Rio

Rhino   R2 70168 The Newer Stuff (Compact Disc)   1989
Awareness AWCD 1014 The Newer Stuff
   Total Control
   Tanya
   I'll Remember You
   Formosa Diner
   Dreamer
   Eldorado to the Moon
   Tahiti Condo
   Chow Mein and Bowling
   Magic
   Cruisin'
   Light
   Carioca
   Rio
   Casablanca Moonlight

Rhino   R2 707163 The Older Stuff -The Best of the Early Years 1991
   Joanne
   The Crippled Lion
   I Fall to Pieces
   Listen to the Band
   Silver Moon
   Propinquity
   I Looked Away
   Nevada Fighter
   Tumbling Tumbleweeds
   Here I Am
   Some of Shelly's Blues
   Born to Love You
   Different Drum
   Harmony Constant
   Continuing
   Prairie Lullaby
   Release
   Roll With the Flow

Pacific Arts Audio PAAD 5000 ...tropical campfires...   1992
Rio Records RIOD/T 2003 ...tropical campfires...
Cooking Vinyl Cookcd 204 ...tropical campfires...   2000
   Michael Nesmith: Guitar & vocals
   John Jorgenson: Guitar & mandolin
   O.J. "Red" Rhodes: Pedal steel guitar
   John Hobbs: Keyboard
   Joe Chemay: Bass
   Luis Conte: Percussion

   Yellow Butterfly
   Laugh Kills Lonesome
   Moon Over the Rio Grande
   One...
   Juliana
   Brazil
   In the Still of the Night
   Rising in Love

Begin the Beguine
I Am Not That
...For the Island
Twilight on the Trail

Rio Records RIOD 2001 The Garden   1994
      Michael Nesmith: 12 string guitar & vocals
      Christian Nesmith: 6 string guitar
      John Jorgenson: 6 string guitar, electric guitar, saxophone, bassoon, mandolin,
                mandocello, oboe and bandurilla
      John Hobbs: Keyboards
      Joe Romano: Trumpet
      John Yoakum: Oboe
      Joe Chemay: Bass
      Sid Page:Violin
      Curt McGetrick: Bass clarinet

      Garden's Glow
      Ficus Carica
      City
      Hills of Time
      Flowers Dancing
      Wisteria
      Life Becoming

BMG 74321 523772 Michael Nesmith Listen to The Band 1997
      CD compilation from the UK

Eagle EAB CD 105 Mike Nesmith The Masters   1998
      CD compilation from the UK

Collectables COL CD 6295 16 Original Classics   1999
      CD compilation

Cooking Vinyl Cook CD 129 Michael Nesmith Live at the Britt Festival 1999
      Michael Nesmith: guitar & vocals
      John Jorgenson: guitar & mandolin
      Red Rhodes: pedal steel guitar
      Joe Chemay: bass
      John Hobbs: keyboards
      Luis Conte: percussion

      Two Different Roads
      Papa Gene's Blues
      Propinquity
      Some of Shelley's Blues
      Joanne
      Tomorrow and Me
      The Upside of Goodbye
      Harmony Constant
      Silver Moon
      5 Second Concerts
      Yellow Butterfly
      Moon Over the Rio Grande
      Juliana
      Laugh Kills Lonesome

I Am Not That
Rising in Love
Rio
Different Drum
I Am Not That (Reprise)

BMG 74321 660442 Magnetic South & Loose Salute 1999
Both albums on one CD plus the bonus track "1st National Dance"

Rio Records 7528-2 Timerider soundtrack   2000
Instrumental film soundtrack composed by Michael
Michael Nesmith: guitar
Joe Chemay: bass
Paul Leim: drums
John Hobbs: keyboards
Steve Forman: percussion
David Mansfield: guitar, mandolin, dobro
Richie Zito: guitar

The Baja 1000
Lost in the Weeds
Somewhere Around 1875
Scared to Death
Silks and Sixguns
Dead Man's Duds
Two Swanns at the Pond
I Want That Machine
Escape to San Marcos
Claire's Cabin
No Jurisdiction
Murder at Swallow's Camp
Claire's Rescue
Up the Hill to Nowhere
Out of Ammo
Reprise

BMG 74321 773822 And the Hits Just Keep on Comin' & Ranch Stash 2000
Both albums on one CD

BMG 74321 822352 Nevada Fighter & Tantamount to Treason   2001
Both albums on one CD plus the bonus tracks Cantata & Fugue in C&W;
Smoke, Smoke, Smoke and Rose City Chimes.

Audiophille APH 102 821 Michael Nesmith Silver Moon 2002
CD compilation from Belgium

BMG 82876533372 The Best of Michael Nesmith   2003
CD compilation from the UK

Audio Books

Videoranch release (no number given) The Long Sandy Hair of Neftoon Zamora 2002
6 CD set with Michael reading his novel.
Music written by Michael Nesmith.
Music performed by Christian Nesmith & Bart Ryan.

Interview Records

US Navy 72-37 Sounds Like The Navy (Interview Record) 1972

Pacific Arts PAC 71300 The Michael Nesmith Radio Special 1979
    contains songs from Infinite Rider on the Big Dogma

Solo Guest Appearances on Others Albums and Various Artists Album

Motown 6059 ML Lionel Richie-Can't Slow Down 1983
    Nesmith is thanked for his work on Richie's "All Night Long" video.

Beechwood BR 2522 Peter Tork-Stranger Things Have Happened 1994
    Nesmith sings background vocals on "Milkshake" and "MGBGT"

Rhino R2 71650 The Colpix-Dimension Story 1994
    Contains "The New Recruit."

Miscellaneous

Prospector 101 The Trinity River Boys 1964
    Limited edition record of band featuring Nesmith, Mike Murphy,
    Johnny Raines and John Kuehne (London)

RCA PRS-345 The Many Moods of Stereo ???
    Early seventies promotional album for RCA stereos contains "Silver Moon."

RCA PRS-387 Fantastic Country Vol.1 ???
    Early seventies promotional album for Salem cigarettes contains
    "Silver Moon."

RCA SRA-5531 The Last of the First 1971
    Japanese compilation of First National Band songs

??? KSP-16985 Michael Nesmith Presents Pacific Artists ???
    German compilation album featuring artists on Pacific Arts record label

Pacific Arts PAC7-1301 Cruisin'/Cruisin' 1979
    12 inch single in plain white sleeve that reads "P.Arts Records & Tapes
    Prime Cuts."

Kid Rhino R2 70403 The Cowboy Album 1994
    Compilation of cowboy songs for children that contains "Prairie Lullaby."

Side Records AZ-5024 Monkey Solo Recordings 1995
    Unlicensed Japanese CD featuring 6 Pre-Monkee Nesmith tracks

Dren Records DNCD015 Papa Nez: A Loose Salute to the Work of Michael Nesmith 2001
    You Told Me - Buddy Woodward
    Nine Times Blue - Sixty Acres
    Different Drum - Frog Holler
    The Girl I Knew Somewhere - Tom Gillam
    Sweet Young Thing - Western Electric

Good Clean Fun - Last Train Home
Texas Morning - Rust Kings
Magic - The Heavy Blinkers
You Just May Be The One - John Jorgenson
Listen to the Band - Meredith Ochs
Sunny Girlfriend - Scott McKnight
Papa Gene's Blues - Two-Fisted Tales
Daily Nightly - Jamie Holiday
St. Matthew - Mark McKay
Some of Shelley's Blues - John Beland
Propinquity - Calico Bind
Here I Am - Simon Raymonde
Hollywood - June Star
Prairie Lullaby - The Mary Janes

Soundtracks

Tam   YX 5002   Blue Angels   1976
            This Japan only soundtrack features one Nesmith composition
            "The World Is Golden Too"

San Andreas SAR 39019 Repo Man   1984
            Mentions Nesmith but contains no Nesmith compositions

Island   91030   Tapeheads   1988
            Mentions Nesmith but contains no Nesmith compositions

Epic   EK 53439 Peter's Friends   1992
            Soundtrack for Kenneth Branagh and Emma Thompson film
            features "Rio"

Appendix 5: Michael Nesmith as Music Producer

Albums

Countryside Records	CS-101	Garland Frady	Pure Country
Countryside Records	CS-102	Red Rhodes	Velvet Hammer in a Cowboy Band
Prodigal	P7-10028	Fresh	Omniverse
Elektra	75061	Ian Matthews	Valley Hi
Charisma	CAS 1090	Bert Jansch	L.A. Turnaround
Proper Records	PRPCD2	Chilli Willi and the Red Hot Peppers	I'll be Home (Nesmith produced two tracks on the cd- I'll Be Home & Friday Song)
Sundazed	SC 11129	Penny Arkade	Not the Freeze

Singles

Dot	17226	Bill Chadwick	Talking To the Wall/If You Have the Time
Dot	17244	The Corvettes	Lion in Your Heart/Back Home Girl
Dot	17283	The Corvettes	Level With Your Senses/Beware of Time
RCA	Unreleased	Bill Chadwick	Tomorrow/Alistair Rascher

Appendix 6: Michael Nesmith as Songwriter

Songs Performed by Others

Texas Re-Cord 1001   Denny Ezba   Sings His Greatest Hits From 4,000 Years
                                         Ago
         Contains "Go Somewhere and Cry."

RCA LSP-4226   Nat Stuckey   New Country Roads
         Contains "Listen to the Band."

Epic KE 33356   Joe Stampley   Joe Stampley
         Contains "I've Never Loved Anyone More."

United Artists UA LA390 Billie Jo Spears   Blanket on the Ground
         Contains "I've Never Loved Anyone More."

Profile PRO 1265   Run DMC   Tougher Than Leather
         Contains "Mary, Mary."

Asylum 7E-1092   Linda Ronstadt   Greatest Hits
         Contains "Different Drum."

Capitol ST-2763   Stone Poneys   Evergreen Vol.2
         Contains "Different Drum."

Liberty LST-7642   Nitty Gritty Dirt Band Uncle Charlie and His Dog Teddy
         Contains "Some of Shelley's Blues" and "Propinquity."

Capitol ST-11564   Linda Hargrove   Just Like You
         Contains "Winonah."

Mercury SRM 1-699   Johnny Rodriguez   My Third Album
         Contains "I've Never Loved Anyone More."

Columbia KC 30105   Andy Williams   The Andy Williams Show
         Contains "Joanne."

ABC Records ABCS-657 Frankie Laine   Take Me Back to Laine Country
         Contains "Pretty Little Princess."

Columbia KC 31354   Earl Scruggs   I Saw The Light With Some Help From
                                       My Friends
         Contains "Some of Shelley's Blues" and "Propinquity."

Epic FE 37108   Charly McClain   Surround Me With Love
         Contains "I've Never Loved Anyone More."

Capitol ST-11685   Linda Hargrove   Impressions
         Contains "If You Will Walk With Me."

Warren County WCR-102 Warren County String Ticklers Live at Waterhole

Contains "Some of Shelley's Blues."

Other Known Nesmith Compositions

The following is a listing of every known Nesmith composition released as well as unreleased. Be aware that there are many duplicate songs where probably the only difference is title.

...For the Island	'Til Then
Admiral Mike	All I Had To Give
All Night Long	All the King's Horses
At the Next Bend In the Road	Auntie and the Municipal
Auntie's Municipal Court	Band 6
Band Six	Beauty and The Magnum Force
Black and Blues	Blue Carioca
Bonnie Jean and the Psychedelic Car	Bound Away
Brand X	Bye Bye Bye
Calico Girlfriend	Calico Girlfriend Samba
Calico Sombra Girlfriend	Candidate
Cantata & Fugue in C&W	Capsule
Carioca	Carlisle Wheeling
Carlisle Wheeling Effervescent Popsicle	Casablanca Moonlight
Circle Sky	Closing Theme
Color of My Skin	Continuing
Conversations	Crippled Lion
Cruisin'	Daily Nightly
Dance	Dance and Have a Good Time
Dance Between the Raindrops	Daughter of Rock and Roll
Dawn Broke Clear in the Morning	Dedicated Friend
Different Drum	Don't Call on Me
Don't Cry Now	Don't Tell Me Everything
Don't Wait For Me	Dr. Duck's Super Secret All Purpose Sauce
Dreamer	Each Man
East O' Texas	Ebanezer
Eclectic Light	Elusive Ragings
Empire	Factions
First National Dance	First National Rag
Flying	Formosa Diner
Found Love	Gabriella
Gas Eat and Arizona	Girl I Knew Somewhere
Go Somewhere and Cry	Goin Down
Going Down	Good Afternoon
Good Clean Fun	Grand Ennui
Great American Thunder Turkey	Happiness
Harmony Constant	Hear Me Calling
Hello Lady	Hello To People A Hundred Years
Here I Am	Hollywood
Horserace	How Can You Kiss Me
I Am Not That	I Won't Be the Same Without Her
I'll Remember You	I've Found a Girl
I've Just Begun To Care	I've Never Loved Anyone More
If You Will Walk With Me	In The Afternoon
Joanne	Journey With Michael Blessing
Joys of Your Youth	Juliana

Just a Little Love	Keep On
Keys to the Car	Kind of Girl I Could Love
Lady Love	Lady of the Valley
Laugh Kills Lonesome	Lazy Lady
Life, The Unsuspecting Captive	Light
Listen to the Band	Listening
Little Red Rider	London Bridge
Looks Like Rain	Lothario In A
Love's First Kiss	Lucy and Ramona and Sunset Sam
Lynn Harper	Magic
Magnolia Simms	Mama Nantucket
Mama Rocker	Marie's Theme
Mary, Mary	Michigan Blackhawk
Moon Over the Rio Grande	More Than We Imagine
Music of the World A Turning	My Share of the Sidewalk
My Song in 7	Naked Persimmon
Nevada Fighter	Never Tell a Woman Yes
Nine Times Blue	Omega
One...	Only Bound
Other Room	Papa Gene's Blues
Popclips Theme	Pretty Little Princess
Propinquity	Release
Rio	Rising In Love
Roll With the Flow	Rollin'
Searchin'	She Calls Herself St. Matthew
Silks and Satins	Silver Moon
Silver Moon Baby	Since I Was in the Army
Sleep	Sleep My Child
Some of Shelley's Blues	Some of Shelly's Blues
Sound of the Sunset, Sound of the Sea	Space Machine
St. Matthew	Sunny Girlfriend
Suzanna Sometime	Sweet Young Thing
Tahiti Condo	Tanya
Tapioca Tundra	Television Song
Tengo Amor	Thank You My Friend
Thanx For the Ride	There's Just A Little Love
Things I've Done	Thirteen Is Not Our Lucky Number
This All Happened Once Before	This Night is Magic
Tommy Blue	Tomorrow and Me
Tonight	Total Control
Twilight on the Trail	Two Different Roads
Upside of Goodbye	Waking Mystery
Walkin' in the Sand	Wanderin'
We Are Awake	Well Well
When I Finally Said Goodbye	Where Has It All Gone
While I Cried	While I Cry
Winonah	Wisdom Has It's Way
Writing Wrongs	Yellow Butterfly
You Are My One	You Just May Be the One
You May Just Be the One	You Told Me
Zilch	

Appendix 7: Michael Nesmith as Live Performer

With The Monkees

Date	Venue	Location
December 3, 1966	Honolulu Intl. Center Arena	Honolulu, Hawaii
December 26, 1966	Denver Coliseum	Denver, Colorado
December 27, 1966	Mid-South Coliseum	Memphis, Tennessee
December 28, 1966	Freedom Hall	Louisville, Kentucky
December 29, 1966	Winston-Salem Coliseum	Winston-Salem, North Carolina
December 30, 1966	Civic Arena	Pittsburgh, Pennsylvania
December 31, 1966	Cincinnati Gardens	Cincinnati, Ohio
January 1, 1967	Municipal Auditorium	Nashville, Tennessee
January 2, 1967	Assembly Center Arena	Tulsa, Oklahoma
January 14, 1967	Olympia Stadium	Detroit, Michigan
January 15, 1967	Public Auditorium	Cleveland, Ohio
January 21, 1967	The Coliseum	Phoenix, Arizona
January 22, 1967	Cow Palace	San Francisco, California
April 1, 1967	The Arena	Winnipeg, Canada
April 2, 1967	Maple Leaf Gardens	Toronto, Canada
May 6, 1967	Field House- State University	Wichita, Kansas
June 9, 1967	Hollywood Bowl	Hollywood, California
June 30-July 2, 1967	Wembley Pool	London, England
July 8, 1967	Sports Coliseum	Jacksonville, Florida
July 9, 1967	Miami Beach Convention Hall	Miami Beach, Florida
July 11, 1967	The Coliseum	Charlotte, North Carolina
July 12, 1967	The Coliseum	Greensboro, North Carolina
July 14-16, 1967	Forest Hills Stadium	New York, New York
July 20, 1967	Memorial Auditorium	Buffalo, New York
July 21, 1967	Memorial Auditorium	Baltimore, Maryland
July 22, 1967	Boston Garden	Boston, Massachusetts
July 23, 1967	Civic Center	Philadelphia, Pennsylvania
July 27, 1967	Rochester War Memorial	Rochester, New York
July 28, 1967	Cincinnati Gardens	Cincinnati, Ohio
July 30, 1967	The Stadium	Chicago, Illinois
August 4, 1967	Municipal Auditorium	St. Paul, Minnesota
August 5, 1967	Kiel Auditorium	St. Louis, Missouri
August 6, 1967	Veterans Memorial Auditorium	Des Moines, Iowa
August 9, 1967	Memorial Auditorium	Dallas, Texas
August 10, 1967	Sam Houston Coliseum	Houston, Texas
August 11, 1967	State Fair Coliseum	Shreveport, Louisiana
August 12, 1967	Municipal Auditorium	Mobile, Alabama
August 13, 1967	Olympia Stadium	Detroit Stadium
August 17, 1967	Mid-South Coliseum	Memphis, Tennessee
August 18, 1967	Assembly Center Arena	Tulsa, Oklahoma
August 19, 1967	State Fair Arena	Oklahoma City, Oklahoma
August 20, 1967	Denver Coliseum	Denver, Colorado
August 25, 1967	Seattle Center Coliseum	Seattle, Washington
August 26, 1967	Memorial Coliseum	Portland, Oregon
August 27, 1967	The Coliseum	Spokane, Washington
May 21, 1968	Valley Auditorium	Salt Lake City, Utah

259

September 18-19, 1968	Festival Hall	Melbourne, Australia
September 21, 1968	Sydney Stadium	Sydney, Australia
September 23, 1968	Festival Hall	Brisbane, Australia
September 27, 1968	Adelaide Centennial Hall	Adelaide, Australia
September 28-29, 1968	Sydney Stadium	Sydney, Australia
October 3-4, 1968	Budokan Hall	Tokyo, Japan
October 5, 1968	Kyoto Kaikan Hall	Kyoto, Japan
October 7-8, 1968	Festival Hall	Osaka, Japan
March 29, 1969	The Coliseum	Vancouver, Canada
March 30, 1969	Seattle Center Coliseum	Seattle, Washington
April 11, 1969	Municipal Auditorium	Birmingham, Alabama
April 12, 1969	Civic Center Arena	Charleston, West Virginia
April 13, 1969	Bell Auditorium	Augusta, Georgia
April 17, 1969	Honolulu Intl. Center Arena	Honolulu, Hawaii
April 26, 1969	Auditorium	Chicago, Illinois
May 3, 1969	The Coliseum	Jackson, Mississippi
May 4, 1969	Coliseum	Houston, Texas
May 9, 1969	Albuquerque Civic Auditorium	Albuquerque, New Mexico
May 10, 1969	Convention Hall	Wichita, Kansas
June 20, 1969	Coliseum, Eastern States Expo.	W. Springfield, Massachusetts
June 22, 1969	First Annual Pops Festival	Milwaukee, Wisconsin
July 18, 1969	4-H Dane County Junior Fair	Madison, Wisconsin
July 19, 1969	Majestic Hills	Lake Geneva, Wisconsin
July 25-26, 1969	Club Forum	Mexico City, Mexico
July 27, 1969	Plaza de Toro	Guadalajara, Mexico
August 1, 1969	Curtis Hixon Hall	Tampa, Florida
August 28-29, 1969	Colorado State Fair	Pueblo, Colorado
October 17, 1969	North Carolina State Fair	Raleigh, North Carolina
November 30, 1969	Oakland Coliseum	Oakland, California
September 7, 1986	Greek Theater	Los Angeles, California
July 9, 1989	Universal Amphitheater	Los Angeles, California
November 20, 1996	Billboard Live	Los Angeles, California
March 7, 1997	Newcastle Arena	Newcastle, England
March 8, 1997	S.E.C.C.	Glasgow, Scotland
March 9, 1997	Waterfront Hall	Belfast, Ireland
March 10, 1997	Point	Dublin, Ireland
March 12, 1997	Cardiff International Arena	Cardiff, Wales
March 14, 1997	Sheffield Arena	Sheffield, England
March 15, 1997	Manchester Nynex	Manchester, England
March 16, 1997	Bournemouth BIC	Bournemouth, England
March 18, 1997	Birmingham NEC	Birmingham, England
March 19, 1997	Wembley Arena	London, England
March 20, 1997	Wembley Arena	London, England

Post Monkees Performances

March 22, 1970	Troubador	Los Angeles, California
September 10, 1970	Inn at the Park Hotel	London, England
October 24, 1970	Round Table	Indianapolis, Indiana
November 20, 1970	KRNT Theater	Des Moines, Iowa
July 9-11, 1971	Troubador	Los Angeles, California
October 6, 1971	Gaslight 1	New York, New York
December 2, 1971	Univ. of California	Riverside, California

December 3, 1971	California State Univ.	Los Angeles, California
December 3, 1971	California State Univ.	Long Beach, California
December 4, 1971	California Poly. Tech.	Pomona, California
December 4, 1971	Valley Junior College	San Fernando, California
December 7, 1971	Pierce Junior College	Woodland Hills, California
December 8, 1971	Palos Verdes High School	Palo Verdes, CA
December 9, 1971	Los Angeles City College	Los Angeles, California
December 10, 1971	San Bernadino Valley College	San Bernardino, California
December 11, 1971	San Diego State	San Diego, California
January 12-19, 1972	Ice House	Los Angeles, California
January 24-25, 1972	McCabes	Santa Monica, California
April 28, 1974	Roundhouse	London, England
March 6, 1975	Victoria Palace	London, England
June 3, 1975	Victoria Palace	London, England
November 21, 1975	Nottingham Poly. Tech.	Nottingham, England
November 22,1975	Essex University	Colchester, England
November 23, 1975	Queen's University	Belfast, Ireland
November 27, 1975	BBC Radio	London, England
November 28, 1975	Brighton University	Brighton, England
November 29, 1975	Sheffield University	Sheffield, England
November 30, 1975	Theatre Royal	Drury Lane, England
November 3, 1977	?	Wollongong, Australia
November 4, 1977	?	Cannberra, Australia
November 5, 1977	?	Newcastle, Australia
November 6, 1977	Her Majesty's Theatre	Brisbane, Australia
November 8, 1977	State Theatre	Sydney, Australia
November 9, 1977	Plaza Theatre	Geelong, Australia
November 10, 1977	Palais Theatre	Melborne, Australia
November 13, 1977	Festival Hall	Adelaide, Australia
November 14, 1977	Dorsett Gardens	Victoria, Australia
November 23, 1977	Perth Concert Hall	Perth, Australia
March 18, 1979	Palomino	Los Angeles, California
August 28, 1979	Old Wardorf	San Francisco, California
August 29, 1979	Whisky	Los Angeles, California
October 4, 1979	Old Wardorf	San Francisco, California
October 5, 1979	California Poly. Tech	Pomona, California
October 28, 1979	Compton Terrace	Phoenix, Arizona
January 25, 1992	Bluebird Cafe	Nashville, Tennessee
February 7, 1992	The Strand	Redondo Beach, California
February 8, 1992	Last Day Saloon	San Francisco, California
February 14, 1992	Nightstage	Somerville, Massachusetts
February 15, 1992	The Cubby Bear	Chicago, Illinois
February 21, 1992	The Lone Star Roadhouse	New York, New York
February 22, 1992	Birchmere	Alexandria, Virginia
February 28, 1992	Variety Playhouse	Atlanta, Georgia
February 29, 1992	Poor David's Pub	Dallas, Texas
June 19, 1992	Peter Britt Pavilion	Jacksonville, Oregon
September 16, 1992	Austin City Limits taping	Austin, Texas
September 17, 1992	Texas Union Ballroom	Austin, Texas
September 27, 1992	Palace of Fine Arts	San Francisco, California
July 16, 1994	The West End	Dallas, Texas
August 18, 1994	River Park	Albany, Oregon
August 20, 1994	Port Marina Park	Hood River, Oregon
January 22, 1995	NAMM Trade Show-Private Show	Anaheim, California
March 18, 1995	Wadsworth Theater	Los Angeles, California

Appendix 8: Wichita Train Whistle Performers

In an Interview in the early Seventies, Michael was asked about the musicians that appeared on the *Wichita Train Whistle Sings* album since there was no personnel list on the original release. Michael was quoted as saying, "It was one of the great stupid mistakes of my life. I just can't imagine that I didn't do that, because it was such an important part of the *Wichita Train Whistle*." For the sake of our readers and as a public service, here is a list of the musicians who appeared on the *Wichita Train Whistle Sings* album.

John Audino: Trumpet
Robert Barene: Violin
Chuck Berghofer: Bass
Louise Blackburn: Trombone
Bud Brisbois: Trumpet
Frank Capp: Percussion
Buddy Childers: Trumpet
Gary Coleman: Percussion
Jim Decker: French Horn
Joseph DiFiore: Violin
Jesse Ehrlich: Cello
Jimmy Getzoff: Strings
Bill Hinshaw: French Horn
Joe Howard: Trombone
Dick Hyde: Trombone
John Kitzmiller: Tuba
Larry Knechtel: Piano
John Lowe: Woodwinds

Leonard Malarsky: Violin
Ollie Mitchell: Trumpet
Jack Nimitz: Woodwinds
Earl Palmer: Drums
Don Randi: Piano
Sam Rice: Tuba
Sid Sharp: Violin: Concertmaster
Tommy Tedesco: Guitar
Jimmy Zito: Trumpet

Isreal Baker: Violin, Concertmaster
Arnold Belnick: Violin
Milt Bernhart: Trombone
Hal Blaine: Drums
James Burton: Guitar
Jules Chaikin: Trumpet
Gene Cipriano: Woodwinds
Buddy Collette: Woodwinds
Vince Derosa: French Horn
Doug Dillard: Banjo
Victor Feldman: Percussion
Justin Gordon: Woodwinds
Jim Horn: Woodwinds
Harry Hyams: Viola
Jules Jacob: Woodwinds
Manny Klein: Trumpet
Ray Kramer: Cello
Edgar Lustgarten: Cello, Concertmaster of Celli
Lew McCreary: Trombone
Alex Neiman: Viola
Barrett O' Hara: Trombone
Dick Perissi: French Horn
O. J. Red Rhodes: Steel Guitar
Ralph Schaeffer: Violin
Kenny Shroyer: Trombone
Tony Terran: Trumpet

Arranged by Shorty Rogers and Michael Nesmith
Produced by Michael Nesmith
Catered by Chasens

Appendix 9: Michael Nesmith as Record Publisher

released on Pacific Arts Corporation label

Number	Artist	Album Name
PAC7-102A	Kaleidoscope	When Scopes Collide
PACR7-105	Swami Nadabrahamananda	Samiji
PAC7-108	Biff Rose	Roast Beef
PAC7-109	Joyce Yarrow	Jumping Mouse
PAC7-110	Henry Wolf & Nancy Hennings	Tibetan Bells II
PAC7-111	Bhagavans Das	Ah
PAC7-112	Rank Strangers	Rank Strangers
PACR7-119	Hamza El Din	Eclipse
PACB7-120	Zytron	Zytron
PAC7-121	Pacific Steel Co.	Pacific Steel Co.
PAC7-122	Celebration	Celebration
PAC7-123	Charles Lloyd	Weavings
PAC7-127	Biff Rose	Thee Messiah Album
PAC7-128	Film Soundtrack	Days of Heaven
PAC7-129	Jet	Jet
PAC7-132	Chris Darrow	Fretless
PAC7-133	dba Success	Success
PACG7-134	Deadly Earnest & The Honky Tonk Heroes	Deadly Earnest & The Honky Tonk Heroes
PACB7-135	Susan Muscarella	Rainflowers
PAC7-136	Trefethen	Am I Stupid Or Am I Great?
PACB7-137	Michael Cohen	Moments
PAC7-138	Michael Chapman	Life On The Ceiling
PAC7-139	Charles Lloyd	Big Sur Tapestry
PAC7-140	The Pirates	Hard Ride
PAC7-142	The Almond Band	Best Of- Live
PAC8-143	Film Soundtrack	The Elephant Man

Overseas Labels That Distributed Pacific Arts Throughout the Years

Australia: Festival Records
Canada: Attic Records
New Zealand: Stetson Records
England: Virgin Records
England: Awareness

263

Appendix 10: Michael Nesmith as Video Publisher

Before you start questioning my sanity about publishing a list of videos, I must tell you that I was asked by a couple of devoted Nesmith fans to compile this list. It is incomplete so any additions will be included in revised editions.

Note: Most of these titles are no longer available for sale

Pacific Arts Video and Pacific Arts Video Records Labels

521	An Evening With Sir William Martin
526	Television Parts Home Companion
527	Firesign Theatre Presents Nick Danger
528	Timerider
529	Elephant Parts
530	Endless Summer
532	My Dinner With Andre
533	To See Such Fun
535	Mr. Mike's Mondo Video
537	Doonesbury Special
539	Koyannisqatsi
540	Rutles: I Love The Rutles
541	Whoops Apocalypse
542	Edie in Ciao! Manhattan
543	James Dean Story
544	Carrott Gets Rowdy
546	Paul Simon Special
547	Say Amen, Somebody
548	Toni Basil: Word of Mouth
549	Dreams Of Gold
550	American Friend
551	Backstage at The Kirov
552	Best Of Blondie
553	Slipstream starring Jethro Tull
554	Happy Hour With The Humans
555	Sherlock Holmes and The Baskerville Curse
556	Huberman Festival (Vivaldi: The Four Seasons)
557	Musicourt
558	Things We Did Last Summer
559	Romance With A Double Bass
560	Down Among The Z Men
561	Nudo Di Donna (Portrait Of A Woman, Nude)
562	Huberman Festival II (Mozart/Handel)
563	Sherlock Holmes and The Sign of Four
564	La Passante
565	Agatha Christie/Partners In Crime: The Crackler
566	Taking My Turn
567	Irezumi (Spirit of Tattoo)
568	Martial Arts: The Chinese Masters

569	Huberman Festival III (Tchaikovsky/Handel)
570	Huberman Festival IV (Mendelssohn/Bach)
571	Huberman Festival V (Bach/Vivaldi)
575	Agatha Christie/Partners In Crime: The Affair of The Pink Pearl
576	Agatha Christie/Partners In Crime: The House Of Lurking Death
577	Agatha Christie/Partners In Crime: Finessing The King
578	Agatha Christie/Partners In Crime: The Clergyman's Daughter
579	Agatha Christie/Partners In Crime: The Sunningdale Mystery
580	Agatha Christie/Partners In Crime: The Ambassador's Boots
581	Agatha Christie/Partners In Crime: The Man In The Mist
582	Agatha Christie/Partners In Crime: The Unbreakable Alibi
583	Agatha Christie/Partners In Crime: The Case of The Missing Lady
584	Brothers Lionheart
585	Heidi
586	Observations Under The Volcano
587	Skyline
588	Chick Corea & Gary Burton: Live In Tokyo
591	Everybody Rides The Carousel
592	Barbara Woodhouse Goes To Beverly Hills
593	Sherlock Holmes and The Valley of Fear
594	Sherlock Holmes and A Study In Scarlet
595	Secret Adversary
596	Yesterday's Witness
597	Zoo-oplis
598	Marty Hogan: Power Raquetball
599	Hank Williams JR: A Star Spangled Country Party
600	Louie Bluie
601	Video Treasures: Briar Rose/Rumpelstilskin
602	Video Treasures: King Thrushbeard/Rapunzel
603	Video Treasures: The Hut in the Forest/Karl Katz
604	Video Treasures: The Fir Tree/The Little Match Girl
605	Video Treasures: The Coming of the Sun/The Robins Red Breast
606	Video Treasures: The Coming of the Corn/Why Monkeys Live in Trees
607	Video Treasures: Why the Loon Calls/The Sleeping Princess
608	Video Treasures: Johnny Appleseed/John Henry
609	Video Treasures: Paul Bunyan/The One Who Wasn't Afraid
610	Video Treasures: Letting in the Jungle/The Coming of Fear
611	Video Treasures: Kaa and the Bandar Log/The Challenge of Shere Khan
612	Video Treasures: The Coming of Mowgli/Tiger, Tiger
613	Video Treasures: The Ugly Duckling/Hansal and Gretel
614	Video Treasures: Pinocchio/Little Red Riding Hood
615	Video Treasures: Peter Pan/Henny Penny
616	Video Treasures: Alice in Wonderland/The Three Little Pigs
617	Video Treasures: Pecos Bill/Casey at the Bat
618	Video Treasures: The Nightingale/Peter Rabbit
619	Video Treasures: The Legend of Sleepy Hollow/The Half Chick
620	Video Treasures: Drakes Tail/The Town Mouse and the Country Mouse
621	Video Treasures: The Enchanted Mule/The Leaves of Autumn
622	Video Treasures: The Snow Queen/Jack and the Beanstalk
623	Video Treasures: Aladdin and the Magic Lamp/The Little Tin Soldier
624	Video Treasures: The Wild Swans/The Little Red Hen
625	Video Treasures: Thumbelina/The Ant and the Grasshopper/The Fox and the Grapes
626	Alsino And The Condor
630	The Official Story (Subtitled)
631	The Official Story (Dubbed)
632	Times Of Harvey Milk

265

633	Jacques Cousteau: The Singing Whale
634	Jacques Cousteau: The Unsinkable Otter
635	Jacques Cousteau: The Smile of The Walrus
636	Jacques Cousteau: A Sound Of Dolphins
637	Jacques Cousteau: Octopus-Octopus
638	Jacques Cousteau: The Dragons of the Galapagos
639	Jacques Cousteau: The Desert Whales
640	Jacques Cousteau: The Flight of The Penguins
641	Jacques Cousteau: The Forgotten Mermaids
642	Jacques Cousteau: Whales
643	Ansel Adams: Photographer
644	Footsteps of Giants
645	Dr. Duck's Super Secret All Purpose Sauce
646	World in Flames
647	Berlin 1945
648	Blitzkrieg
649	Warlords
650	Men of Bronze
651	Vagabond
652	Salvador Dali: A Soft Self Portrait
653	Kitchen: Two Moon July
654	Kitchen: Media- Zbig Rybczynski
655	Kitchen: Robert Wilson's Stations
656	High & Low
658	Colonel Redl
659	Dim Sum
660	Great Wall
661	Sacrifice
662	Wim Wenders: State of Things
663	Wim Wenders: Alice in the Cities
664	Wim Wenders: The Goalie's Anxiety
665	Wim Wenders: Scarlet Letter
666	Summer
667	Macarthur's Children
668	Wim Wenders: Tokyo Ga
669	Wim Wenders: Wrong Move
670	Wim Wenders: Lightning Over Water
671	Wim Wenders: Kings of the Road
672	Best of the Festival of Claymation
673	Square Dance
674	El Amor Brujo
679	Heaven
680	King: Montgomery to Memphis
681	Drive to Win
682	Freedom Beat
683	Radio Bikini
684	State of the Art of Computer Animation
685	Half of Heaven
686	Painting With Light
687	Animal Wonders: 7 Cassette Boxed Set
688	Animal Wonders: The Little Marsupials/The Kangaroos
689	Animal Wonders: Crocodiles/Reptiles
690	Animal Wonders: The Bandicoots/World of the Koala
691	Animal Wonders: Platypus/The Islands
692	Animal Wonders: Silver Gulls/Mallee Fowl
693	Animal Wonders: The Tiny Carnivores/Wombat

694	Animal Wonders: Fauna of Australia
695	Coming Up Roses
696	Zed & Two Naughts
700	Distant Harmony: Pavarotti In China
702	Le Grand Chemin
705	Border Radio
706	Loose Connections
707	Funhouse: Eric Bogosian
708	Nezmuzic
709	Wheels: The Joy of Cars
710	Space: The frontiers and Beyond
711	Wings: The Jet Age
712	Aretha Franklin: Queen of Soul
713	A.C. Clarke: The Journey Begins
714	A.C. Clarke: UFO's/Strange Skys
715	A.C. Clarke: Monsters of the Deep/Monsters of the Lakes
716	A.C. Clarke: Missing Ape Man/Dragons, Dinosaurs & Snakes
717	A.C. Clarke: The Great Siberian Explosion/ Out of the Blue
718	A.C. Clarke: Ancient Wisdom/Giants For The Gods
719	A.C. Clarke: Riddle of the Stones/Cabinet of Curiosities
721	Agatha Christie's Murder By The Book
722	Quicksilver: Mad Max
723	Quicksilver: Tahitian Dreams
724	Quicksilver: Performers II
725	Quicksilver: Edie Aikay/Big Wave Contest
726	Tapeheads
729	A.C. Clarke: Mysterious World 7 cassette boxed set
731	Where The Heart Roams
739	Sirius Puppy Training
746	Look What I Made (without FunKit)
750	A.C. Clarke: Warnings From The Future
751	A.C. Clarke: From Mind To Mind
752	A.C. Clarke: Things That Go Bump In The Night
753	A.C. Clarke: The Roots Of Evil
754	A.C. Clarke: Stigmata: The Wounds of Christ
755	A.C. Clarke: Ghosts, Appartions and Haunted Houses
756	A.C. Clarke: Fairies, Phantoms & Fantastic Photography
757	A.C. Clarke: Have We Lived Before?
758	A.C. Clarke: Messages From The Dead
759	A.C. Clarke: Metal Bending, Magic and Mind Over Matter
760	A.C. Clarke: Walking On Fire
761	A.C. Clarke: An Element of the Divine
762	A.C. Clarke: Strange Powers: The Verdict
763	A.C. Clarke: Strange Powers 13 Cassette boxed set
767	Agatha Christie 12 Piece for Retail
768	Agatha Christie 24 Piece for Retail
769	Agatha Christie 12 Cassette Collection
770	Look What I Made with FunKit
771	Bruce Brown Collection: Slippery When Wet
772	Bruce Brown Collection: Surf Crazy
773	Bruce Brown Collection: Barefoot Adventure
774	Bruce Brown Collection: Surfing Hollow Days
775	Bruce Brown Collection: Waterlogged
776	Bruce Brown Collection: Surfin' Shorts
777	Bruce Brown 7 Cassette Collection
788	Carriers: The Langley/The New Weapon

789	Carriers: Rehearsal for War/Coral Sea: Holding the Line
790	Carriers: Midway: The Tide Turns/The Escort Carrier
791	Carriers: Wave of Victory/Kamikaze
792	Carriers: Lessions of War/Korea
793	Carriers: Vietnam: Dixie Station, Yankee Station/Vietnam: A Different Kind of War
797	Carriers 6 Cassette Video Collection
806	Computer Visions
808	On Any Sunday
817	Flight: F-15 Eagle
818	Flight: F-105 Thunderchief
819	Flight: B-25 Mitchell
820	Flight: P-51 Mustang
821	Flight: F-4 Phantom (II)
822	Flight: B-26 Marauder
823	Flight 6 Cassette Video Collection
824	Flight: Special Edition: F-15 Eagle
826	What Kids Want to Know About Sex and Growing Up
835	What Kids Want to Know About Sex and Growing Up 36 Piece for Retail
836	What Kids Want to Know About Sex and Growing Up 50 Piece Parents Brochures
837	What Kids Want to Know About Sex and Growing Up 12 Piece for Retail
838	Fear in the Dark
840	Michael Nesmith: Live at The Britt
853	John Bradshaw: On Surviving Divorce
859	Seventeenth Annual Telluride Bluegrass Festival
5032	Diana: A Portrait
5033	Diana: A Model Princess
5034	Diana 24 Piece for Retail
5036	Kurt Vonnegut's Monkey House
5040	Tanner 3 Cassette Set
5044	Flashing On The Sixties
5045	Flashing On The Sixties Book & Video Combo
5046	Comic Book Confidential
5057	Def Comedy Jam Audio & Video Combo
5058	Def Comedy Jam
5059	Def Comedy Jam Audio
5060	Def Comedy Jam 2
5061	Def Comedy Jam 2 Audio
5062	Def Comedy Jam 2 Audio and Video Combo
5068	Television Parts 4 Cassette Collection (Never Released)
5069	Television Parts Volume 1 (Never Released)
5070	Television Parts Volume 2 (Never Released)
5071	Television Parts Volume 3 (Never Released)
5072	Television Parts Volume 4 (Never Released)

PBS Home Video

The following is a listing of the PBS Home Video line. I was asked to list these as well since Nesmith was in charge of their initial distribution. Please note that some of these titles have been re-released by Turner Home Video and they look similar to the Pacific Arts releases and the only difference is the Turner logo on the box.

100	Frugal Gormet: Colonial Christmas With Friends
101	MacNeil/Lehrer: My Heart, Your Heart
102	Amazing Grace
103	Nature: The Volcano Watchers

104	This Old House: Creating a New Kitchen I
105	This Old House: Creating a New Kitchen II
110	Leo Buscaglia: Loving Relationships
117	Walk Through The 20th Century: The Democrat & The Dictator
123	Walk Through The 20th Century: The Second American Revolution, Parts I &II
131	Walk Through The 20th Century: The 30 Second President
135	Creation of the Universe
136	God And Politics: The Kingdom Divided
137	God And Politics: The Battle For the Bible
138	God And Politics: On Earth As It Is In Heaven
146	Creativity With Bill Moyers: John Huston
174	We Shall Overcome
213	Zora Is My Name
214	Wall Street Week: An Investment Primer: Stocks, Bonds & Gold
215	Wall Street Week: An Investment Primer: Mutual Funds, Options, etc...
216	Newton's Apple: Dinosaurs, Bulletproof Glass, Whales, Sharks, etc...
247	MacNeil/Lehrer: 15 Years of MacNeil/Lehrer
248	Nature: Hawaii: Island of the Fire Goddess
249	Nature: Rainforest Selva Verde: Green Jungle
250	American Patchwork: Cajun Country: Don't Drop The Potato
251	Newton's Apple: Skiing, Blimps, Beavers, Falcons, Baseball Bats, etc...
254	PBS 12 Pack for retail
255	PBS 24 Pack for retail
256	PBS 12 Pack for retail
257	PBS 24 Pack for retail
258	NBR: How Wall Street Works
260	American Patchwork: Land Where The Blues Began
261	American Patchwork: Jazz Parades: Feet Don't Fail Me Now
262	Winds of Change: A Matter of Promises
263	Odyssey: Myths and Moundbuilders
264	Tale of Two Cities
265	Jeeves and Wooster: Jeeves' Arrival
271	World of Ideas with Bill Moyers: Islamic Mind: Seyyed Hossein Nasr
273	Geronimo & The Apache Resistance
274	Spirit of Crazy Horse
275	Seasons of the Navajo
276	Astronomers: Where Is The Rest of the Universe?
277	Astronomers: Searching For Black Holes
278	Astronomers: A Window to Creation
279	Astronomers: Waves Of the Future
280	Astronomers: Stardust
281	Astronomers: Prospecting For Planets
282	Astronomers 6 Cassette Collection
283	Astronomers 24 Unit for Retail
287	Nature: Man's Best Friend
288	Nature: Death Trap
289	Nature: Cats
290	Nature: The Holy Land
294	Nature: Land of the Kiwi
296	Nature: Secret Weapons
298	Nature 24 Piece for Retail
300	American Patchwork: Appalachian Journey
301	American Patchwork: Dreams and Songs of the Noble Old
303	I, Claudius 7 Cassette Collection
304	Kids Ask About War
305	American Indian 5 Cassette Collection

306	Civil War 9 Cassette Collection
308	I, Claudius: Touch of Murder/Family Affairs
309	I, Claudius: Waiting in the Wings/What Shall We Do About Claudius?
310	I, Claudius: Poison Is Queen/Some Justice
311	I, Claudius: Queen of Heaven/Reign of Terror
312	I, Claudius: Zeus, By Jove/Hail Who?
313	I, Claudius: Fool's Luck/God in Colchester
314	I, Claudius: Old King Log
315	And A Nightingale Sang
316	Heat of the Day
317	Real Charlotte
318	Talking With David Frost: General H. Norman Schwarzkoph
319	Winds of Change: A Matter of Choice
320	Frontline: Vietnam Memorial
322	Newton's Apple: Mummies, Bicycles, Tigers, Helium Chat, Owls, etc...
323	Newton's Apple: Artificial Heart, Penguins, Fire, Lie Detector, etc...
324	Newton's Apple: Boomerangs, Muscles & Bones, Einstein, Bears, etc...
325	Newton's Apple: Plastic Surgery, Tornadoes, Hi-Speed Bicycles, etc...
326	MacNeil/Lehrer: Eat Smart
327	NBR: Guide To Retirement Planning
336	Jeeves and Wooster: Golf Tournament/The Gambling Event
338	Jeeves and Wooster: Hunger Strike/The Matchmaker
343	Civil War: The Cause, 1861
344	Civil War: A Very Bloody Affair, 1862
345	Civil War: Forever Free, 1862
346	Civil War: Simply Murder, 1863
347	Civil War: The Universe of Battle, 1863
348	Civil War: Valley of the Shadow of Death, 1864
349	Civil War: Most Hallowed Ground, 1864
350	Civil War: War Is All Hell, 1865
351	Civil War: The Better Angels of Our Nature
355	NBR: Guide To Buying Insurance
359	20 Years of Listening To America with Bill Moyers
360	Fit or Fat For the 90's
361	A. Einstein: How I See The World
365	LBJ
372	Leo Buscaglia: Together
373	Leo Buscaglia: Speaking of Love
374	Empire of the Air: The Men Who Made Radio
375	LBJ Twin Pack
388	Do You Mean There Are Still Real Cowboys?
389	Buckaroo Bard
390	Cowgirls
391	On The Cowboy Trail
392	Austin City Limits: Salute to the Cowboy
393	God and Politics 3 Cassette Collection
395	Can Tropical Rainforests Be Saved?
399	Mikhail Gorbachev: The Rise and Fall
403	American Cowboy 5 Cassette Collection
404	Crosby, Stills and Nash: Acoustic
406	Spaceflight: Thunder in the Skies
407	Spaceflight: The Wings of Mercury
408	Spaceflight: One Giant Leap
409	Spaceflight: The Territory Ahead
410	Spaceflight 4 Cassette Collection
414	A Dangerous Man

415	Lodz Ghetto
417	Millennium: Shock of the Other/Strange Relations
418	Millennium: Mistaken Identity/An Ecology of Mind
419	Millennium: The Art of Living/Touching the Timeless
420	Millennium: A Poor Man Shames Us All/Inventing Reality
421	Millennium: The Tightrope of Power/At the Threshold
422	Millennium 5 Cassette Collection
423	Eyes On the Prize: Awakenings
424	Eyes On the Prize: Fighting Back
425	Eyes On the Prize: Ain't Scared of Your Jails
426	Eyes On the Prize: No Easy Walk
427	Eyes On the Prize: Mississippi: Is This America?
428	Eyes On the Prize: Bridge to Freedom
437	Eyes On the Prize 6 Cassette Collection
439	Eyes On the Prize Commemorative Edition
440	Reading Rainbow: Rumplestiltskin/Snowy Day: Stories and Poems
441	Reading Rainbow: Dive to the Coral Reef/ The Magic Schoolbus: Under the Earth
442	Reading Rainbow: Mummies Made in Egypt/Bringing the Rain to Kapiti Plain
443	Reading Rainbow: Legend of the Indian Paintbrush/The Lifecycle of the Honeybee
444	Reading Rainbow: The Bicycle Man/The Adventures of Taxi Dog
445	Reading Rainbow: OPT: An Illusionary Tale/A Three Hat Day
447	Reading Rainbow 6 Cassette Collection
448	Reading Rainbow book and video combo
452	Reading Rainbow 12 Pack for retail
457	Eyes on the Prize Display art
458	Animal Olympians
459	Marine Life Miracles
1000	Traffik
1001	A Very British Coup
1016	Surviving Columbus: The Story of the Pueblo People
1018	Lincoln: The Making of a President
1019	Lincoln: The Pivotal Year
1021	Lincoln: Now He Belongs To The Ages
1022	Lincoln 4 Cassette Collection
1027	A Decade of Hard Choices: A Retrospective with Fred Friendly
1029	The Dinosaurs 4 Cassette Collection
1031	The Dinosaurs: Flesh on the Bones
1032	The Dinosaurs: The Nature of the Beast
1033	The Dinosaurs: The Death of the Dinosaurs
1035	The Dinosaurs: The Monsters Emerge
1036	George Washington: The Man Who Wouldn't Be King
1037	Lincoln: I Want to Finish This Job
1038	In Country
1046	Last Stand at Little Big Horn
1047	Berkeley In the Sixties
1052	Celebrating the American Family
1053	Tribal Legacies 4 Cassette Collection
1055	Eyes on the Prize II 4 Cassette Collection
1056	Eyes on the Prize II: The Time Has Come/Two Societies
1057	Eyes on the Prize II: Power!/The Promised Land
1058	Eyes on the Prize II: Ain't Gonna Shuffle No More/A Nation of Law?
1059	Eyes on the Prize II: The Key to the Kingdom/Back to the Movement
1061	The Incas
1062	Maya: Lords of the Jungle
1063	Lincoln and the War Within
1064	Encounters With Whales

271

1068	Leo Buscaglia: Born for Love
1091	Beyond Fit or Fat 4 Cassette Collection
1096	Covert Bailey's Fit or Fat: The Target Diet
1097	Covert Bailey's Fit or Fat: Potbellies and Thunder Thighs
1098	Covert Bailey's Fit or Fat: How to Get Fit Fast
1099	JFK, Hoffa and the Mob
1101	The Secret File on J. Edgar Hoover
1103	The Best of PBS 5 Cassette Collection
1104	Portraits of Greatness 4 Cassette Collection
1105	Maya Angelou
9972	The Civil War 9 Cassette Collection

Pacific Arts Video Laser Discs

L PAV 528	Timerider
L PAV 651	Vagabond
L PAV 708	Nezmuzic
L PAV 726	Tapeheads
L PAV 5001	Elephant Parts/Live at the Britt (Released twice with different covers. The second issue has a card signed by Michael.)
L PAV 5003	On Any Sunday
L PAV 5005	Agatha Christie: Murder By the Book
L PAV 5006	Ansel Adams: Photographer
L PAV 5007	A.C. Clarke's Strange Powers Vol.1
L PAV 5008	A.C. Clarke's Strange Powers Vol.2
L PAV 5009	A.C. Clarke's Strange Powers Vol.3
L PAV 5010	A.C. Clarke's Strange Powers Vol.4
L PAV 5011	A Doonesbury Special
L PAV 5012	The Eagle Has Landed
L PAV 5014	Le Grand Chemin
L PAV 5015	My Dinner with Andre
L PAV 5016	The Official Story (Subtitled)
L PAV 5017	Painting with Light
L PAV 5018	State of the Art of Computer Animation
L PAV 5019	State of Things
L PAV 5020	Timerider
L PAV 5021	Edie in Ciao! Manhattan
L PAV 5022	Down Among The "Z" Men
L PAV 5024	Space: The Frontiers and Beyond
L PAV 5025	A.C. Clarke's Mysterious World Vol.1
L PAV 5026	A.C. Clarke's Mysterious World Vol.2
L PAV 5027	A.C. Clarke's Mysterious World Vol.3
L PAV 5028	Agatha Christie/Partners in Crime:Unbreakable Alibi/Case of the Missing Lady
L PAV 5029	Agatha Christie/Partners in Crime: The Ambassador's Boots/The Man in Mist
L PAV 5030	Agatha Christie/Partners in Crime: The Cracler/The Affair of the Pink Pearl
L PAV 5031	Agatha Christie/Partners in Crime: The House of Lurking Death/Finessing King

PBS Home Video Laser Discs

L PBS 306	The Civil War

L PBS 361	A. Einstein: How I See The World
L PBS 374	Empire of the Air
L PBS 1002	Eyes on the Prize I 3 Disc Collection
L PBS 1003	Crosby, Stills & Nash:Acoustic
L PBS 1004	Geronimo/The Spirit of Crazy Horse
L PBS 1005	Amazing Grace
L PBS 1006	American Patchwork: Land Where Blues Began/Jazz Parades
L PBS 1007	LBJ
L PBS 1008	The Astronomers Collector's Edition
L PBS 1009	A Walk Through The 20th Century: The Democrat & The Dictator
L PBS 1011	We Shall Overcome
L PBS 1012	Zora is My Name
L PBS 1013	Newton's Apple
L PBS 1014	MacNeil/Lehrer: 15 Years of MacNeil/Lehrer
L PBS 1022	Lincoln 2 Disc Collection
L PBS 1029	The Dinosaurs
L PBS 1049	The American Cowboy Collection
L PBS 1051	The American Indian Collection
L PBS 1055	Eyes on the Prize II 4 Disc Collection
L PBS 1110	I, Claudius 7 Disc Collection
L PBS 1111	The Frugal Gourmet:Colonial Christmas

Hi-Top Sports Audio Books

HITC 2-7201	Bad Boys
HITC 2-7202	Beisbol
HITC 2-7203	Between the Lines
HITC 2-7204	Daly Life
HITC 2-7205	A Day in the Season of the LA Dodgers
HITC 2-7206	Super Bowl Chronicles Volume I
HITC 2-7207	Black Diamonds
HITC 2-7208	Darryl
HITC 2-7209	The History of the Pacific Coast League
HITC 2-7210	Best in the Game
HITC 2-7211	Super Bowl Chronicles Volume II
HITC 2-7212	Super Bowl Chronicles Volume III
HITC 2-7213	Against the World
HITC 2-7214	Super Bowl Chronicles Volume IV
HITC 2-7219	Ladies of the Court

Appendix 11: Michael Nesmith as Video Performer

Home Videos Starring Nesmith

1980	Pacific Arts PAVR-521 An Evening with Sir William Martin
1981	Pacific Arts PAVR-529 Michael Nesmith in Elephant Parts
1983	Pacific Arts/Sony (no number given) Michael Nesmith in Rio & Cruisin' Video 45
1985	Pacific Arts PAVR-526 Michael Nesmith in Television Parts Home Companion
1986	Pacific Arts PAVR-645 Michael Nesmith in Dr. Duck's Super Secret All-Purpose Sauce
1987	Pacific Arts (no number given) OverView January 1987
1989	Pacific Arts PAV 708 Nezmuzic
1989	Pacific Arts PAV 710 Space The Frontiers and Beyond (Nesmith provides narration for this documentary)
1992	Pacific Arts PAV 840 Michael Nesmith Live at the Britt Festival
1996	Rhino R3 2284 33 1/3 Revolutions Per Monkee
1997	Rhino R3 2327 Hey, Hey We're The Monkees (Monkees documentary originally aired on the Disney Channel)
1997	Rhino R3 2284 Justus (30 minutes of Monkees videos from the Justus CD)

Misc Home Videos

1989	Tapeheads, 30 minute promo tape hosted by Nesmith

DVD's Starring Nesmith

With The Monkees

2000	Rhino R2 4460 Head
2003	Rhino R2 976076 The Monkees Season 1 Nesmith provides commentary for the episodes; Here Come the Monkees – The Pilot, I've Got a Little Song Here and Monkees on Tour.
2003	Rhino R2 970128 The Monkees Season 2 Nesmith provides commentary for the episodes; Fairy Tale & Monkees Blow Their Minds.

Solo works of Michael Nesmith

1998	DVD International DVDI 0714 Michael Nesmith in Elephant Parts Contains 'Nez Explains It All' commentary.
2001	Anchor Bay DV11270 Michael Nesmith Live at the Britt
2003	Anchor Bay DV11901 Michael Nesmith in Elephant Parts Contains different Nesmith commentary.
2003	Videoranch release Michael Nesmith in Television Parts Home Companion

Miscellaneous

2000	New Concorde NH20787 Daydream Believers The Monkees' Story contains commentaries with Peter Tork, David Jones and Micky Dolenz.
2000	Anchor Bay DV11229 Repo Man contains commentary with Alex Cox, Nesmith, Victoria Thomas, Sy Richardson,

Zander Schloss and Del Zamora.
2001   Anchor Bay DV11238 Tapeheads
        contains commentary with Bill Fishman, Catherine Hardwicke and Nesmith.
2003   Anchor Bay DV11686 Square Dance
        contains director Daniel Petrie commentary
2004   Anchor Bay DV11400 Timerider
        contains director William Dear commentary

Music Videos Starring Nesmith

1977   Rio
1979   Cruisin'
1981   Magic
1981   Light
1981   Tonight
1984   Eldorado To The Moon
1985   I'll Remember You
1985   Chow Mein and Bowling

Music Videos Produced/Directed by Nesmith

1980   Kim Carnes "More Love" (EMI)
1980   Sean Tyla "Breakfast In Marin" (Polydor)
1980   Poco "Under The Gun" (MCA)
1980   Trefethen "The Last Bosenians" (Pacific Arts)
1982   Rosanne Cash "I Don't Know Why You Don't Want Me" (CBS Records)
1982   Rosanne Cash "I Wonder" (CBS Records)
1982   Juice Newton "Love's Been A Little Bit Hard On Me (CBS Records)
1983   Lionel Richie "All Night Long" (Motown Records)
1995   Jonatha Brooks and The Story "Nothing Sacred" (GRP Records)

275

Appendix 12: Michael Nesmith as Film Maker/Performer

1968   **Head**

Michael Nesmith	The Monkees
Micky Dolenz	
David Jones	
Peter Tork	
Annette Funicello	Minnie
Timothy Carey	Lord High 'n' Low
Logan Ramsey	Officer Faye Lapid
Abraham Sofaer	Swami
Vito Scotti	I. Vitteloni
Charles Macaulay	Inspector Shrink
T. C. Jones	Mr. & Mrs. Ace
Charles Irving	Mayor Feedback
William Bagdad	Black Sheik
Percy Helton	Heraldic Messenger
Sonny Liston	Extra
Ray Nitschke	Private One
Carol Doda	Sally Silicone
Frank Zappa	The Critic
June Fairchild	The Jumper
Terri Garr	Testy True
I. J. Jefferson	Lady Pleasure
Victor Mature	The Big Victor
Director	Bob Rafelson
Producers	Bob Rafelson & Jack Nicholson
Writers	Bob Rafelson & Jack Nicholson
Executive Producer	Bert Schneider

1974   **Northville Cemetary Massacre**

a.k.a. Freedom R.I.P.
a.k.a. Harley's Angels

David Hyry	Chris
Carson Jackson	Deke
Jan Sisk	Lynn
Herb Sharples	John Tyner
Len Speck	Armstrong
J. Craig Collicott	Putnam
Scorpions Motorcycle Club of Detroit	Themselves
Director	William Dear & Thomas L. Dyke
Producer	William Dear & Thomas L. Dyke
Writers	William Dear, Thomas L. Dyke & Jim Pappas
Executive Producer	Robert H. Dyke
Music Composer	Michael Nesmith

1983   **Timerider: The Adventures of Lyle Swann**

Fred Ward	Lyle Swann

Belinda Bauer		Claire Cygne
Peter Coyote		Porter Reese
Richard Masur		Claude Dorsett
Tracey Walter		Carl Dorsett
Ed Lauter		Padre
L. Q. Jones	Ben Potter	
Chris Mulkey		Daniels
Macon McCalman		Dr. Sam
Jonathan Bahnks		Jesse
Laurie O' Brien		Terry
William Dear		Third Technician
Michael Nesmith		Technician

Director	William Dear
Producer	Harry Gittes
Writers	Michael Nesmith & William Dear
Executive Producer	Michael Nesmith
Music Composer	Michael Nesmith

1984 **Repo Man**

Harry Dean Stanton	Bud
Emilio Estevez	Otto
Tracey Walter	Miller
Olivia Barash	Leila
Sy Richardson	Lite
Susan Barnes	Agent Rogersz
Fox Harris	J. Frank Parnell
Tom Finnegan	Oly
Del Zamora	Lagarto
Eddie Velez	Napo
Vonetta McGee	Marlene
Rodney Bingenheimer	Club Owner

Director	Alex Cox
Producer	Jonathan Wacks & Peter McCarthy
Writer	Alex Cox
Executive Producer	Michael Nesmith

1987 **Square Dance**

Jason Robards	Dillard
Jane Alexander	Juanelle
Winona Ryder	Gemma
Rob Lowe	Rory
Deborah Richter	Gwen
Guich Koock	Frank
Elbert Lewis	Beecham
Charlotte Stanton	Aggie
J. David Moeller	Dub Mosley
Dixie Taylor	Dolores

Director	Daniel Petrie
Producer	Daniel Petrie
Writer	Alan Hines
Executive Producer	Charles Haid & Jane Alexander

(Michael Nesmith and NBC provided the money for this production.)

277

1987   **Burglar**
    Whoopi Goldberg   Bernice Rhodenbarr
    Bobcat Goldthwait   Carl Heller
    G. W. Bailey   Ray Kirschman
    Lesley Ann Warren   Dr. Cynthia Sheldrake
    James Handy   Carson Verrill
    Anne DeSalvo   Detective Todras
    John Goodman   Detective Nyswander
    Elizabeth Ruscio   Frankie
    Vyto Ruginis   Graybow
    Larry Mintz   Knobby
    Michael Nesmith   Cab Driver

    Director   Hugh Wilson
    Producer   Michael Hirsh & Kevin McCormick
    Writer   Joseph Loeb III & Matthew Weisman

1988   **Tapeheads**
    John Cusak   Ivan Alexeev
    Tim Robbins   Josh Tager
    Mary Crosby   Samantha Gregory
    Clu Gulager   Norman Mart
    Katy Boyer   Belinda Mart
    Jessica Walter   Kay Mart
    Sam Moore   Billy Diamond
    Junior Walker   Lester Diamond
    Doug McClure   Sid Tager
    Connie Stevens   June Tager
    Susan Tyrrell   Nikki Morton
    King Cotton   Roscoe
    Don Cornelius   Mo Fuzz
    Michael Nesmith   Skip
    Lyle Alzado   Thor Alexeev
    "Weird Al" Yankovic   Himself

    Director   Bill Fishman
    Producer   Peter McCarthy
    Writer   Bill Fishman & Peter McCarthy
    Executive Producer   Michael Nesmith

Appendix 13: Michael Nesmith as Television Actor

The Monkees

Songs listed as included in the show are the songs used in the original NBC broadcasts. Later episodes repeated on CBS and in syndication had some songs replaced with later recordings.

Season One

1. Royal Flush (9-12-66)
    The Monkees rescue the Princess of Harmonica from her evil uncle the Archduke Otto.
    "Take A Giant Step"
    "This Just Doesn't Seem To Be My Day"
    "Last Train To Clarksville"
    Director: James Frawley
    Writers: Peter Meyerson & Robert Schlitt

2. Monkee See, Monkee Die (9-19-66)
    The Monkees spend the night in a haunted house in order to collect an inheritance.
    "Tomorrow's Gonna Be Another Day"
    "Last Train To Clarksville"
    Director: James Frawley
    Writer: Treva Silverman

3. Monkee vs. Machine (9-26-66)
    The Monkees go job hunting in a computerized toy factory
    "Last Train To Clarksville"
    "Saturday's Child"
    Director: Bob Rafelson
    Writer: David Panich

4. Your Friendly Neighborhood Kidnappers (10-3-66)
    A crooked publicity man kidnaps the Monkees to stop them from winning a talent contest.
    "Last Train To Clarksville"
    "(I'm Not Your) Stepping Stone"
    Director: James Frawley
    Writer: Dave Evans

5. The Spy Who Came In From The Cool (10-10-66)
    The Monkees get mixed up with a spy ring who want the microfilm hidden in Davy's maracas.
    "Last Train to Clarksville"
    "(I'm Not Your) Stepping Stone"
    "The Kind of Girl I Could Love"
    "All The King's Horses"
    Director: Bob Rafelson
    Writers: Gerald Gardner & Dee Caruso

6. The Success Story (10-17-66)

The Monkees try to convince Davy's visiting grandfather that his grandson
is wealthy and successful
"I Wanna Be Free"
"Sweet Young Thing"
Director: James Frawley
Writers: Gerald Gardner & Dee Caruso & Bernie Orenstein

7.   Monkees In A Ghost Town (10-24-66)
Stranded in a ghost town, the Monkees meet up with a band of gangsters.
"(Theme From) The Monkees" (with Rose Marie)
"Tomorrow's Gonna Be Another Day"
"Papa Gene's Blues"
Director: James Frawley
Writers: Robert Schlitt & Peter Meyerson

8.   Don't Look A Gift Horse In The Mouth (10-31-66)
Davy is given a horse, which the Monkees have to hide from the landlord.
"Papa Gene's Blues"
"All The King's Horses"
Director: Bob Rafelson
Writer: Dave Evans

9.   The Chaperone (11-7-66)
Micky must pose as a female chaperone so Davy can date General
Vandenburg's daughter.
"This Just Doesn't Seem To Be My Day"
"Take A Giant Step"
Director: Bruce Kessler
Writers: Gerald Gardner & Dee Caruso

10.   The Monkees (Pilot) (also titled: Here Come the Monkees) (11-14-66)
The Monkees are hired to play at a sweet sixteen party and they help the
birthday girl with her studies.
"I Wanna Be Free"
"Let's Dance On"
Director: Mike Elliot
Writers: Paul Mazursky & Larry Tucker

11.   Monkees A La Carte (11-21-66)
The Monkees save an Italian restaurant from being taken over by the
Purple Flower Gang.
"(I'm Not Your) Steppin' Stone"
"She"
Director: Jim Frawley
Writers: Gerald Gardner, Dee Caruso & Bernie Orenstein

12.   I've Got A Little Song Here (11-28-66)
Mike is conned by a phony song publisher.
"Gonna Buy Me A Dog"
"Mary, Mary"
Director: Bruce Kessler
Writer: Treva Silverman

13.   One Man Shy (12-5-66)
Peter falls in love with a debutante who has a wealthy boyfriend.
"I'm a Believer"

"You Just May Be The One"
Director: James Frawley
Writer: Gerald Gardner, Dee Caruso & Treva Silverman

14.   Dance, Monkees, Dance (12-12-66)
The Monkees wind up signing lifetime contracts for lessons at a
local dance school.
"I'll Be Back Up On My Feet"
"I'm A Believer"
Director: James Frawley
Writer: Bernie Orenstein

15.   Too Many Girls (12-19-66)
A stage mother pushes her daughter into a showbiz career via
a duo act with Davy
"I'm A Believer"
"Different Drum" parody
Director: James Frawley
Writers: Dave Evans, Gerald Gardner & Dee Caruso

16.   Son Of Gypsy (12-26-66)
A band of gypsies force the Monkees to steal the `Maltese Vulture'
to free Peter who was kidnapped.
"I'm A Believer"
Director: James Frawley
Writers: Gerald Gardner, Dee Caruso & Treva Silverman

17.   Case Of The Missing Monkee (1-9-66)
Peter is kidnapped when he searches for a kidnapped scientist.
"(I'm Not Your) Steppin' Stone"
Director: Bob Rafelson
Writers: Gerald Gardner & Dee Caruso

18.   I Was A Teenage Monster (1-16-67)
The Monkees are hired by a mad scientist to teach his creation to play music.
"Your Auntie Grizelda"
"Tomorrow's Gonna Be Another Day"
"Monkees Theme"
Director: Sidney Miller
Writers: Gerald Gardner, Dee Caruso & Dave Evans

19.   Find The Monkees (1-23-67)
The Monkees try to audition for a TV producer but things keep going wrong.
"Sweet Young Thing"
"Papa Gene's Blues"
"I'm A Believer"
Director: Richard Nunis
Writers: Gerald Gardner & Dee Caruso

20.   Monkees In The Ring (1-30-67)
A crooked boxing promoter tries to turn Davy into a boxer.
"Laugh"
"I'll Be Back Up On My Feet"
Director: James Frawley
Writers: Gerald Gardner & Dee Caruso

21. The Prince And The Pauper (2-6-67)
Davy is the dead ringer of a shy young prince who is the victim of a
murder plot.
"Mary, Mary"
Director: James Komack
Writer: Peter Meyerson

22. Monkees At The Circus (2-13-67)
The Monkees try to help an unsuccessful circus.
"She"
"Sometime In The Morning"
Director: Bruce Kessler
Writer: David Panich

23. Captain Crocodile (2-20-67)
The Monkees appearance on a children's show is sabotaged by the
jealous host.
"Valleri"
"Your Auntie Grizelda"
Director: James Frawley
Writers: Gerald Gardner & Dee Caruso

24. Monkees A La Mode (2-27-67)
A fashion magazine runs an inaccurate article on the Monkees.
"Laugh"
"You Just May Be The One"
Director: Alex Singer
Writers: Gerald Gardner & Dee Caruso

25. Alias Micky Dolenz (3-6-67)
Micky must impersonate his lookalike, the famous gangster 'Baby Face'.
"The Kind Of Girl I Could Love"
"Mary, Mary"
Director: Bruce Kessler
Writers: Gerald Gardner & Dee Caruso

26. Monkee Chow Mein (3-13-67)
The Monkees battle Dragonman to free Peter who was kidnapped by a
Chinese gangster. Monkeemen come to the rescue
"Your Auntie Grizelda"
Director: James Frawley
Writers: Gerald Gardner & Dee Caruso

27. Monkee Mother (3-20-67)
The Monkees get a new roommate in the form of a middle aged widow
named Millie.
"Sometime In The Morning"
"Look Out (Here Comes Tomorrow)"
Director: James Frawley
Writers: Peter Meyerson & Bob Schlitt

28. Monkees On The Line (3-27-67)
The Monkees cause a lot of trouble as they take over a telephone
answering service.
"Look Out (Here Comes Tomorrow)"
Director: James Frawley

Writers: Gerald Gardner, Dee Caruso & Coslough Johnson

29.   Monkees Get Out More Dirt (4-3-67)
      The four Monkees compete for the love of April Conquest, the owner
      of the local laundromat.
      "The Girl I Knew Somewhere"
      "Monkees Theme" (snippet)
      Director: Gerald Shepard
      Writers: Gerald Gardner & Dee Caruso

30.   Monkees in Manhattan (4-10-67)
      The Monkees go to New York and save a producer from bankruptcy.
      "The Girl I Knew Somewhere"
      "Look Out (Here Comes Tomorrow)"
      "Words"
      Director: Russell Mayberry
      Writers: Gerald Gardner & Dee Caruso

31.   Monkees At The Movies (4-17-67)
      Getting bit parts in a beach movie, the boys incur the wrath of the
      movie's star Frankie Catalina.
      "When Love Comes Knockin' At Your Door"
      "Valleri"
      "Last Train To Clarksville"
      Director: Russell Mayberry
      Writers: Gerald Gardner & Dee Caruso

32.   Monkees On Tour (4-20-67)
      A documentary look at the behind-the-scene madness of a
      Monkees concert in Phoenix, Arizona.
      "Randy Scouse Git"
      "Words"
      Medley: "Last Train To Clarksville"
                 "Sweet Young Thing"
                 "Mary, Mary"
                 "Cripple Creek"
                 "You Can't Judge A Book By It's Cover"
                 "I Wanna Be Free"
                 "I Got A Woman"
                 "(I'm Not Your) Steppin' Stone"
      Director: Bob Rafelson
      Writer: Bob Rafelson

Season 2

33.   It's A Nice Place to Visit (9-11-67)
      The Monkees go to Mexico where they are forced to join a bandit
      gang to free kidnapped Davy.
      "What Am I Doing Hangin' Round?"
      Director: James Frawley
      Writer: Treva Silverman

34.   The Picture Frame (9-18-67)
      Believing they are making a movie, the Monkees rob a bank.
      "Pleasant Valley Sunday"
      "Randy Scouse Git"

Director: James Frawley
Writer: Jack Winter

35.   Everywhere A Sheik Sheik (9-25-67)
       Davy is kidnapped and finds himself engaged to marry an Arabian princess.
       "Love Is Only Sleeping"
       "Cuddly Toy"
       Director: Alex Singer
       Writer: Jack Winter

36.   Monkee Mayor (10-2-67)
       Mike runs for mayor to stop his neighborhood from being torn
       down for the sake of progress.
       "No Time"
       "Pleasant Valley Sunday"
       Director: Alex Singer
       Writer: Jack Winter

37.   Art, For Monkees Sake (10-9-67)
       Peter's paintbrush talents get him kidnapped at an art gallery and he
       is forced to reproduce a work of art.
       "Randy Scouse Git"
       "Daydream Believer"
       Director: Alex Singer
       Writer: Coslough Johnson

38.   I Was A 99 Pound Weakling (10-16-67)
       Micky takes a body building course to impress a beach beauty.
       "Sunny Girlfriend"
       "Love Is Only Sleeping"
       Director: Alex Singer
       Writers: Gerald Gardner, Dee Caruso & Neil Burstyn

39.   Hillbilly Honeymoon (10-23-67)
       Davy is kidnapped and expected to marry young Ella Mae when
       the Monkees get stuck in a family feud.
       "Papa Gene's Blues"
       Director: James Frawley
       Writer: Peter Meyerson

40.   Monkees Marooned (10-30-67)
       After Peter trades his guitar for a buried treasure map, the Monkees
       become marooned on a desert island.
       "Daydream Believer"
       "What Am I Doing Hangin' Round?"
       Director: James Frawley
       Writer: Stanley Ralph Ross

41.   Card Carrying Red Shoes (11-6-67)
       A visiting Russian ballerina with microfilm hidden in her shoes tries to defect.
       "She Hangs Out"
       Director: James Frawley
       Writer: Lee Stanford

42.   Wild Monkees (11-13-67)
       The Monkees are forced to imitate a gang of bikers when they encounter

a real motorcycle gang.
"Goin' Down"
"Star Collector"
Director: Jon C. Anderson
Writers: Stanley Ralph Ross & Corey Upton

43.   A Coffin Too Frequent (11-20-67)
        The Monkees are forced to witness a man's return from the dead as a
        mad scientist takes over the house.
        "Daydream Believer"
        "Goin' Down"
        Director: David Winters
        Writer: Stella Linden

44.   Hitting The High Seas (11-27-67)
        When the Monkees sign on as shiphands they find themselves under the orders
        of a pirate captain.
        "Daydream Believer"
        "Star Collector"
        Director: James Frawley
        Writer: Jack Winter

45.   Monkees In Texas (12-4-67)
        During a visit to Mike's aunt, the Monkees becomes involved a feud over
        land and oil.
        "Words"
        "Goin' Down"
        Director: James Frawley
        Writer: Jack Winter

46.   Monkees On The Wheel (12-11-67)
        The Monkees become involved with crooked gamblers while in Las Vegas.
        "The Door Into Summer"
        "Cuddly Toy"
        Director: Jerry Sheppard
        Writer: Coslough Johnson

47.   The Christmas Show (12-25-67)
        The Monkees try to teach a cold-hearted child the true spirit of Christmas.
        "Riu Chiu"
        Director: Jon Anderson
        Writers: Dave Evans & Neil Burstyn

48.   Fairy Tale (1-8-68)
        In this spoof of fairy tales, Peter tries to save Princess Gwen
        (Michael in drag).
        "Daily Nightly"
        Director: James Frawley
        Writer: Peter Meyerson

49.   Monkees Watch Their Feet (1-15-68)
        Aliens invade Earth and replace Micky with a double who has backwards feet.
        "Star Collector"
        Director: Alex Singer
        Writer: Coslough Johnson

50. The Monstrous Monkee Mash (1-22-68)
     The Monkees battle vampires, werewolves and a Frankenstein like creature
     to save Davy.
     "Goin' Down"
     Director : James Frawley
     Writers: Neil Burstyn & David Panich

51. The Monkees Paw (1-29-68)
     A bad luck but reasonably priced monkey paw causes Micky to lose his voice.
     "Words"
     Director: James Frawley
     Writer: Coslough Johnson

52. The Devil And Peter Tork (2-5-68)
     Peter trades his soul to the devil for the ability to play the harp, but Mike
     wins it back in court.
     "Salesman"
     "No Time"
     Director: James Frawley
     Writer: Robert Kaufman

53. Monkees Race Again (2-12-68)
     Davy races the Monkeemobile against the baron and his Clutzmobile.
     "What Am I Doing Hangin' Round"
     Director: James Frawley
     Writer: Dave Evans & Elias Davis & David Pollock

54. Monkees In Paris (2-19-68)
     Frustrated by the same old scripts, the Monkees go to Paris.
     "Don't Call On Me"
     "Love Is Only Sleeping"
     "Star Collector"
     Director: Bob Rafelson
     Writer: Bob Rafelson

55. The Monkees Mind Their Manor (2-26-68)
     Davy inherits a castle in England but must win a singing contest before
     claiming it.
     "Star Collector"
     Director: Peter H. Thorkelson
     Writer: Coslough Johnson

56. Some Like It Lukewarm (3-4-68)
     Davy dresses in drag so the Monkees can win a battle of the bands contest.
     "The Door Into Summer"
     "She Hangs Out"
     Director: James Frawley
     Writers: Joel Kane & Stanley Z. Cherry

57. Monkees Blow Their Minds (3-11-68)
     Oraculo, the great mentalist, hypnotizes Peter and Mike so they will join
     his act.
     "Valleri"
     "Daily Nightly"
     Director: David Winters
     Writer: Peter Meyerson

58.   Mijacogeo (3-18-68)
        The evil wizard Glick tries to control the world with Frodis, an
        alien he captured.
        "Zor And Zam"
        Director: Micky Dolenz
        Writers: Jon Anderson & Micky Dolenz

Michael Nesmith in Television Parts

Pilot episode directed by William Dear
Airdate: March 7, 1985
Special Guests: Martin Mull, Garry Shandling, Jim Stafford, The Funny Boys: Jonathan
Schmock and James Vallely.

Second episode directed by Alan Myerson
Airdate: June 14, 1985
Special Guests: Jay Leno, Arsenio Hall, The Coyote Sisters.

Third episode directed by Alan Myerson
Airdate: June 21, 1985
Special Guests: Dick Cavett, Whoopi Goldberg, Martin Mull, Dirkson von Mast.

Fourth episode directed by Alan Myerson
Airdate: June 28, 1985
Special Guests: Lois Bromfield, Jimmy Buffett, Garry Shandling,

Fifth episode directed by Alan Myerson
Airdate: July 5, 1985
Special Guests: A. Whitney Brown, Jerry Lee Lewis, Jerry Seinfeld.

Last three episodes edited into 90 minute slot directed by Alan Myerson
Airdate: July 27, 1985
Special Guests: Jimmy Buffett, Rosanne Cash, The Funny Boys: Jonathan Schmock and James
Vallely, Whoopi Goldberg, Bobcat Goldthwait, Arsenio Hall, Jay Leno, Jerry Lee Lewis, The
MFQ (Modern Folk Quartet), Martin Mull, Taylor Negron.

TV Specials

Hey, Hey, It's The Monkees
Airdate: February 17, 1997
Starring: Michael Nesmith, Peter Tork, Micky Dolenz & David Jones
TV special written & directed by Michael Nesmith

Appendix 14: Bibliography

BOOKS

Beck, Marilyn. *Marilyn Beck's Hollywood*. New York: Hawthorn Books, 1973.
Blaine, Hal and David Goggin. *Hal Blaine and The Wrecking Crew*. California: MixBooks, 1990.
Crevelt, Dwight and Louise Crevelt. *Slot Machine Mania*. Michigan: Gollehon Books, 1989.
Dolenz, Micky and Mark Bego. *I'm A Believer- My Life of Monkees, Music, and Madness*. New York: Hyperion, 1993. Cooper Square Press, 2004.
Jones, Davy. *Davy Jones: Daydream Believin'*. Hercules Promotions, 2000.
Jones, Davy and Alan Green. *They Made A Monkee Out of Me*. Pennsylvania: Dome Press, 1987.
Harper, Colin. *Dazzling Stranger - Bert Jansch and the British Folk and Blues Revival*. Great Britain: Bloomsbury Publishing Plc, 2000.
Hopkins, Jerry . *The Rock Story*. New York: Signet Books, 1970.
Lefcowitz, Eric. *The Monkees Tale (Revised Edition)*. San Francisco: Last Gasp, Inc, 1989.
Marcus, Greil. *Dead Elvis*. New York: Anchor Books, 1991.
McGilligan, Patrick. *Jack's Life- A Biography of Jack Nicholson*. New York: W. W. Norton & Company, 1994.
McGrath, Tom. *MTV-The Making of a Revolution*. Philadelphia: Running Press, 1996.
Miller, Edwin. *Seventeen Interviews Film Stars and Superstars*. New York: Macmillan Company, 1970.
Murray, Charles Shaar. *Crosstown Traffic: Jimi Hendrix and the Rock n' Roll Revolution*. New York: St. Martins Press, 1989.
Nance, Scott. *Music You Can See: The MTV Story*. Las Vegas, Nevada: Pioneer Books, 1993.
Pollock, Bruce. *When the Music Mattered*. New York: Holt, Rinehart and Winston, 1984
Reilly, Edward and Maggie McManus and William Chadwick. *The Monkees- A Manufactured Image*. Ann Arbor, Michigan: Pierian Press, 1987.
Shore, Michael. *The Rolling Stone Book of Rock Video*. New York: Rolling Stone Press, 1984.
Smith, Joe. *Off The Record*. New York: Warner Books, 1988.
Vare, Ethlie Ann and Greg Ptacek. *Mothers of Invention- From the Bra To The Bomb, Forgotten Women And Their Unforgettable Ideas*. New York: William Morrow and Company, 1988.
Wiseman, Rich. *Neil Diamond: Solitary Star*. New York: Dodd, Mead & Company, 1987.

MAGAZINES

"Aussie Imposters At Work." *Billboard*, May 10, 1980.
"Chrysalis Titles To Pacific Arts." *Billboard*, February 4, 1984.
"Comedy...The Cure." *Cinetex Report*, August, 1989.
"Elektra Bows Country Label." *Billboard*, January 20, 1973.
"Elephant Parts Video Movie Filmed In California." *Billboard*, April 4, 1981.
"MCA Distributing, Pacific Arts Pact." *Billboard*, November 6, 1982.
"Meet Tackles Video Issues In Nashville." *Billboard*, December 5, 1981.
"Michael Nesmith: The Maverick Makes Good." *People*, August 12, 1985.
"Michael Nesmith Is Innocent." *Mojo*, November, 1994.
"Michael Nesmith: It Is What It Is" *Songwriter's Monthly*, December, 1996.
"Montieth Riverpark To Be Closed Thursday Until 4." *The Albany Democrat-Herald*, August 17, 1994.
"Nesmith & Cody Coming." *Melody Maker*, November 8, 1975.

"Nesmith & Island Ink Distribution Pact." *Billboard*, September 25, 1976.

"Nesmith Cuts 6 Sides With A 'Triple Header' Sound." *Billboard*, June 22, 1968.

"Nesmith Launches Countryside Label." *Variety*, February 7, 1973.

"Nesmith Readies 'Swann' Music." *Billboard*, January 9, 1982.

"Nesmith Sues Island." *Record World*, October 15, 1977.

"Nesmith's Britt Concert To Become Video Album." *The Mail Tribune*, June 11, 1992.

"Overdrive Meets Mike Nesmith." *Overdrive*, September, 1971.

"Pacific Arts In U.K., Australia Distribution Deals." *Billboard*, August 18, 1984.

"Pacific Arts Video Calls It Quits." *Video Business*, May 6, 1994.

"Pacific Arts Releases New Nesmith Single." *Billboard*, October 9, 1982

"Polygram Has Rights To Elephant Parts." *Variety*, November 13, 1981.

"Random Notes." *Rolling Stone*, December 23, 1971.

"Random Notes." *L.A. Herald-Examiner*, May 1, 1981.

"RCA on Coast Talent Push on Campus Concerts." *Billboard*, November 20, 1971.

Review: "The Prison." *Melody Maker*, November 15, 1975.

Review: "And the Hits Just Keep On Comin'." *Billboard*, August 5, 1972.

Review: "Pretty Much Your Standard Ranch Stash." *Billboard*, October 6, 1973

Review: "Michael Nesmith & The First National Band: Complete." *Dirty Linen*, April/May, 1994.

Review: "Television Parts." *Variety*, March 13, 1985.

Review: "Gaslight I Concert." *Variety*, October 6, 1971.

Review: "State Theatre, Sydney Australian Concert." *Variety*, November 16, 1977.

Review: "Michael Nesmith In Elephant Parts (LaserDisc)." *Billboard*, June 12, 1982

Review: "...Tropical Campfires..." *The Hard Report*, February 26, 1993.

"Shoot 'Monkees' Around Nesmith, Under Knife." *Variety*, May 23, 1967.

"Trapped." *Forbes*, April 15, 1973.

"Varied Prices For Nesmith's Album." *Billboard*, February 14, 1976.

"Vidpix Talks To Video Visionary Michael Nesmith." *Vidpix*, Vol 3, No. 9.

Ambrose, Chris. "Michael Nesmith." *Tokion*, September/October 2003.

Arar, Yardena. "Ex-Rock Star Visualizes A New Art Form." *Arizona Republic*, September 23, 1981.

Auerbach, Matthew. "Nesmith Dusts Off Gems." *New York Daily News*, February 24, 1992.

Baltin, Steve. Review: "The Garden." *Cashbox*, February 18, 1995.

Battaglio, Stephen and Mary Huhn. "Monkee Nesmith to Publish Video Mag." *Adweek*, September 8, 1986.

Behrens, Steve. "PBS Partner In Home Video Seen Ailing." *Current*, June 28, 1993.

Behrens, Steve. "Producers, PBS claim Pacific Arts Owes Them $2 Million-Plus." *Current*, February 20, 1995.

Behrens, Steve. "Nesmith Reply Blames PBS For Video Labels Failure." *Current*, April 3, 1995.

Beller, Miles. Review: "Austin City Limits." *Hollywood Reporter*, January 21, 1993.

Beltane, Dave. Review: "...Tropical Campfires..." *Dirty Linen*, June/July, 1993.

Beltane, Dave. Review: "The Prison, The Garden,etc..." *Dirty Linen*, June/July, 1995.

Berman, Marc. "Michael Nesmith: Hey, Hey, He's Much More Than a Monkee- A Barrelful More." *Video Review*, June, 1987.

Bessman, Jim. Review: "Lone Star Roadhouse Concert." *Billboard*, March 14, 1992.

Bianculli, David. "Best of PBS-On Video." *New York Post*, July 25, 1990.

Bierbaum, Tom. "Nesmith Testing 'Symbiosis Of TV and Homevid." *Variety*, June 28, 1985.

Black, Louis. "The Nesmith Legacy-A Singer And His Songs." *Austin Chronicle*, September 11, 1992.

Blackwell, M.I. "Debut of 'OverView' May Be it's Swansong." *Dallas Morning News*, March 16, 1987.

Blenkle, Joe. "Nesmith's Latest Looks at Beginnings." *Orangevale News*, December 22, 1993

Blowen, Michael. "Ex-Monkee Nesmith Has Seen The Future." *The Boston Sunday Globe*. February 5, 1989.

Bohn, Jeff. Review: "The Older Stuff." *The Cosmic American Music News*, Winter/Spring, 1992.

Boissonade, David. "Mike Nesmith." *Music Collector*, August, 1991.

Boyd, Deanna. "Life After The Monkees." *The Albany Democrat-Herald*, August 16, 1994.

Bronson, Harold. "Instant Replay: Does Anyone Dare Remember The Monkees ?" *Coast*, September, 1971.

Bronson, Harold. "Mike Nesmith-The Monkees, Hendrix, Zappa, Easy Rider...To First National Band." *Hit Parader*, February, 1972.

Bronson, Harold. "Michael Nesmith-No More Monkee Business." *Rock Magazine*, May 21, 1973.

Brown, Joe. "The Niches Of Nesmith." *The Washington Post*, February 21, 1992.

Brumley, Al. "A Monkee At Heart." *Dallas Morning News*, November 20, 1994.

Burton, Charlie. Review: "Nevada Fighter." *Rolling Stone*, July 22, 1971.

Carafelli, Carl. Review: "The Garden." *Goldmine*, March 31, 1995.

Chase, Donald. "On the Set of 'Square Dance.' *New York Daily News*, September 14, 1986.

Clark, Randy. Review: "...Tropical Campfires..." *Cashbox*, December 26, 1992.

Clayton, John. "Nesmith Today." *Ballroom Blitz*, August, 1977.

Cling, Carol. "Nesmith Takes His Hat Off to New Video." *Las Vegas Review-Journal*, September 12, 1986.

Crook, David. "Ex-Monkee Nesmith: Video's New-Wave Guru." *Los Angeles Times*, April 30, 1981.

Curry, Jack. Review: "Television Parts." *USA Today*, March 7, 1985.

Daly, Tom. "The Monkees' Mike Nesmith-His Desperate Search For The Father Who Deserted Him!" *TV and Movie Screen*, January, 1967.

Darling, Cary. "No Regrets For Pacific Arts In Shift From Vinyl To Video." *Billboard*, February 27, 1982.

DeYoung, Bill. "Michael Nesmith." *Music Players Magazine*, September 3-16, 1992.

DiMartino, Dave. Review: "...Tropical Campfires..." *Entertainment Weekly*, January 29, 1993.

Doggett, Peter. "Too Much Monkee Business?" *Record Collector*, August, 1997.

Doke, Mike. "Hellecasters, Nesmith Add To Apple Jam's Diversity." *Hood River News*, August 20, 1994.

Doke, Mike. "Apple Jam Charms 2,000 Eager Fans." *Hood River News*, August 24, 1994.

Duff, S.L. "Jimi and the Monkees." *Guitar World*, March, 1988

Edgers, Geoff "Think Diffident" *Wired*, December, 2000.

Eller, Claudia. "Nesmith Goes From Monkees To Mogul." *Hollywood Reporter*, March 19, 1987.

Ervolino, Bill. "Daydream Believer." *New York Post*, March 15, 1989

Everett, Todd. "Hey, Hey, Here's The Monkees." *L.A. Herald-Examiner*, July 11, 1989.

Fong-Torres, Ben. "Mike Nesmith Shakes The Monkee From His Back." *GQ*, August, 1984.

Forman, Bill. "Sound & Vision." *43rd Annual Grammy Awards program*, 2001.

Foster, Madge. "Meet The Monkee Baby (Why No Doctor Was At His Birth.)" *TV Picture Life*, February, 1967.

Freedland, Nat. "Nesmith to Begin Elektra C&W Label." *Billboard*, July 15, 1972

Freeman, Paul. "Monkees Are Only A Minor Part Of Life For Nesmith." *Milwaukee Journal*, May 5, 1992.

Fricke, David. Review: "Infinite Rider On The Big Dogma." *Rolling Stone*, November 15, 1979.

Frieden, Jack. Review: "...Tropical Campfires..." *The Virginian-Pilot and The Ledger-Star*, December 4, 1992.

Gans, David. "Mike Nesmith interview." *Mix*, April 1982.

Gelman, Morrie. "PBS Annual Meet to Key on Funding For Programs." *Variety*, June 14, 1990.

Gilbert, Calvin. "He's a Believer." *The Nashville Banner*, February 27, 1995.

Goebel, Nancy. "The Unlimited Potential of Bette Graham." *Texas Woman*, July, 1979.

Golden, Christie. Review: "Nezmuzic" *Orbit Video*, May, 1989.

Golden, Mike. "Evolution Of A Monkee." *Gallery*, May, 1990.

Goldman, Stuart. "Nesmith Takes a Commercial Tilt." *Los Angeles Times*, August 31, 1979.

Grein, Paul. "Five Artists Gaze Into The Video Future." *Billboard*, November 22, 1980.

Grove, Martin. "Hollywood Report." *Hollywood Reporter*, December 23, 1988.

Gullo, Jim. "Monkee Business- Mike Nesmith Takes Home Video Seriously." *Premiere*, January, 1989

Gutman, Barry. "Nesmith to Publish Electronic Video Magazine." *Video Insider*, September 8, 1986.

Gutman, Barry. "Nesmith's First All- New Album In 13 Years Plus." *Philadelphia Inquirer*, January 14, 1993.

Gutman, Barry. Review: "Nesmith Live At The Britt Festival" *Pulse*, May, 1993.

Hartigan, Brian. "Michael Nesmith: The Solo Years." *Goldmine*, March 16, 1984.

Hartigan, Brian. Review: "Television Parts Home Companion." *Goldmine*, August15, 1986.

Henderson, Bill. "An Interview with a Soundtrack." *Street Life*, December 27, 1975.

Hendryx, Kevin. Review: "The Newer Stuff." *The Austin Chronicle*, February 2, 1990.

Hendryx, Kevin. Review: "The Older Stuff." *Music City Texas*, December, 1991.

Hendryx, Kevin. Review: "...Tropical Campfires..." *Music City Texas*, November, 1992.

Hibbert, Tom. "Hey Hey, We're a Symbolic Uniquity." *Mojo*, March, 1997.

Hilburn, Robert. "Mike Nesmith-He's Down, But Not Out." *Los Angeles Times*, January 15, 1972.

Hinckley, David. "No More Monkee-ing Around." *New York Daily News*, November 26, 1988.

Hirschberg, Lynn. "Michael Nesmith-A Video Visionary Leaps Into The Future." *BAM*, August 14, 1981.

Hochman, Steve. Review: "Wadsworth Theater Concert." *Los Angeles Times*, March 20, 1995.

Hooker, Michael. Review: "The Prison." *Los Angeles Times*, April 16, 1976.

Hoppe, Christy. "Little Known AG Hopefuls Turn to TV." *Dallas Morning News*, February 2, 1990.

Hughes, Mike. "He's Not Monkeyin' Around." *Lansing State Journal*, August 7, 1990.

Jackson, Blair. "The Quotable Mr. Nesmith." *BAM*, August 3, 1979.

Jones, Allan. "Nesmith-Prisoner of Love." *Melody Maker*, December 6, 1975.

Jones, Allan. "Nesmith: And the Hits Just Keep On Comin." *Melody Maker*, April 9, 1977.

Katz, Cynthia. "The Video Music Mix." *Videography*, May, 1982.

Kaye, Roger. "But Where Is Mike Nesmith?" *Fort Worth Star Telegram*, June 22, 1986.

Kessler, Ken. "Mike Nesmith Exploits The Evolution of Dolby Surround On His Latest CD." *HI-Fi News & Record Review*, March, 1993.

Kirk, Cynthia. "Pacific Arts Corp. Drops Out Of Record Biz, Focuses On Video." *Variety*, October 14, 1981.

Kirk, Cynthia. "Pacific Arts Unveils First Project Slate." *Variety*, March 19, 1982.

Kirk, Cynthia. "Pacific Arts Wins A Bout In 'Elephant Parts' Piracy Bout." *Variety*, May 26, 1982.

Kozak, Roman. "Industry Ripe for Change, Ex-Monkee Nesmith Claims." *Billboard*, April 2, 1977.

Kweder, Kenn. "A Monkee's Work is Never Done - Ask Michael Nesmith." *Happytimes*, March 25, 1977.

Lake, Steve. "Nesmith Shakes Off a Ghost." *Melody Maker*, May 4, 1974.

Lake, Steve. "Tantamount To Reason." *Melody Maker*, April 12, 1975.

Lake, Steve. "Silent Tribute to Nesmith." *Melody Maker*, April 12, 1975.

Lantos, Jeffrey. "The Evolution Of A Monkee." *American Film*, July/August, 1985.

Lappen, John. Review: "Wadsworth Theater Concert." *Hollywood Reporter*, March 20, 1995.

Lehecka, Mike. Review: "The Garden." *Request*, April, 1995.

Leogrande, Ernest. "A Monkee Speaks." *NY Daily News, March 30, 1977.*

Lewis, Randy. Review: "...Tropical Campfires..." *Los Angeles Times*, June 24, 1993.

Liebenson, Donald. "Michael Nesmith and Pacific Arts- A Decade of Innovative Video Programming." *Video Alert*, July/August, 1989.

Lieck, Ken. Review: "The Garden." *Austin Chronicle*, February 17, 1995.

Lilienthal, Lisa. "Pacific Arts Exits Video Business, Blames PBS." *Video Store*, May 15-21, 1994.

Lindholm, Jeffrey. "Michael Nesmith-Many Lives Since." *Dirty Linen*, October/November, 1992.

Lyon, Richard. "Mike Nesmith: 'I Won't Settle For Just One Woman'." *Movie Mirror*, September 1967.

MacDonald, Jay. "Ex-Monkee Nesmith Manages to Keep a Low Profile." *Country Style*, March 24, 1977.

Maddux, Cathy. "Concert Collection Hits All-Time Low." *The Albany Democrat-Herald*, August 19, 1994.

Mahler, Richard. "Former Monkee Creates Video Magazine." *Electronic Media*, March 9, 1987.

Margulies, Lee. "A Monkee Shines Anew." *US*, May 11, 1982.

Maurstad, Tom. "No More Monkee Business." *Dallas Morning News*, February 28, 1992.

McCullaugh, Jim. "Nesmith's Pacific Arts Preps For Coming Videodisk Market." *Billboard*, March 1, 1980.

McCullaugh, Jim. "Nesmith Quits Disk Business, Entering Video." *Billboard*, February 7, 1981.

McCullaugh, Jim. "Former Disc Execs Find Excitement In Home Video." *Billboard*, June 12, 1982.

McCullaugh, Jim. "Pacific Arts Embarks On New Ventures." *Billboard*, May 2, 1987.

McCullaugh, Jim. "Nesmith Says Vid Mags Aren't Monkee Business." *Billboard*, July 1, 1989.

McDonough, Jack. "Pacific Arts Steps Up Activity." *Billboard*, September 8, 1984.

McDowell, Mike. "Michael Nesmith." *Ballroom Blitz*, March, 1977.

McDowell, Mike. "An Exclusive Interview With Michael Nesmith." *Blitz*, September/October , 1978.

McGowan, Chris. "Pacific Arts Enrolls 'Dr. Duck' In College." *Billboard*, January 24, 1987.

McKissick, Heather M. "Michael Nesmith Opens Season 18 of Austin City Limits." *San Antonio Focus*, January, 1993.

McLeese, Don. Review: "...Tropical Campfires..." *Request* January, 1993.

McLeese, Don. "ACL Still Hasn't Reached It's Limits." *Austin American-Statesman*, January 14, 1993.

Millard, Bob. "Ex-Monkee Business." *Dallas Times Herald*, June 21, 1990.

Miller, Ron. "TV Parts Gets More Tinkering." *Philadelphia Inquirer*, July 5, 1985.

Moen, Debi. "Michael Nesmith's Multi-Purpose Club Tour." *Performance*, March 20, 1992.

Morgenthaler, Eric. "At Council Of Ideas, It Is Helpful To Be A Daydream Believer." *Wall Street Journal*, July 29, 1994.

Mulkern, Lou. "Back Page." *Video Business*, June 9, 1989.

Nesmith, Michael. "Sure Sign That The Video Revolution Is Here Now." *Variety*, October 26, 1982.

O'Hare, Kevin. Review: "...Tropical Campfires..." *Sunday Republican*, January 17, 1993.

O'Rourke, P.J. "Baja Diary." *Car and Driver*, March, 1983.

O'Rourke, P.J. "Intellectual Victory." *Car and Driver*, July, 1984.

Okamoto, David. Review: "...Tropical Campfires..." *CD Review*, March, 1993.

Orlando, Greg. Review: "...Tropical Campfires..." *The Review*, February 5, 1993

Owen, Stacy. Review: "...Tropical Campfires..." *Guided Tour*, March, 1993.

Patterson, Rob. "From Pop Star To Video Visionary." *Austin Chronicle*, March 11, 1994.

Popson, Tom. "Hey, Hey: It's The Monkees--Michael Nesmith A Believer In CD, Video Reissues." *Chicago Tribune*, December 8, 1994.

Porter, Bob. "Small Film Takes Cue From Big Lone Star Setting." *Danville Herald*, September 7, 1986.

Quantick, David. "People Said They Monkeyed Around." *Q*, April, 1997.

Rense, Rip. "Rock 'N' Pictures." *L.A. Herald-Examiner*, October 2, 1981.

Rhodes, Joe. "Monkee Business: Video Capitalist Nesmith Cashes In." *Dallas Observer*, March 5, 1987.

Rich, Andrew. "Local Company Sues Ex-Monkee." *Minneapolis/St. Paul CityBusiness*, April 8, 1987.

Riemenschneider, Chris. "Dallas Native, Former Monkee Michael Nesmith Remains A Manufacturer Of Dynamic Duos." *Dallas Morning News*, July 15, 1994.

Roby, Steven. "Time Has Come Today." *Straight Ahead*, April/May, 1994.

Runkle, Patrick. "Papa Nez Kicks Back." *Artist Pro*, May/June, 2003

Saporita, Jay. "Is There Life After Super Stardom? *The Aquarian Weekly*, May 25, 1977.

Schembri, Jim. "Not Monkeing Around." *The Age*, October 7, 1988.

Schiff, Allen. "Mike Nesmith The Strange Power He Has Over The Monkees." *TV and Movie Screen*, October 1967.

Schulze, Stewart. "Video Mags Turn New Media Page. *Boston Herald*, March 18, 1990.

Schwed, Mark. "Soon You Can Set Your Sights on the Sounds." *NY Daily News*, December 22, 1981.

Sciarra, Dean (with Michael J. Ferguson). "Hey, Hey, He's No Monkee." *The Planet*, March 22, 1977

Seay, Davin. "Michael Nesmith's Flow Charts for the Future." *BAM*, August 3, 1979

Seidenberg, Robert. "Monkee Business-Mike Nesmith's Chart-Proof Music." *Entertainment Weekly*, April 1, 1994.

Shales, Tom. Review: "Television Parts." *The Washington Post*, March 7, 1985.

Sharbutt, Jay. "NBC To Shift 'Television Parts' In Survival Bid." *Los Angeles Times*, June 28, 1985.

Sharpe, Tom. "Putting Heads Together." *The Santa Fe New Mexican*, July 24, 2000.

Slotek, Jim. "Hey, Hey He's Free." *Toronto Sun*, April 10, 1993.

Smith, Russell. "Dallas Native Michael Nesmith Stepped In To Save the Project." *Dallas Morning News*, June 29, 1986.

Smith, Russell. "Monkee Business Over, Michael Nesmith Swings Into Filmaking Industry." *Chicago Tribune*, July 31, 1986.

Smith, Stacy Jenel. "Home -Video Industry Not Monkee Business." *Tampa Tribune*, August 26, 1981.

Snyder, Michael. "Making Monkee Business For the '90s." *San Francisco Chronicle*, December 27, 1994.

Sutherland, Sam. "Nesmith's Pacific Arts: A Unique Small Label." *Record World*, October 7, 1978.

Sutherland, Sam. "Pacific Arts Eyes New Projects." *Billboard*, September 11, 1982.

Sutherland, Sam. "Nesmith Brings Video To NBC." *Billboard*, November 26, 1983.

Tamarkin, Jeff. "Michael Nesmith." *Goldmine*, December 27, 1991.

Terrell, Steve. "Panel: Government Must Change." *Santa Fe New Mexican*, July 18, 1994.

Terrell, Steve. "From Monkee to Foundation Head." *Santa Fe New Mexican*, July 18, 1994

Tobler, John. "Monkee in the Countryside." *Melody Maker*, 1973

Tobler, John "Interview with Michael Nesmith." *Zig Zag #39*, 1973.

Tobler, John. "On The Road to Rio." *Zig Zag*, May, 1977.

Trakin, Roy. "Michael Nesmith- Monkee to Mogul." *Music Connection*, September, 1986

Tutellan, Louise. "Monkeying Around With Movies, Video." *USA Today*, January 23, 1983.

Van Matre, Lynn. "This Man Used to be a Monkee" *Chicago Tribune*, January 23, 1983.

Vaughn, Andrew. "Michael Nesmith." *Record Collector*, November, 1991.

Webb, Dewey. "Reading Between the Electronic Lines." *New Times*, February 18, 1987.

Weber, Bruce. "Monkees Fix Rerun Music." *Billboard*, April 12, 1969.

Weideman, Paul R. "Learning Is Top Global Issue." *Los Alamos Monitor*, July 17, 1996.

Willman, Chris. "Nesmith Goes Out On A Limb For The Monkees." *Los Angeles Times*, July 11, 1989.

Writer, Larry. "The King Of Con." *Who*, June 14, 1993.

Young, J.R. Review: "Tantamount To Treason." *Rolling Stone*, April 13, 1972.

Zacks, Richard. "Finding the Real Thing at VSDA Means Cutting Through the Hype." *New York Daily News*, September 7, 1986.

Zuckerman, Faye. "Mixed Bag From Pacific Arts." *Billboard*, January 26, 1985.

The Author and her subjects

Shown with the author:
Davy, Micky, Victoria
Kennedy, Michael and Peter.

Photo by Henry Diltz.

CPSIA information can be obtained at www.ICGtesting.com
Printed in the USA
BVOW021825260812

298853BV00006B/44/A